TiMBiT NATiON

A Hitchhiker's View of Canada

John Stackhouse

RANDOM HOUSE CANADA

Published in 2003 by Random House Canada, a division of Random House
of Canada Limited, Toronto. Distributed in Canada by Random House of
Canada Limited.

www.randomhouse.ca

Random House Canada and colophon are trademarks.

NATIONAL LIBRARY OF CANADA CATALOGUING IN PUBLICATION

Stackhouse, John, 1962–
      Timbit nation : a hitchhiker's view of Canada / John Stackhouse.

Based on a series of articles written for the Globe and mail.

ISBN 0-679-31167-X

      1. Stackhouse, John, 1962–   —Journeys—Canada. 2. Canada—
Description and travel. I. Title.

FC75.572 2003   917.104'648   C2002-905014-6
F1017.572 2003

Timbit is a trade mark of The TDL Group Ltd.
      Reprinted by permission of the TDL Group Ltd.

Design by Daniel Cullen

Printed in Canada

10 9 8 7 6 5 4 3 2 1

For my parents,
Margaret and Reginald,
and the Canada they helped build

Introduction

I decided to hitchhike across Canada when my editor at the *Globe and Mail* asked what would be the best way to see the country. I had just returned from nearly eight years of living overseas, in New Delhi, as a correspondent for the newspaper, and he figured I might see my own country differently. "See Canada as a foreigner sees it," he suggested. He had imagined me taking the train, not realizing that VIA Rail had been relegated to the back roads of travel. I didn't buy into the train myth anyway. Like every good Canadian high school student in the 1970s, I had read *The Last Spike*, memorized arcane details about John A. Macdonald's national dream and concluded it was very nineteenth century. I didn't know anyone who took the train anywhere. My Canada lived on the highway, and by the highway.

Long before *The Last Spike* was published, one of my favourite storybooks was about a family's driving trip along the Trans-Canada Highway, from sea to sea. The route had just been completed, in the early sixties, and the images of a diverse land, from rocky shores to barren prairie, mountains and crowded cities, all linked by one highway, were awesome to a young imagination.

I could not have realized it at the time, but this one road was quietly uniting the country in ways the railway never did. In the emerging era of the middle class—the motoring class—the Trans-Canada enabled ordinary Canadians to see Canada. Like most families of my generation, before the dawn of discount airlines, vacations took us along parts of the great highway in Ontario, Quebec and the Maritimes. When I was old enough to travel alone but too young to afford a car, I began hitchhiking on the same road. My student poverty aside, hitchhiking in the 1980s seemed innately Canadian.

There was no better way to see a country and meet its people than to beg for rides along the way, to have long conversations (sometimes very long) with strangers, to test public generosity, to overcome fears, within oneself and in others, and to see the road, and feel it. Standing on a remote rural road, you could see the vastness of what it was attempting to connect. On a suburban on-ramp, you could feel the pulse of a society as it rushed from office to mall to home. And climbing into the cars of that society—at the invitation of a stranger who had everything to lose, as did you—you could sense the openness of a nation, along with its fears and prejudices. In short, you could stand on the roadside and put an entire nation on the couch. Over the years, I came to see hitchhiking as the most genuine form of travel. Through it, I was forced to meet new people and new ideas. It was wildly unpredictable, maddeningly erratic, hilariously entertaining and slightly dangerous—all in all, what a great journey should be.

The Canadian road only added to the allure. The long, lonely stretches of Prairie highway. The womb of a wooded back road in Ontario. The coastal routes of Nova Scotia that hug the shore so closely they blend with the surf.

With exceptions like Ontario's 400 series of highways, the Trans-Canada and its tributaries seem designed not to remove travellers from their country so much as to make them part of it. In the United States, by contrast, there are so many highways they intersect and overlap with such fury that nothing seems to stand between A and B except four lanes. In Europe, the M's of England and autobahns of Germany are more efficient still, like those old vacuum chutes in offices that take a tube from one floor to another with utter disregard for everything in between.

But for all the marvels of our roads, never had I attempted the width of the country, a course that meanders nine thousand kilometres, which was what my editor, after hearing my description of the road, wanted me to do. It would be like circling France three times. It would also be more dangerous and considerably more difficult than when I had last hitchhiked, in the mid-eighties. Hitching was once a Canadian rite of passage, like renting vacation property in the American South. Now I feared it had become a national scourge. So reluctant were people to pick up strangers that I had some doubts anyone would be able to complete the journey. I feared that Canadians, like the Americans I had met hitching from Vancouver to San Francisco in 1986, had become too distrusting of strangers, too paranoid of random crime, too, well, American in our fears. But that was the point of the journey, to pry into the Canadian psyche.

I agreed with my editor to set off in the summer of 2000, when Canada would be in bloom and Canadians eager to talk about their new century.

——— ——— ———

Hitchhiking as a reporter, there would be benefits I had not enjoyed as a student. A company credit card, for instance. And the security blanket of being able to tell strangers I was with a nationally known organization.

There were also the exceeding ambitions of a newspaper deadline. I was given one month to cross the country, which pretty much ruled out the Far North. I would also have to write a daily diary for the paper, which meant carrying a laptop computer and stopping at a motel or bed and breakfast every night to write, rewrite and transmit my copy.

Appearance was another factor. The ruffled reporter look had to go. I got a haircut and packed two changes of perma-press clothes that would both allow me to travel with one small backpack and look clean-cut every day. With a small laptop, a sleeping bag, the Lonely Planet guide to Canada and a few blank notebooks, there wasn't room for more.

Before setting out, though, my biggest concern was a route. Most people who travel across the country by road begin their journey at either end of the impressively long Trans-Canada. If they start in the east, choosing to follow the sun and Canada's modern history, their trip invariably is launched in St. John's, Newfoundland, on the farthest reach of the Avalon Peninsula. In the summer, you can see tourists and travellers there every morning, snapping a commemorative picture by their recreation vehicle or symbolically dipping a bicycle wheel in the Atlantic. At the other end of Canada, in Tofino, across six time zones and a stretch of nationhood surpassed only by Russia, the same models of RVs and bicycles can be seen on the Pacific coast.

Rather than at a highway's terminus, I wanted to begin my cross-Canada odyssey where my family had landed in what would become this country. More than two centuries ago, in 1783, Joseph and Robert Stackhouse arrived at the mouth of the Saint John River, aboard one of the first refugee boats to reach the continent's north-east coast. The brothers had come from America where their regiment, the 1st New Jersey Volunteers, had been routed in the war of independence. Their family farm in New Jersey had been lost to rebel forces. They had nothing else to lose by venturing to New Brunswick, except maybe their lives. In revolutionary New York, even those weren't safe.

That October, Robert and Joseph, along with their wives and children, their father James and 350 other Loyalists, boarded the *Duke of Richmond* in New York, among the last of six major fleets to leave that year for New Brunswick and Nova Scotia.

Any refugee today would recognize their flight of fear, just as they would the unwelcoming conditions at the other end. The remaining colonies were already overwhelmed with newcomers. The rocky shores around Fort Howe, in what is now Saint John, had to settle four thousand displaced people in conditions so squalid and deprived that when the *Duke of Richmond* entered the Saint John River, the people onshore fired cannons at the ship to drive it away. The captain wisely chose to land on the other bank.

For that first winter, the men were each given one tattered blanket normally reserved for horses, and a daily ration for each family of a pound of flour, a half-pound of salted beef and a pat of butter. Eventually, the Stackhouses and their children began to clear trees for their own homes and got jobs in the shipyards that sprang up easily in the woods around the harbour.

A century later, according to the *Directory of New Brunswick*, there were Stackhouses listed as shipbuilders, wharf builders, ship carpenters and one assistant engineer in the fire department. This emerging nation had some spunk. My family began to move up the Saint John River to clear land for farms. There was no glamour or glory in it, though, and not enough to make ends meet. My father's father, Edward, spent his boyhood summers on road gangs, with his own father, in lieu of paying municipal taxes. They had too little cash to do otherwise. At the age of thirteen, Edward packed it in and walked to Maine, where he worked in logging camps before making his way across the northeastern United States and Ontario, finally settling in Toronto.

I prepared to set off from Saint John, New Brunswick, a pulp and paper town that had been for the last several generations enveloped by fog and forgotten by history. From there, I could head east to Newfoundland, north into Labrador and straight west to Vancouver Island, following parts of the Trans-Canada and, for diversions, secondary highways, rural roads and, where none of those existed, sea routes.

The journey seemed entirely Canadian, for the emergence of the affordable family car and a national highway had changed the country as much as the canoe and railway once did. It was not just the advent of middle-class comfort, but the creation of an accessible nation. It was not just about shortening distances geographically but about shrinking them socially, which was always part of the Canadian dream.

But in the summer of 2000, the national dream that had brought two brothers here on an unwelcome boat, pushed their descendants up a river and across half a country, and propelled future generations to new dreams was being tested anew. Even before I set out for Saint John, I feared the notions of Canada that had been passed down to me were just about gone, and a very different nation lay ahead.

Prelude

To get to my starting point, I had to take a small regional jet from Toronto to Saint John. Only in Canada would fifteen hundred kilometres be considered "regional." Yet the two cities and their provinces had become so different and disparate they were not just in different regions; they could be in different countries. That was the new Canada.

Nowhere could this be more evident than in the main terminal of Toronto's Lester B. Pearson International Airport, where I got to stand with thousands of travellers headed to every part of the continent and the world. Terminal Two used to be Air Canada's showpiece for domestic travel, the hub of cross-country air routes. But a new continental economy had transformed it. Most of the morning's flights were headed for places like Los Angeles, Dallas, Raleigh, Chicago and Newark, not far from Robert and Joseph Stackhouse's old regimental base in New Jersey. Saint John, on the other hand, seemed like a curiosity, the kind of quaint name you might see on a sign pointing down an old country highway.

This was hardly fair for a city that is positively ancient by North American standards. The explorer Samuel de Champlain sailed into

Saint John harbour in 1604, nearly two centuries before the *Duke of Richmond* landed. The area was so promising, with a big river, forests and an excellent harbour, that Thomas Haliburton, a writer in the early nineteenth century, predicted Saint John "will be the largest city in America, next to New York."

Something quite different awaited, as my airplane approached this fabled land of plenty. At first, I thought I might be able to see Saint John harbour, but did not count on such a thick fog. There was not so much as a glimpse of land until we were on it, giving the feeling that instead of the plane touching down, New Brunswick had risen up into the clouds to meet us. It wouldn't take much to do that. Saint John airport was smaller than a typical city bus terminal, and with much less traffic. The whole place seemed isolated and remote, as if cast aside by its country nearly four hundred years after the first European set foot here.

By the time I found my backpack and left the terminal, I realized it would be a mistake to hitchhike in the thick fog. I also wanted to get to the Museum of New Brunswick, with its rich Loyalist files, and then to the original Stackhouse home, where I hoped to begin my journey proper. Behind me, the terminal was empty and ready to be padlocked for the rest of the day, or maybe a week. In front of me was Lloyd, the last taxi driver, apparently tipped off by an insider to the fact that one remaining passenger needed to make the long haul into the city. Lloyd said he had been waiting three hours for a fare, and was clearly in no hurry. Once we were clear of the airport, he steered his big old LTD onto the highway, taking to the open road at the very speed he had reached in the parking lot. Over a small rise, the fog began to lift, and still Lloyd kept his leisurely pace.

For a time, I assumed he wanted me to enjoy the New Brunswick countryside, or at least the woodlands between Saint John airport and the city, of which there were plenty. But I began to notice another feature of the countryside, a name that kept reappearing. There was a turnoff for an Irving tree plantation, followed by signs for the Irving Nature Park, more signs for "Irving, the tree-planting company," and one of the big Irving gas stations that, according to the latest edition of *Canadian Business* magazine, were as common in New Brunswick as covered bridges.

On the airplane I had read the magazine's annual rich list, which ranked the three Irving brothers—J.K., Arthur and Jack—as the second wealthiest family in the country. Although they are low-key and restrict their business pretty much to one province, and a relatively poor one at that, their family fortune was put at a little over $6 billion. Only media magnate Kenneth Thomson, partial owner of my employer, The Globe and Mail, was richer, with $23 billion to his name.

It was an exaggeration only in degree to say the Irvings owned the place. The province's forests, where my grandfather once chopped wood, fed the Irvings' mills and the mills fed their newspapers. Their chain of gas stations was as ubiquitous as McDonald's, while their Saint John oil refinery, with a billion dollars of new equipment, was the biggest of its kind in Canada. No one had to ask why the industry section at the New Brunswick Museum was named for the family.

Beyond the Irving gas station, Lloyd had to follow a detour around an impressive road construction crew that had enough equipment to build a big-city expressway. There was no traffic in sight. It was just part of the region's make-work economy, Lloyd said. After twelve weeks on the site, the workers would be eligible for "employment insurance," the latest euphemism for pogey, which was all that buffered the four Atlantic provinces from outright poverty.

We eventually reached the city, with the taxi meter at a point where Lloyd could think about a new set of tires. Instead, he made me an offer. For another five dollars, he would show me the real Irving domain.

With no need to slow down from the highway, he carefully steered his LTD up a series of winding roads to the leafy hilltop neighbourhood of Mount Pleasant, where some of the trophies of

Atlantic Canada's first fortunes stood. Although most of the stately homes had been converted to apartments because, as Lloyd put it, "there aren't many rich folk left in Saint John," there was the Irving home, stately and secure behind a defensive line of tall hedges. The front lawn was the size of an inner-city park.

According to Lloyd, the stone and brick mansions on Mount Pleasant Avenue were pretty much the high point of Saint John. Over the course of three generations, from my grandfather's time, the city's population had shrunk, from 150,000 to 120,000, while the Toronto area's population grew from 750,000 to three million.

Lloyd had joined the exodus to Toronto, only to return "for a woman." Actually, the woman ditched him, but there was their seven-year-old daughter. I asked him if there was any other reason to stay. He thought long enough to reach the next stop sign, which felt like a Maritime afternoon, and then shook his head. "The men here are drunk, and the women are big and hairy," he said. "There aren't a lot of pretty people here."

Since time was ticking and his meter wasn't, Lloyd suggested we move on. And for a moment he seemed to approach the speed limit as we drove down from Mount Pleasant to the scraggy western shore of the harbour—the place where my family's journey to Canada ended, and where I wanted this new journey to begin.

After getting out at the New Brunswick Museum, I spent a couple of hours in the archives sifting through United Empire Loyalist files to find Robert Stackhouse's discharge papers—the one document that got us to Canada. I felt odd holding a document two hundred years older than I was, wondering how Robert felt, on October 10, 1763, holding the same paper in a besieged New York City. Could he have known what lay ahead on this rocky hillside? Could he have understood the mission he was about to embark on, to create a new nation right next to a triumphant America? Could he have envisioned a Canada that would abut three seas, that would become America's closest friend, that would remain loyal to the Crown and that would conquer the world in every worthy aspect of human development?

Holding this very paper that discharged him from the New Jersey Volunteers, could Robert Stackhouse have even imagined a Canada? Was he content trading in life, liberty and happiness for peace, order and good government? Or was he, in 1763, like so many Canadians in the summer of 2000, not quite sure of his destination?

Perhaps, unlike the Americans he was leaving behind, he did not see nationhood as a destination at all, but rather a journey—grinding, tumultuous, unpredictable, magnificent. And one that had to be taken. Perhaps like three centuries of people who have journeyed to Canada, he knew the road here never really ends.

⸺ ⸺ ⸺

To begin the journey properly, I took a city bus to Saint John's Lower West Side and walked to the corner of Prince and Ludlow. I wasn't yet ready to hitchhike, not without seeing the spot where the first Stackhouse home was recorded in Canada. The landing site was seedy in an old-town kind of way, a gentle slope of old houses, abandoned shops and cluttered yards divided by an expressway that allowed people to commute from downtown Saint John to the suburbs without so much as glancing at the Lower West Side. The expressway accounted for one side of Prince and Ludlow. On the other corners were a parking lot and a dilapidated clapboard house. When I crossed from the bus stop and knocked on the door, an older male voice shouted for me to come in.

Ian Donald was sitting in the living room, in a wheelchair. His brother Bruce was in the kitchen making coffee. Like a good many people in the Maritimes, they didn't blink at the thought of inviting a stranger through the door. I introduced myself and asked Bruce if he knew of any Stackhouses in the area. He scratched his head. He and Ian grew up in this house, which had been built in 1845. They didn't remember anyone by this name. But there were several old houses across the street, at least before the bulldozers came. In 1967, to celebrate Canada's centenary, the province cleared a row of houses to make way for the expressway, which had become the newest form of nation building. One of the fallen houses must have been ours at one time.

Ian said the neighbourhood had not been the same since the expressway allowed a new generation to move to the suburbs. "The core of the old communities has deteriorated. It seems in this country, transportation has been given priority rather than the preservation of old houses and buildings."

"I don't know hardly anyone around here," said Bruce, a retired salesman. "They're all strangers. I said this the other day at Tim Hortons. I don't know anyone here."

"You used to know the butcher, the baker. You knew everyone," Ian said, interrupting his brother.

"You see these old communities, the cores that were the lifeblood of communities, are all boarded up," Bruce said. "We found this all over here. The malls are on the outskirts."

"The hospitals are out there too," Ian complained.

"That expressway out there did it," Bruce said, grabbing hold of the conversation again. "It moved people to the suburbs. It changed our world here."

Ian, who had been in a wheelchair since the early seventies, moved across the living room to an old wooden chest. He rummaged through the contents, pulling out a photograph of the old house where he said some Stackhouses might have lived. He suggested I lift the tattered curtain to see the throughway that had taken its place.

Perhaps it was not surprising that one of the earliest European settlements in Canada—really, the gateway to a new nation—was now a four-lane road. We long ago became a nation of suburbs, defined by big-box malls and car dealerships more than by forests and water. I was heading straight into it, eager to voyage through treacherous intersections, climb towering overpasses and follow majestic stretches of dotted white lines.

Thanking the Donald brothers for the coffee, I took my backpack and walked toward a toll bridge that crossed the narrows carrying the

Saint John River into the Bay of Fundy. I could not see five feet in front of me for all the fog, let alone downtown Saint John across the river. But at least my journey had begun.

1

Tokin' Joe

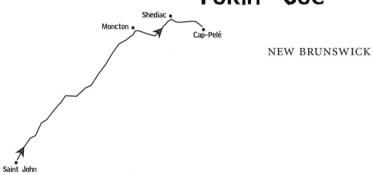

NEW BRUNSWICK

By the time I got over the bridge to downtown Saint John, it was early evening. In the fading light, I followed the music to a strip of bars, outdoor patios and what looked to be a beach planted in the middle of the city. It was. Right next to the harbour, the city had laid out a stretch of sand where scores of fit, attractive young things, as tanned as one could get in Canada's fog capital, were playing volleyball in the mist. Dowdy old Saint John—staging ground for the United Empire Loyalists, hometown to monopolist capitalism—had found itself a bit of cool.

I sat down at a table with a group of players, who were resting between games, and explained that I was hitchhiking across Canada to see how the nation was changing. Okay, I hadn't put out my thumb yet, but I was on the move.

One of the players, Curtis Baxter, was the very opposite of the Donald brothers, and not just because of his boyish freckles and red hair. At thirty-nine, with two kids and a career in digital technology, he had only opportunities to fret over. The son of an army officer, he grew up all over Canada, attending the University of Western Ontario before returning to his home province with his wife.

Although the young couple could have taken any number of jobs in Ontario or the United States, they joined New Brunswick

Telecom—he as a technical manager, she as a database manager—just as the company was starting to go big with broadband. This was encouraging, because so much other news about Saint John was depressing. Apart from the Irvings' new refinery and Moosehead Brewery, which was Saint John's real pride, the place seemed to be in terminal decline. Back on the Lower West Side, a soap factory and nail factory had closed. The city's big sugar refinery, with 250 jobs, had also shut down. Even the dry docks, among the world's biggest, were losing ground to foreign competition and in danger of collapse.

Curtis, on the other hand, described a new economy and needed only to point to the three volleyball courts in the sand for evidence. The team he had just played against was made up entirely of Russian software programmers, hired by a local company. Several other squads came from call centres, the biggest industry to hit Saint John and its provincial rival, Moncton, in years. The centres, which can operate pretty much anywhere in the world, staff hundreds of Canadian telephone operators who take calls for mail orders and consumer product complaints from around the continent. The Russians were brought in to make the computers run faster.

New Brunswick was a natural location because, as an officially bilingual province, its people were probably more comfortable in Canada's two official languages than anyone else in the country. This new wired world allowed Curtis and his wife together to earn about $130,000 a year—enough to enjoy a big house in the very suburbs that the Donald brothers so disliked, and plenty of toys and free time to go with it. There was a new Future Shop out where they live (the first in the Saint John area), as well as an expanded Wal-Mart, a new Canadian Tire and talk of a Chapters or Indigo. In Atlantic Canada, this was progress, and Curtis was proud of it. He would no longer have to drive to Fredericton to buy a book.

In the United States, he and his wife could more than double their gross income, but for the longest time they had said no. They bought into the myths of Canada. They knew the "I am Canadian" beer commercials by heart. And they figured lower salaries and higher taxes were just part of the price for peace, order and good government—or in a new millennium, good roads, public education and free health care.

That is, until their fourteen-year-old explained one evening why he had no homework. No after-school assignments were given any more since the local school did not have enough textbooks to go around. So Curtis and his wife put their boy in a private school—the antithesis of their "I am Canadian" beliefs—and began to wonder where exactly their tax money was going. Was it just to those road builders who went on "employment insurance" for much of the year?

Curtis began to talk with American companies and learned they would pay his health insurance premiums. While on business trips, he started to visit suburbs around Boston and California's Silicon Valley, and saw how friendly and safe their neighbourhoods were. The myopia of America—the Californians who didn't know the difference between New Hampshire and New Brunswick—bothered him less and less, while misty Saint John began to lose some of its appeal.

This was the brain drain at work, tugging at good Canadians like Curtis, encouraging them to take their journey elsewhere. "We keep hearing there's no brain drain, but I know Rod and Cameron and Bruce and the other Rod have all left, and I don't think they're coming back," Curtis said. "I know people working in the next desk, and suddenly they're working in Bermuda, making $75,000 U.S. and it's tax-free. It's something I think about all the time."

Curtis faced that fundamental Canadian dilemma: he could go to the United States, for the sake of opportunity, or stay in Canada, for the sake of something less tangible. He told me about his brother-in-law in Fredericton, a loader who made perhaps $40,000 a year. Although the man couldn't afford to send his children to private school, they had the same opportunities as Curtis's son. That was the Canadian way, and Curtis's dilemma. Sitting at the edge of Saint John harbour, I wondered if he had very different thoughts than Robert and Joseph Stackhouse did as they waited in New York harbour in 1763—except this time the revolution was going on north of the border.

Cool evening air was beginning to settle over the artificial beach, which was now barely visible in the mist. Hoping for an early start the next day, I said goodbye to Curtis and his friends, and took one final look at the Russians leaping and spiking the ball with the greatest of ease, against a squad from some unfortunate call centre. Barking to each other in Russian and across the net in English, they seemed more at ease in Saint John than the frustrated Baxters or the nostalgic Donalds were.

——— ——— ———

Almost from the moment I left my downtown hotel the next morning, my journey felt doomed. I had naively thought I could walk to the edge of Saint John, only to learn that as Canada's oldest city it was no hamlet. It was an old town that sprawled, and sprawled.

I found a city bus headed for the suburbs.

"Do you stop at Highway 1?" I asked the driver.

He looked at me as if I had just drifted up on the beach and told me to take a seat at the back. He would tell me when we got to the mall. At the edge of every Canadian city and town, there's a mall. I could walk from there, the driver said.

He did not tell me it would be a two-kilometre walk, instead estimating the distance as "not far." I could not see far enough in the morning fog to doubt him.

When I reached the on-ramp, half an hour later, I was starting to worry about other things, such as the first metaphysical question of hitchhiking: Where do you stand? I decided to start at the bottom of the on-ramp, where vehicles stopping for gas or food would not have to slow down to get a good look at me as they returned to the highway. A few waved politely. I noticed they had New Brunswick plates, not like the big American RVs sailing by, each with enough room to house a small African village. Forty-five minutes passed. The fog cover turned to sun. I still had no ride. I began to think seriously about moving to another on-ramp so I could hitchhike to the bus station. But then Gerry stopped. I knew he was Canadian even before he apologized for his old blue Pontiac and its trailer of lawnmowers, ladders and hedge clippers. He spoke like a Maritimer, and drove like one too. Slowly.

Gerry's bare chest was checkered with leaf bits and so tanned I had to wonder if he really did work in these parts. There was no time to probe him on that. He was going down the road a couple of exits, to the airport turnoff, but at least, he said, he would get me to the land of long-distance drivers, the real McCoys of the highway compared with these short-hop commuters who had passed me by. In his experience, the spot where I had been standing was the worst for hitchhiking this side of the Bay of Fundy.

Up on the highway, I noticed more of the big-game vehicles he had talked about—the domineering SUVs, the sleek extended pickup trucks, even the motorhomes that rumbled along like herds of elephants—and how many were not American. They carried licence plates from New Brunswick, one of the perpetually poor provinces that, when asking for federal money, likes to call itself "have not." Most of the motorhomes, I noticed, had bicycles strapped to their rears. Many of the New Brunswick cars did too.

Gerry once built a motorhome, like the ones passing us on the inside lane. When he drove it onto the highway for the first time, he went straight into a ditch. He said he had been pushed by another vehicle. Whatever the cause, when the homemade motorhome had finished its third roll, its roof and two sides were gone. That was the last time Gerry drove one, but the accident didn't change his opinion of New Brunswick highways, which he said were far better than Toronto's. He'd never seen anything like the drivers in Toronto. "Those drivers there are crazy! Jesus!" he exclaimed, when I told him where I was from. Just the mention of the city turned his gardener's tanned face white. "They all go one-thirty, one-forty on the 401." I glanced at his digital speedometer. It read eighty-nine.

Just before we reached his exit, Gerry pointed to the ditch where he had rolled his motorhome. "Imagine rolling over three times," he said, still looking at the gully in disbelief. He advised me to steer clear of motorhomes. I told him that if I had to wait another forty-five minutes, I'd be willing to accept a ride on one of his lawnmowers. A motorhome would be a dream.

"You'll have no problem getting a ride to Sussex," he said, referring to the next town where Highway 1 joins the Trans-Canada (which, in a very Canadian way, sports the number 2 in New Brunswick).

Just before he pulled away, Gerry gave me one last bit of hopeful Maritime advice: "You can throw a rock at anyone who passes you."

Gerry was right. A few minutes after parking my bag on the on-ramp, an Irving refinery worker stopped and offered me a ride up the highway to Sussex, where I didn't have to wait long for another lift, in a beat-up old van.

The driver was alone, dressed in white shorts and a T-shirt, looking like he was barely out of high school. A couple of tennis bags sat between the driver's seat and the front passenger seat. Nick said he was on his way to a tennis tournament in Moncton, which was what Maritime kids like him did. A century ago, my grandfather couldn't find a future here. Today, kids got to turn down job offers and dream wildly about their futures.

Nick was a second-year economics student at Acadia University in Nova Scotia, and home in Saint John for the summer, teaching tennis. The previous summer, he planted trees in British Columbia but found the work too hard, so he quit and played his guitar outside a casino in central British Columbia. After making $800 in a few weeks, he headed home.

Once we were on the highway, I began to appreciate Nick's choice in clothes. Braced for the fog, I was dressed in jeans, a denim shirt and a rain jacket, and was dripping in sweat. Not only had the fog given way to a warm August sun that was beating down on the van, the windows didn't work. Nick apologized when I tried to roll mine down. The air vents, he said, were broken.

Unlike the big new superhighways, the roads of southern New Brunswick do not blow through a place, but rather bend and dip and politely ease their way around dairy farms and small towns. Highway 1 felt like it was staying true to the original trail as it followed the gentle curves of Kings County (this being the one bordered by Charlotte, Queens and Albert counties). Southern New Brunswick can be like that. At times, the entire road looked like an intrusion, even at a hundred kilometres an hour, which Nick, clearly living on the irrational edge of youth, dared to cross.

I told him I had noticed a Saint John newspaper article about a serious worker shortage in the area's famous blueberry patches. For people with strong backs, there was work picking blueberries, at least for a few weeks in late summer. A good picker, the article said, could make a hundred dollars in a morning. Yet in this region of chronic unemployment, there was no lineup for the jobs. Farmers were going to Maine for volunteers.

It was like that for most of his friends, Nick explained as we started to race by local traffic at a good Ontario clip. His voice had none of Gerry's salty lilt. In the Maritimes, he said, jobs were easy come, easy go. After graduation, none of his friends knew what they would do, or much cared. One of his classmates expected to inherit a job at the family's molasses company. The rest assumed they would find something at one of the call centres or the computer companies that had come to the Maritimes with them. Or they'd move to Toronto.

Most of these kids were two or three generations removed from poverty. They weren't rich, not like the Irvings, but they weren't unemployed fishermen or cranky natives, which was what the rest of Canada often equates with the Maritimes. Nick was part of a rapidly growing middle class in the region. His father was an accountant, his mother a schoolteacher, and they had saved enough to pay his $5,000-a-year tuition fee, as well as his room and board. His summer earnings were pocket money.

Unfortunately, this growing urban bourgeoisie had not found its place in the Maritimes. For generations, the region had been a resource-producing hinterland for central Canada. But now, with a new service economy and loads of bright young people coming through university, the Maritimes had grander ambitions than sawing wood and catching fish. It wanted to be part of a much bigger world, and was changing to get there. In the down-home capital of Canada, where hitchhikers were expected to stone cars that passed them by, satellites were swamping the Maritimes' folk culture and the Internet was silencing its chatty lilt.

On a gorgeous sunny driving day, I began to notice the road looked empty. All the American vehicles were gone, as were the local motorhomes. East from Saint John, those not headed in a hurry for Moncton had turned off the highway for what Nick described as a stunning stretch of road along the Bay of Fundy. As we rounded another bend in Kings County, Nick cranked up his radio. A Moncton station was playing "Purple Haze." He was eager to play Hendrix on his steering wheel. And so we drove on in silence as Nick's stifling van shook with bass riffs recorded fifteen years before he was born.

Once a gateway to Nova Scotia and Prince Edward Island, Moncton had come to pride itself on being the capital of the new Maritimes. This was a remarkable comeback for a city of a hundred thousand people that appeared doomed more than a decade earlier, in 1988, when its biggest employer, the Canadian National Railway yards, shut down the bulk of its operations and laid off 4,500 people.

The decision, it turned out, liberated Moncton from generations of government dependency. The call centre boom I had witnessed in Saint John was far bigger in Moncton, where the three thousand new telecommunications jobs nearly offset the CN closing. The Atlantic Lottery—as lowbrow as an economic prospect could be, but surprisingly high-tech—became another major employer when it moved its headquarters there.

The credit had gone almost entirely to a former premier, Frank McKenna, who preferred to go out and hustle the private sector rather than whine to Ottawa for more handouts. He once said New Brunswick needed two things to move ahead—direct flights to New York City and a *Globe and Mail* bureau—figuring they would generate more investment than any of his own sales pitches.

McKenna's new style of Maritime politics was nothing more than a realization that the rest of Canada was changing. With federal budgets under severe pressure in the 1990s, there was no chance for new money for the poorer provinces, not when hospitals and schools were being closed in the richer ones where most of the country's taxpayers and voters live. The scaling down of equalization payments—a founding tradition in Canada that takes money from Ontario and Alberta to prop up just about everyone else—had hit the Maritimes like a perfect storm. There was even talk of ending employment insurance. So much had changed that the latest issue of *Atlantic Progress,* a regional business magazine, declared "the old politics of economic equalization are now as out of fashion as the pet rock and the Hoola Hoop."

Nick pulled off the highway at the Moncton exit leading to Magnetic Hill, the city's most bizarre tourist attraction, on the outskirts of town next to farmland. For generations, the hill had been a tourist draw, convincing drivers they could put their cars in neutral and roll up a hill, as if being pulled by a gigantic hidden magnet. I had been here as a child and was eager to see it again, but as I walked to the gate at the bottom of the fabled hill, I met only perplexed looks from two young ticket collectors. They were charging two dollars per vehicle to defy gravity. They had no idea what to do with a pedestrian, so they waved me through. And why not? I mean, how much metal could I have in my pack?

Inside the gate, I counted twenty cars from out of province, and one Pro Deco-Habitat van from Jonquière, Quebec, lined up to test the hill. Most of them must have known the amusement was based on a simple optical illusion: the hill appeared to be going up, when in fact it was headed down. But they were willing to give it a try, at least for the photograph that had to be taken of each vehicle coasting up the hill. Give credit to Moncton. The Magnetic Hill illusion was enough to support an entire tourist complex, including a small zoo, water park, restaurants, stores and a miniature train.

After a quick walk down Magnetic Hill, I found the local crowd at a nearby Tim Hortons—one of sixteen in the city, according to my guidebook. This was the New Brunswick that intrigued me, not the struggling farmers or angry fishermen but the vibrant middle class that was on the move, creating jobs, redefining their province and hanging out at donut shops. These were the people who had just elected a new Conservative premier, Bernard Lord, not so much because of his ideology but because he had promised to cut the previous government's one-dollar toll on a new stretch of the Trans-Canada Highway.

The standard-bearer for this new motoring class sat at the next table. She was a biker who, along with her boyfriend, was on her way to a motorcycle weekend outside Halifax. Both worked as letter carriers and were dressed in biker's leather that did not bother them in the August heat as they drank a coffee. They also were not suffering. Aside from a couple of big Harleys parked outside, Judy owned a twenty-two-foot sailboat and had enough leisure time to play in two baseball leagues. She was going to tell me more about this new age of comfort when her cell phone rang. As she gabbed, her boyfriend said I could see what she was talking about in downtown Moncton, because it was Friday night and every Friday night there was a parade of vehicles along Main Street.

I took a city bus downtown, dropped my bag at a bed and breakfast and headed for the parade. Sure enough, at ten in the evening on Main Street, there was a long jam of spiffy sports cars, roadsters, motorcycles and jazzed-up SUVs. The line of fine vehicles—longer than anything I had seen at Magnetic Hill—stretched through two red lights, and from there to the edge of the downtown core.

From what I could tell, the car owners did nothing more than cruise up one side of Main Street and down the other, eagerly pumping money into Irving Oil as they revved their engines at each intersection. On both sides of the road, outdoor bars and rooftop patios were jammed with spectators drinking beer and gawking at cars. Up a side street, I found a street festival with several local rock bands playing, and bars advertising wet T-shirt and homemade bikini contests. It was hard to miss the air of contentedness, the feel of a society that, perhaps like that of the 1950s, had all that it could want. Except, that is, for the mosquitoes.

At the far end of Main Street, where it took on the more interesting name of Champlain Street and opened up to two big shopping malls and parking lots where the fancy cars could turn around, the tidal bed of the Petitcodiac River was a breeding ground for insects. How anyone could have decided to place the grandiose Château Moncton hotel and conference centre there was a greater mystery than Magnetic Hill. But the little faux castle, where leaders of the French-speaking world met in 1999, was built next to a riverbed that is relieved twice daily by tidal flows, exposing it again and again to the impressive efficiency of insect breeding.

Unfortunately, when I followed a pleasant little walkway along the river, I caught the evening ebb, when mosquitoes were multiplying furiously. In less than a minute on the boardwalk outside the hotel, I had half a dozen bites, each as vicious as those in any northern forest. Flailing my arms, I retreated quickly to Main Street and the cover of exhaust fumes. I wanted to be up early the next morning anyway, for the Moncton farmers' market.

⸻

It must be said that real Canadian farmers are more inclined to spend their weekend mornings at Wal-Mart than at a farmers' market, so I was not surprised to reach Moncton's Saturday market and find nothing but casually dressed city folk selling pickles, candies, kebabs, baked goods and some locally grown produce. The vegetables were kept to the side, like something destined for a remainder bin. This only meant the city's tastes were changing, Dina Zahir explained, as she sold homemade koftas in the indoor market's central aisle.

I was as shocked as anyone to see koftas in Moncton, but at eight in the morning Dina was already doing a brisk business. Her past struggles and future hopes said a good deal about her evolving city and about the Maritimes too, and how it had changed since my grandfather's day. Dina was an Afghan refugee who had immigrated to Canada the previous year after a seven-year wait for a visa in India, where she and her family had lived in exile. She is the sort of woman who once made Afghanistan the jewel of central Asia. She had trained as an economist in Russia and worked under the Communist government in Kabul until it fell in 1992, when she and her husband and two children fled to New Delhi.

They ended up in Moncton for no other reason than a Canadian immigration officer in New Delhi said it was a good place to live. Moncton? Dina had never heard of it. She certainly did not know there was only one mosque and no other Afghans in the city. But at least, she said, "it's safe," which was no small observation for someone coming from Kabul. She intended to stay, hoping to see her two children through university in Moncton. She was also studying at a local college, with plans to become an accountant. The kofta business paid for her tuition.

Canada's image as a haven of multiculturalism focused mostly on the big three cities, Toronto, Montreal and Vancouver, which often act like they're the only destination for immigrants. But as I could see up and down the aisles of the Moncton farmers' market, the country's diversity was becoming more widespread. In the stall next to Dina, a Lebanese woman named Fahda was busy selling her own kebabs. "I love it here," she said. Her only complaints regarded the weather and mosquitoes.

Despite their very different heritages, the two women attended the same mosque, where Lebanese, Egyptians, Pakistanis and Indians alike—along with the lone Zahirs of Afghanistan—formed a single congregation that blended streams of Islam, languages and styles of worship. Quite unintentionally, Moncton's only mosque was bringing together the world in ways that bigger cities, with their ethnic ghettos, had not. Oddly, little Moncton was becoming cosmopolitan.

——— ——— ———

Still dozy from Friday night on Main Street and an early start at the farmers' market, I headed back to the highway on a city bus, nodding unquestioningly to the driver who said I should get off at the closest intersection to downtown. I should have remembered that downtown on-ramps are the bubonic plague of hitchhiking. You can wave hundred-dollar bills at passing cars and none will stop. Most are going to the next interchange, or maybe the one after that. And those headed out of town, well, they're at the start of their journey and have better things to consider than appraising a person on the roadside—like which CD to play. Besides, they might well ask, what kind of bum needs a ride from downtown on a Saturday morning? Isn't that where the shelters and drunk tanks are?

After half an hour on the central Moncton on-ramp, I started to walk. The last straw was watching another hitchhiker do the same. He looked like he had been walking from Saint John. When I caught up with him on the gravel shoulder, we stood together long enough to be nearly knocked over as a convoy of trucks blew by, leaving a hurling wind in their wake. We agreed to split up.

Still walking a few kilometres later, I saw a big-box mall on the horizon that told me I must be close to the city's edge. It was the crossover of the Trans-Canada and the coastal road, which I wanted to follow to Prince Edward Island. I had seen the new New Brunswick, with its digital ambitions and immigrant dreams. I wanted to see some of the old.

Now a hundred metres ahead of the other hitchhiker, I knew I had the upper hand. Drivers who felt guilty about passing him would surely stop for me. I dropped my backpack and put out my thumb, only to see in a few minutes the other hitchhiker sailing past in the passenger seat of a pickup truck. He did not glance at me.

It was approaching noon and I was ready to head back to the farmers' market, to take up kebab-selling, when an old two-door Chevy pulled over. The driver said he was going to Shediac—"the Lobster Capital of Canada," according to my guidebook. I couldn't think of an older slice of New Brunswick, the Donald brothers' house excepted.

Serge was going home for the weekend. At twenty-seven, he was living in Moncton and studying civil engineering, while his wife, who worked as a waitress in a restaurant on Main Street, supported their two children. She was pulling in about $800 a week.

We drove along the divided highway to Shediac at a ferocious speed, Serge assuring me that no police would be on the road at this time of day. "There are too many girls in bikinis at the beach," he said. We were there in ten minutes.

The beach at Shediac has for at least a century been a magnet to girls, and lots of other people, from Quebec. People flock there every summer for the abundant sandbars and warm, shallow seawater (about twenty degrees Celsius in July and August), French-speaking waitresses, and lobsters, which were thought to be so abundant they could roll onto the beach like seashells.

At the main entrance to the town, a giant lobster set the tone. Tourists were lined up to be photographed next to one of the dangling claws before buying the latest catch at a drive-through window. The lobster frenzy continued along the main street, where every other shop sold something to do with the creature. There were lobsters by the pound, lobster on pizza, lobster sandwiches and plates of lobster for $25. I saw everything except lobster ice cream, but I admit I didn't look very hard. Lobster seemed to flow in the veins of Shediac, which made one small fact all the more curious.

According to Serge, there were just about no lobsters left in the warm waters that stretched from the town's wharf to the horizon.

The collapse of the lobster fishery was a well-told political story, blamed on native fishermen, white fishermen, foreign boats, global warming—just about anything, depending on who was doing the blaming. As he gave me a quick tour, Serge said he wasn't sure who was responsible, but he knew it had ended generations of lobster fishing in his family. He was not complaining, either.

He first learned to trap lobsters with his grandfather, a legendary Shediac fisherman who drank daily until his death, at the age of eighty-seven. And they weren't nips of brandy. The old man, an Acadian, put back "a pint of the hard stuff" every day, Serge boasted. But even in his grandfather's last years, Serge could see that the lobster catch was waning. He also began to notice how tourism was quickly outpacing the old fishery. After finishing high school, he took up construction work, renovating local houses for the influx of Québécois and American visitors. His older brother had also forgone the family fishing trade to start his own business fixing high-performance boat engines. Both young men owned their own houses. Serge had two.

On the main street of Canada's lobster capital, I noticed a steady stream of Mercedes-Benzes, all with Quebec licence plates. Down on the wharf was a different picture. There, Serge showed me lobster crates stacked high on the docks when they should be out in the water. The season had been delayed again for a lack of supply. I asked about the shops and restaurants we had passed. The lobsters for sale in Shediac, Serge said softly, as if not to incite a mass panic, came from New England.

None of the locals appeared to mind, though. The wharf was thriving with new businesses—bars, ice-cream stands and boat tours among them. "I'd like to move back," Serge said. "The pace is easy here." He figured a civil engineering degree would help him do more than renovate houses. He could set up his own building business, on land, which had always been more profitable than a life on the water.

Serge dropped me at the giant lobster—"largest in the world," one sign read—and pointed to a nearby on-ramp to the coastal highway. If I was lucky, he said, I would get a quick ride to Prince Edward Island. I had been on the move for four hours and covered only twenty-two kilometres. Had I walked, I would have been four kilometres closer to P.E.I. by now. I definitely did not feel lucky.

It didn't take me long to realize that Serge had, unintentionally I think, given me a bum steer. The on-ramp from Shediac was a kilometre before the highway forked to Moncton in one direction and toward P.E.I. in the other. When a couple of cars stopped and offered me a lift back to the very spot where I had started that morning, I realized I was going backwards. I took my bag and walked along the highway's edge to the next interchange, where in a few minutes an old Pontiac pulled over. I was moving again.

Dressed in shorts, a singlet and Adidas sandals, the Pontiac's driver looked fit and tanned, especially for a trucker. Guy said he was in the lobster business, driving truckloads of them up and down the coast. But today he was off duty and on his way to Cap-Pelé, another seaside town crowded with Québécois and New Englanders, an odd mix one finds only on the Northumberland Strait and in Miami Beach. He confirmed the rumour about Shediac's missing lobsters. Just the other day, he had brought a full truckload from Maine to a Shediac restaurant that was desperate for a fresh "catch of the day."

In our short ride, Guy told me how he managed to look more like a fisherman than a trucker. At Cap-Pelé, there was a new board-walk, where he could exercise among the throngs of Québécois who have given up suntanning for walking and running. He also ate nothing but local food. New England lobster, he sneered, twitching his handlebar moustache—he wouldn't touch the muddy creatures.

Doubling my distance for the day, the thirty-kilometre jump to Cap-Pelé felt extraordinary, until Guy directed me to the most forsaken hitchhiking spot I had ever seen. His turnoff was in the middle of nowhere, a narrow exit surrounded by forest and a thin strip of divided highway that carried so little traffic it felt like it was closed for the weekend. When a car or truck passed—every five minutes or so—it went hurtling by at such a speed that I had to cover my mouth to avoid swallowing a trail of summer dust. Suddenly, New Brunswick drivers seemed very fast.

I was forty-three kilometres from Confederation Bridge, the engineering wonder that links the mainland to Prince Edward Island. Too far to walk, and yet no hope of turning back. Even Cap-Pelé was a few kilometres off the highway, scuttling any hope of a quick drink. At points like this I was beginning to curse my decision to bring a guidebook as my sole piece of reading material. By Newfoundland, I'd be ready for something like the *Canadian Encyclopedia*. I was about to turn my attention to roadside mind games—singing tunes from *Oklahoma,* followed by a reverse listing of Stanley Cup winners—when a dark green van pulled onto the shoulder, skidding to a halt about fifty metres beyond me. I grabbed my bag and ran toward it, fearing that as soon as I got within spitting distance the driver would speed off.

As I reached the van, a side door slid open. A man in his thirties sat in the driver's seat. A woman of about the same age was in the front passenger's seat. The middle bench had been removed, leaving a metal floor covered with empty food packages. Everything else about the van told me to pass on the ride. I was outnumbered. All the windows except the front were tinted, allowing no one outside to see me in the back. From the roadside, I could also see an empty beer can next to the driver's seat. Worst of all, the driver was not committed to a destination. He wanted to know first where I was going.

Every basic rule I knew about hitchhiking safety was being broken. So I still don't understand why I hopped in. Perhaps it was
because I knew I couldn't get beyond the '87 Edmonton Oilers, or
bear the thought of another round of "The Surrey with the Fringe
on Top." Whatever the reason, I said hello to Joe and Judy and slid
the door shut.

I had yet to reach the back bench when Joe, the driver, tore
ahead. He still had two wheels on the shoulder as the speedometer,
as far as I could see, passed eighty. "I was doin' her pretty good last
night, John," Joe shouted from the front. "I went to bed about the
time I usually get up, so there's still some intoxicants in me."

I thought about asking Joe to stop, but then looked through the
front and rear windows. There wasn't a vehicle in either direction.
Besides, Joe had just put in a CD of the Celtic band Kilt playing a
cover version of the Kiss classic "I Was Made for Loving You." If my
number was up, at least I wouldn't have Shirley Jones in my head.
And if it wasn't, we'd be on the island in less than half an hour.

Once Joe was on the highway, I realized why he had stopped for
me. Judy wanted nothing to do with him. She said they were on their
way from Moncton to Prince Edward Island for a long weekend of
watching the Tall Ships. "And partying," Joe added.

Feet perched on the dashboard, Judy, a nurse, kept to her John
le Carré novel, du Mauriers and coffee, while Joe proceeded to
work off his hangover by telling me his life story. Born in a small
town outside Bathurst, in northern New Brunswick, he had lived
in Moncton for five years, working most of the time as a vending
machine operator. That explained the missing middle seat. He
had removed it to make room for boxes of potato chips and
chocolate bars.

Sensing Judy would be more illuminating, I asked her why she
stayed in the Maritimes, when nurses had their pick of jobs all over
the continent. She said she had just turned down a $10,000 signing
bonus from a hospital in Toronto, and a $1,500 bonus to go to the
United States just for three months. She liked the laid-back lifestyle,

and cheap housing, of Moncton, and she could get to beautiful Prince Edward Island in less than an hour. In Toronto, she couldn't get past the suburbs in that time.

I noticed Joe did not appear happy about spending part of his weekend listening to people talk about the brain drain, in his van no less. His brain was suffering enough already. He reached behind Judy's seat, where there was a small cooler, and fished out a can of Guinness, which he offered me. I declined, figuring I might as well confirm his beliefs about English Protestant Toronto. He was blessed with strong Irish blood, he said, and always happy to down another pint.

As Judy returned to her book, Joe cranked up the Kilt CD—they were on to Newfoundland folk tunes—and blissfully sped along the empty highway, singing at full volume with each tune. I sat silently in the back seat, staring at the windshield straight ahead and wondering if my backpack, fixed strategically on my lap, would see me through a crash.

Before I could worry more about fatal collisions, though, I noticed a sign for the Confederation Bridge, and a long line of cars ahead of us. The approach road to the bridge had narrowed to two lanes, just as traffic was backing up, but that did not worry Joe. He lit up a joint and took to the lane of oncoming traffic, passing three cars in the time it took him to exhale a good toke. "Let's let her rip," he shrieked. We missed the first oncoming car by a few metres.

I glanced at Judy. She had barely looked up from her book. Her feet were still on the dashboard. Strangely, she looked bored.

As we approached the next group of cars in front of us, Joe took another quick toke. He seemed angry. "I hate lookin' at bicycles," he cursed. A van in front of us had two bikes strapped to its rear. I was expecting Joe to ram the bikes when he quickly swerved into the lane of oncoming traffic to overtake the van and another car. Once we were back in our proper lane, he finished the joint and offered an explanation of his contempt for bike-toting vans. "You can't always see the brake lights," he said, looking at me in the rear-view mirror. "It's a bit of a safety hazard, if you ask me."

Up ahead, traffic on Confederation Bridge had come to a stop to allow a construction crew to do some midsummer work on an addition to the bridge. A new scenic lookout was supposed to make more room for camera-wielding tourists who in the first two years of operations had caused an inordinate number of accidents. Joe put the van in park and suggested we get out for a better view of the bridge while we waited.

When it opened in 1997, the bridge, at thirteen kilometres, was the world's longest, connecting Cape Jourimain in New Brunswick with Borden-Carleton on the island. It consists of forty-four spans, some rising the equivalent of twenty storeys above the straits below. It cost the Canadian government, which built it, $900 million. But more than any other reason, the bridge had made history because it ended the physical isolation of the very province where Canada, the nation, was born.

I was leaning against the bridge's rails, staring through an afternoon haze at the island's snowy white beaches, when Joe urged me to look the other way. The bucolic shores of New Brunswick, he said, where Acadians had turned swampland into wheat fields, had become an ideal spot for growing pot. Actually, Joe continued, correcting himself, the best spots for that were in the basements of Moncton, where a thriving hydroponics industry had found its ultimate cash crop in the form of marijuana. Anyone could now go to Toronto, buy some marijuana plants and bring them home to a basement farm, he explained. "You can clear a hundred thousand dollars a year," he said. "Easy."

I wasn't sure if he was making me a business proposition or simply offering a helpful tourist tip, but Joe lit another joint and continued to describe Moncton's real new economy. The biggest danger, he said, was a recent spate of police busts on home-based operations, apparently for political reasons. What would all these self-starters do, he wondered, for employment? And what would the province's youth turn to for stimulation?

"The worst thing they did was crack down on grass," he said. "All those kids, they turned to the hard stuff. There was nothing else for them. I don't like the hard stuff. I've done heroin. Didn't like it. I just like something to make me numb."

Joe flicked the remains of his joint into the Northumberland Strait, twenty storeys and $900 million below us. I thought about walking the rest of the way to the island, until I remembered that it would be illegal, and there was a good chance I'd be ticketed. There'd be no chance of hitching a ride from here, either. I was stuck with Tokin' Joe.

As traffic resumed and followed the towering bridge down to the island, Joe stayed politely in line, all the time trying to humour Judy. "Hay, hay, hay," he blurted out as we reached land and saw a freshly harvested field. She looked up briefly before returning to her book.

In another field, not far from the bridge, I noticed a tractor pull and leapt at my opportunity. "Hey Joe," I shouted above the full volume of Kilt. "Do you mind pulling over? There's a tractor pull going on. I've always wanted to see one."

Joe glanced at me in the rear-view, unable to hide his disappointment. He had been looking forward to a good bender with me in Charlottetown. Now, and he didn't have to say this, he'd be stuck with Judy. Or rather, she'd be stuck with him.

I apologized to Joe and thanked Judy for her company. I think I was out of the van before it came to a complete stop, but not before Joe could give me a quick list of tips for hitchhiking. "Always ask the driver first where he's going," he said. "If he says he's just driving, don't get in. I'd just shut the door and wait for another ride. He may be a predator. You should also wait for a ride to a major destination. Never take a ride that's going to drop you in some rural place, like the place where we picked you up. You could have been there for days."

I sensed that Joe was genuinely concerned for my safety and I felt a tinge of regret as I watched his green van pull away. It wasn't just the loss of a good ride. Staring at the fields, I realized I had given up a Saturday night in Charlottetown for a tractor pull in Crapaud.

2

The Crapaud
Women's Institute

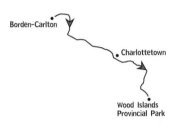

Borden-Carlton

Charlottetown

Wood Islands
Provincial Park

Crapaud, P.E.I., was a very different place from where I had come. There were no billboards, for one, at least not like in other provinces. On the island, every billboard had to be approved by the government and adhere to a provincial colour code. Everything else had the feel of a small town too—local licence plates with only five characters, for instance, like those outposts that need only four digits for a telephone number.

Walking down a dirt road to a field of parked vehicles, almost all of them pickup trucks, I reached the South Shore Tractor Pull, which promised to be everything the Moncton call centres were not. It seemed like the sort of down-home tradition that Maritimers believed could withstand the great tides of economic and social change in their region. It looked like the sort of activity that kept communities together, that kept young people from drifting to the city. It was also the sort of event that new Maritimers like Dina Zahir must have thought was imported from another planet.

As I approached the main event, the ground outside the bleachers rumbled slightly. I could hear a tractor's engine roar its last breath as it clawed its way through the final inches of mud, and then a loud cheer from the crowd. In a few moments, an announcer read out the result and suggested it had not been very good. "That's tractor pull for you," he told the crowd. "You miss a gear and it all changes."

I paid ten dollars for an entry ticket, said no to a one-dollar pair of earplugs and made my way to the front side of the bleachers that had been erected in a farmer's field. The last available seats were up in the back row, by a family with three young boys who were cheering for the next contestant as if their favourite hockey team had just taken to the ice. At the far end of the field was a lineup of tractors, most of them looking spiffy and souped-up, awaiting their shot at the title. When it came their turn, each would be saddled with a category of weights that it had to haul through mud until the tractor could move no more. But before the next tractor could run the course, we had to wait for a steamroller to run over the lanes, smoothing the ground like a Zamboni at the rink.

The boys beside me ate ice-cream sandwiches and watched, making sure the steamroller didn't miss a single rut or groove left by the last tractor. Then, when the steamroller was safely off the mud track, an umpire in front of our bleacher waved a flag, signalling for the next contestant to fire his engine just loud enough to buckle the middle spans of Confederation Bridge. I instantly regretted not buying the earplugs.

The tractor, with four tonnes of weights hooked to its rear, roared down the track, spraying a cloud of red dust in its wake. Shifting gears as he raced ahead, the driver not only had to keep moving forward; he needed to delicately balance his machine on all four wheels to prevent the most common catastrophe known to tractor pulling, when one wheel assumes too much weight and digs itself quickly and irretrievably into a rut. The tractor looked like a bull charging a red cape as it barrelled ahead, nimbly jumping a foot to the left and then back to the right when it needed to regain its balance. Like every other machine in the competition, it also looked like it had never seen a real potato field.

Dirt continued to spray in every direction until the entire crowd, except for me, turned their faces away from the tractor and covered their snacks. And to think I could have hit the Tall Ships with Joe. Dirt continued to billow at the crowd as the tractor, spinning its big rear wheels, frantically scratched a few more inches out of the track. It was over. With not another inch to be gained, the driver turned off his engine, leaving the field to its serenity. The dust settled. Spectators politely brushed their shirts and shook their billed caps. I alone had to wipe my face.

The driver climbed out of his tractor to watch a couple of field judges measure the last forward movement of his front wheels, and then a great cheer went up, led by the boys beside me. Their tractor was the new leader.

After watching a few unsuccessful attempts to break the new mark, with my ears throbbing and nostrils plugged with dirt, I decided to retreat to the car park. The tractor teams were there preparing for the next weight category. At the far end of the first row of trucks, I found a man lounging in the front seat of his cab while his two boys fiddled with a rear tire on their tractor, which was perched on a trailer. The man looked like he would be willing to entertain a few dumb questions.

Ricky Springer had come to the South Shore Tractor Pull with his wife and two sons because that's what they did most weekends in summer. During the week, he worked as a food inspector in Waterville, New Brunswick, up the Saint John River, near the Maine border, about fifteen kilometres west of where my grandfather was raised. But on his days off in August, Ricky liked little more than a good tractor pull. For him, it was the hockey of summer, an exhibition of human spirit so essential to his way of life that every year on their wedding anniversary he gave his wife tractor-pull tickets. (He always remembered the date because it was when he took up pulling, on their tenth anniversary.)

"I've always been involved in motor sports," he explained when I asked why he would haul his tractor and family five hundred kilometres just to watch people get stuck in the mud. "In high school, I drag-raced a little on weekends. In drag racing, it's kind of winner takes all. Here, you can finish in fifth place and still get something."

This was no leisure pursuit, not when the Springers spent every weekend driving across the Maritimes and sometimes into Maine. Ricky had won the Maritimes' 5,800-pound division—the lightweight of tractor pulls—in five of the past eight years. This weekend, he figured he and his boys, Adam and Ryan, would earn enough prize money to pay for the family's gas, food and hotel.

Ricky himself had grown up on a farm, but like my grandfather and so many other young people in rural New Brunswick he did not see a good future on the land. He chose to finish high school, study at college and move to a nearby town, where he had a salary and steady hours for six months of the year. The remaining months, he worked on the family farm, where he had built a house near his parents'.

He knew his sons would not find many prospects there. The neighbours were all selling their land or borrowing $500,000 to buy more property and expand. The most profitable farms in western New Brunswick were the big corporate operations, and they mostly grew potatoes for the McCain family and their frozen french fry empire based in Florenceville, on the Saint John River.

Quietly, beginning in the 1970s, this movement away from family farming had produced the biggest shift Canada had seen in a century. Nearly a million Canadians like Ricky Springer had given up on the land. According to Statistics Canada, 313,000 Canadians now derive their primary income from farming, down from 1.2 million when Ricky's dad was a kid in the Second World War. At least one reason was obvious. After inflation, net farm incomes were one-quarter what they were in 1975. And it was true across the country, from the potato farmers of New Brunswick to the dairy herders of Ontario and the wheat growers of Saskatchewan.

It is all the more amazing, then, to consider that food production is at record levels, as we consume sandwiches, milkshakes and potato chips at rates my grandfather, the lumberjack, could not have imagined. The humble french fry has become a huge global industry, consuming eighty-five per cent of all potatoes harvested in North America. The McCains, the people who make a good chunk of those fries, had become billionaires off our changing diet, and transformed Florenceville as a result. They brought in international standards, a slick marketing machine and a hyper-efficient production line that helped make some local farmers very rich. Those were the ones who went deeper into debt to buy more land and machinery, bulking themselves up into a corporate operation.

Ricky admitted he was not aggressive enough to do that, to bet his parents' farm on a global market, but he was proud of the McCains nonetheless. After a century of economic and human migration from New Brunswick to Ontario, they had created a global company in his neck of the woods, right on the land my grandfather had helped clear before he packed up for Toronto. Ricky also saw how free trade with the United States had led to far more demand for their french fries than they had had from any previous deal with Ontario and Quebec. The McCain business was going so strong, Ricky said, they couldn't get enough workers for a new data centre in Florenceville.

As a food inspector, Ricky was now part of this Maritime middle class that was lifting the region out of poverty, but also placing it on the endless track of commercialism that he saw threatening the spirit of the Saint John River valley. When he was a kid, he worked summers hauling big square hay bales. Now he saw kids turning down farm jobs for easier shifts at the fast-food restaurants in town, if they worked at all. Nick the tennis pro sprang to mind.

"The fifties and sixties were relatively hard times," Ricky continued. "I remember the big thing as a kid was going to town on Friday night to get the groceries. That was it. That was our entertainment." A memorable car trip would be to Perth, a town forty-five minutes away by road.

These days, Ricky took his family out for dinner one night a week and went on road trips several times a month. The boys played hockey all over the province, and he was putting in extra hours to pay for twelve-year-old Ryan's goaltender equipment as well as a special new hockey stick for fourteen-year-old Adam. He had to drive an hour to Fredericton to buy Adam that one.

"Everyone wants better for their kids than they had for themselves. Oh my Lord, that's just human nature," Ricky said a bit sheepishly.

We were sitting in the front seat of his pickup truck, gabbing like old friends, which is what people in the Maritimes do, even when they're with strangers. This weekend was special for the Springer family, a passage of sorts, because it was Adam's first time at the wheel in competition. The two boys were still behind the truck, fiddling with the wheel alignment. I asked Ricky to explain the skills he had tried to pass on to Adam and wondered how they might draw on their Waterville spirit.

"Oh my Lord, tire pressure is crucial," he started. Get the pressure wrong and you'll be spinning your wheels faster than a potato dicer. "You also have to keep your weight balanced," he added. Get the weight on the wrong wheel and there you go, straight off course. Avoid the brakes, too. Just tapping on the brakes could cost you ten feet. "Oh my Lord, ten feet can drop you from first to last," Ricky exclaimed. He said "Oh my Lord" a lot.

Most importantly, Ricky concluded, you have to study the mud like a farmer studies his soil. If you don't know every soft patch, dip and rut, you might as well drive blindfolded. "Drag racing, you just release the brake and go. This is a balancing act. Every track is different. This track is different than it was last night." Just last night, Adam, in his very first competition, had veered into a dip that his father, before the race, had urged him to avoid. The boy came second.

Ricky put it down to the soft, sandy P.E.I. soil, which required a different pace of gear shifting.

Smart driving used to make all the difference in tractor pulls, but technology was fast becoming the key to victory. Ricky first got into tractor pulling with a used frame and engine he bought from a junkyard. Today, he was thinking of buying a new $10,000 engine just to stay with the pack. He knew his main competitors were buying new engines, especially automatics that could eliminate the human error he sometimes encountered with his slipper clutch. "I have to decide whether to spend the money or settle for seconds," he said.

Buying his way to the podium was not what Ricky wanted from tractor pulls, just as he didn't like to have to fork out a thousand dollars to dress his son in goalie equipment. At times like these, the hard times of the sixties, when you drag-raced on the road and played hockey on a pond, seemed appealing. He just hoped his summer sport would not lose its essential good.

Last Saturday night, he explained, his voice softening for a moment with emotion, he found himself in the garage with Adam. "Oh my Lord, I was thinking, 'Jesus, how many fourteen-year-olds are home with their fathers on a Saturday night?' To have that kind of relationship, it kind of chokes you up.

"You don't need alcohol. You don't need drugs when you're drivin' one of these things," Ricky continued, with pride returning to his voice. "I know where my young feller is on a Friday or Saturday night. He's down in the shed working on the tractor."

We could have talked for the rest of the day, but Ricky had to excuse himself to prepare for the next competition. As I returned to the bleachers, I looked back to see him talking with Adam and Ryan about the intricacies of a front axle. The boys were spellbound.

— — —

Not quite ready for another mouthful of dust, I skirted the bleachers to an ice-cream stand that was run by the Crapaud Women's Institute. The very name reminded me that I was on an island. In more than geography, and in more ways than a bridge can ever change, Prince Edward Island is different from the rest of the Maritimes, and very different from the rest of Canada. To begin with, just about every community on the island has a Women's Institute, a group of twenty or thirty women who raise money for hospitals, run social events and advise the provincial government on a range of issues. They are the Green Gables.

I found Anna Stewart, president of the Crapaud Women's Institute, behind the ice-cream counter, serving an unending line of dusty spectators, all to raise money for some local cause. When I asked if she could spare a few minutes, she handed her scoop to another lady, wiped her hands on her apron and sat down to explain that this was what they did every summer, as religiously as Ricky hauled his tractor around three provinces and New England.

Through special events, bake sales, fundraising dinners and fun nights, the Crapaud Women's Institute raised a few thousand dollars a year for the Queen Elizabeth Hospital in Charlottetown and to send patients to other provinces for additional care. The group also helped the local community put on something most nights of the year, whether it be a village meeting, a card party or an adult-learning class in the local school.

Anna said the community classes were unique to P.E.I., where during the winter schools were kept open one evening a week for adult classes given by local volunteers. Anna had taught sewing in the local school for twenty years, from New Year's to Easter. Her neighbours gave lessons in guitar playing, conversational French and cooking to two hundred Crapaud adults.

Jokingly, I said I would hate to own the local cable licence. Imagine your entire market being in a classroom during sweeps week. But Anna took me quite seriously. The Women's Institutes worked diligently to protect their communities from unwanted out-side forces. It's what islanders had to do, she said. Two years earlier, a band of Women's Institutes pressured the provincial government to ban video gambling machines from corner stores. Taking on a five-year-old industry that generated lots of profits was no easy feat, politically. But "it was ruining families and lives," Anna said. "People became addicted."

The women won. The machines were banished from the island.

Anna was not sure why her group was so grandly called an *institute*, when *association*, *movement* or *revolutionary force* might do. They had no letterhead or alumnae group, not even a building to call their own. The name at least gave an air of permanence to the ice-cream vendors.

But there was one issue on which the women were divided: the bridge. Even before Confederation Bridge opened in 1997, there were apocalyptic predictions for the island's culture. At one point, Friends of the Island, a group whose mission was to block the bridge at all costs, took the federal government to court, claiming the bridge would harm the local fishery. A judge threw out the case, arguing a narrow stretch of concrete could not do much harm to the lobsters of Northumberland Strait. Maybe he knew there were no lobsters left.

Tourism was changing the island anyway. For decades, P.E.I. had attracted planeloads of visitors from Japan, where Anne of Green Gables enjoys a cult-like following among young women who know a thing or two about cultural repression. As many as ten thousand Japanese tourists a year come to the island, often to be wed at Silver Birch in Park Corner where Anne's creator, Lucy Maud Montgomery, was married in 1911.

And this is what tourism had done: Not far from Montgomery's one-time home on the north shore, someone had built a Ripley's Believe It or Not Museum and a life-size replica of the space shuttle. What the space shuttle had to do with the island was unclear, but it attracted a good many more visitors than the P.E.I. Potato Museum, way up the road in O'Leary. Tactless or not, the attractions all pre-dated The Bridge, which was why Anna shook her head at the fuss. She knew that nothing short of quarantine would keep away summer hordes from her island's beaches and the benevolent Gulf Stream current that warms its sea waters. Of course, the Trans-Canada

Highway, which runs by her house and the small coffee shop she owns, had seen a big increase in traffic. Bridges tend to do that. But it also meant she and her husband, a developer, could get off the island whenever they wished. No longer did they have to wait hours, sometimes days during a storm, for a ferry to New Brunswick.

Not all members of the Crapaud Women's Institute agreed. Some had suggested the bridge would bring dereliction and vice from the mainland. In Joe and Judy, they had a case. Others talked of wild New Brunswick drivers running down their dogs or, worse, their cows. I'm not sure those women had spent much time on Highway 1, the go-slow road in Kings County, but Anna listened to them, to a point.

"The one criticism people made the most was the bridge would change the island's way of life," she said, as we sat in the shade of her ice-cream stand. "As far as I can tell, it hasn't changed a thing. We're still islanders, even though there's a bridge. We have boundaries. You're constantly keeping those boundaries in the back of your mind. All island people, I think, are like that. I think it makes you more close-knit. You have to live on an island, probably, to understand it."

The idea of invisible boundaries was something most Canadians never had to worry about. There was almost something class-like about it, that idea of knowing one's place. It was enough to drive many people away, but it also brought a large number back. Anna's own son, who had moved to southern Ontario for university and stayed on to work for a large multinational company, would not stay away from P.E.I. forever, she said. "They all come back. The island draws them back. The island. The island."

Back at the main field, the tractor events were over, and they were on to four-wheel-drive trucks. I decided to move on, walking down the dirt road to the Trans-Canada, where it was getting late in the afternoon and traffic was thinning. Fortunately, hitchhiking is considered a form of public transport on the island, and a car stopped

within a minute of me putting out my thumb. It was a four-by-four
Jeep Cherokee with leather seats and a good stereo—the perfect
antidote to a dusty afternoon of tractor pulls. When the driver, a
farm equipment dealer named Jimmy, said he was going only fifteen
kilometres, I wanted to cry.

From the comfort of Jimmy's Jeep, I could appreciate the
island's rolling pastoral beauty as it eased from one picture-book
scene into another. Herds of black-and-white dairy cows. Emerald
green pastures. Clapboard cottages by the sea. A golf course for
every six thousand people. This was more than the work of a wise
law against garish billboards. This was a place without an apparent
worry in the world.

But P.E.I. could be deceptive. Almost 130 years after the island
joined Confederation, it was little more than a dependency, an outpost that without tourism and federal transfer payments would sink
into the economic sea. The island's population had been stuck at
140,000 since the 1930s. One-quarter of them depended on government for their employment. Equalization—a polite word for the
federal welfare guaranteed to the poorest provinces—remained the
island's biggest source of revenue.

Jimmy was trying to forge a different path on the island, by
making farm equipment for U.S. buyers. The free trade deal had
opened up that market, while the bridge allowed him, and his
equipment, to get across the water and onto the road to Maine at a
much faster clip. But much of the rest of the place, as pleasant as it
looked from a cruising position, appeared to be living in the past.

When Jimmy dropped me on the roadside, I had to wait for a
long line of tourist vehicles to pass, as I was unable to make eye contact with drivers seated so high in their vans and motorhomes.
There were licence plates from British Columbia, Texas, California
and, curiously, Hawaii before a local car came into view and
stopped. A young swimming instructor, who was on her way home
from work, offered to take me to the edge of Charlottetown, where
she told me I would find that familiar, dispiriting strip of big-box

stores. Tourists may flock to the quaint craft shops, the swim teacher said. Locals preferred Home Depot.

A few minutes up the road, she apologized for having to drop me in such a bland place. Had she not been headed to her cottage for the night, she said, she would have shown me the city, which is what islanders apparently do with out-of-province hitchhikers. When I reached a bed and breakfast, after a couple of quick rides, the homeowners also said they were sorry for not being able to show me around town. They were on their way out the door for an evening at the racetrack, which, if you had seen the local production of *Anne of Green Gables* ("Canada's favourite musical") a hundred times, was the last decent nightlife left in Charlottetown. Sadly, Festival of the Fathers—a re-enactment of the original Confederation conference, with street musicians, dances and a ten-tavern pub crawl—was not on until later in the month.

——— ——— ———

Before the bridge was built, the farthest the residents of Tignish could drive from their homes on the northern tip of the island was 143 kilometres—and then they were on their way home again. Distances in the province were so short that you could live happily on the island buying a new car every couple of decades or so. I learned this from Gerry and Louise, an older couple who picked me up early Sunday morning on the outskirts of Charlottetown. They had come to the capital for breakfast and a bit of a drive. But as much as they liked to cruise around the island, Gerry and Louise had put only 165,000 kilometres on their '86 LTD.

What the islanders lacked in distance, they made up for with speed. I was barely buckled into the back seat when I noticed the old speedometer passing 140. It settled down at 180. The LTD's cassette deck, blaring a Best of the Seventies tape, was on high volume. "You probably noticed even we old guys on the island like to go fast," Gerry said, taking another drag from his Export A.

Gerry and Louise, both chain-smokers in their sixties, were very different islanders from the ones I had met at the tractor pull. I suspected Louise, who sat silently, locked in her smoke-shrouded bubble, had little time for a local Women's Institute. I was not sure Gerry, who hacked violently when he wasn't inhaling, had darkened the doors of many golf clubs, either, even though he said he worked at one as a groundskeeper.

But he loved to gab, and that made him a good Maritimer. He said he left the island no more than once a year, usually to go to New Brunswick "just to poke around." The bridge made no difference to his plans. No matter how he got to the mainland, he felt uncomfortable there. Once, many decades ago, he went as far as British Columbia and decided never to go west again. "Didn't like it at all," he said. "The people were too crabby, too cranky."

Ahead of us on the two-lane road, I saw another car, with what looked like a Nova Scotia plate. I wasn't sure if Gerry saw it too. He certainly didn't slow down as the LTD hurtled like a tidal wave toward the little compact. "Look at that guy in front of us," he cursed. "Nova Scotia. From the big city and he's slowin' us down."

We passed the car at one-eighty.

Interprovincial rivalries were no small affair in the Maritimes, where the old Acadian contempt for Haligonian bluenoses and P.E.I. disdain for all things on the mainland remained a strong undercurrent in every conversation. The bridge wouldn't change that, Gerry said. There may be more traffic on the road and more golfers on his course, but the local people had not changed, he said. They remained islanders.

"We and the Newfies are pretty much the same: happy-go-lucky people," he said. "New people who come here, if there's a storm and you can't move for a few hours, they get upset. We don't."

"Bad, Bad Leroy Brown" was playing on the car stereo when Gerry pulled over to the side of the road. "Well, this is where you'll have to get out," he said. I looked around. There were fields and woods on both sides of the road, and one building: a two-room shack on the other side. The only diversion that might cause any car to slow down was the shack's grassy driveway.

I was trying to figure out what I had said to deserve being dumped on the open road when the LTD drove onto the shack's front lawn, which was as crowded with cars as the field at the tractor pull. I remembered Gerry saying he liked to fix them up for sale, but the market these days was not so good, not when his neighbours could drive to the mainland, buy one and be home for lunch.

While I appreciated some fresh air after the smoke-filled LTD, I soon began to curse myself for forgetting Tokin' Joe's advice the previous day, that I should turn down rides to obscure rural areas. The first wave of cars passed me at such a clip that I had to hold on to my backpack for balance. About ten minutes passed before another car came and went. And then, every few minutes, one would blow by me at a hundred or more.

During the intervals, I watched crickets hop onto the highway and just as quickly jump back to safety in the tall roadside grass. This was pretty much all there was to look at. While P.E.I. is known the world over for its marathon stretches of wild, white beaches, rolling green pastures and finely manicured golf courses, the southern interior was not going to make many travel brochures. Slow-growth forests and unruly patches of wild grass looked like all the sandy soil could support. Even the junk on Gerry and Louise's front yard began to look rustic.

As I continued to stare at their modest house and its small front door, I wondered if I would be knocking on it for lunch. The rising heat was doing other strange things to my mind. After an hour or so on the open road, I began to record in my notebook the reaction of each driver. Out-of-province vans passed most frequently, usually with a man in the driver's seat and, in the front passenger's seat, a big unfolded map framed by female knuckles. Seldom did the man's lips seem to be moving. In some cars, the driver would lift all his fingers from the steering wheel, without losing his grip, as if to motion an apology. Others would point to a turn ahead, indicating they would soon be going in a different direction. Why people felt the need to gesture an excuse to a stranger baffled me, especially as they passed at such speeds, but it did look like a very Canadian thing to do. At least no one gave me the finger on Prince Edward Island.

Slowly it dawned on me that standing opposite a country shack would not exactly instill confidence in many drivers. So I took my pack and walked a kilometre down the road to a small intersection where I could stand by a side road and hope for traffic to emerge at a speed that would allow the driver to come to a halt in this province. More critically, there was a stretch of shoulder wide enough for a truck, which was where Alec pulled over.

After Anna of Green Gables and the car-happy hillbillies, Alec was just the sort of islander I was eager to meet. He came from somewhere else. In fact, he came from many places somewhere else. I knew this the moment he drove off at a reasonable speed. Alec was content never to pass a hundred. Born in Scotland and raised in Montreal, he had spent most of his working life on the West Coast as a computer technician, before taking an early retirement and moving the entire width of the country for another coast with cheaper real estate. Perhaps to Gerry he was crabby and cranky, but to me Alec was perfectly pleasant. He had chosen the southern tip of P.E.I. for his retirement because it was laid-back, had a decent climate and wasn't too far from a good airport, in Charlottetown.

"I look at a place in terms of convenience," he said. "I'm thirty minutes from the airport here, and then eight hours to anywhere in Canada. Same in Vancouver and I'd pay ten times more for a property."

It took a Scot to find value in an eight-hour journey. Unfortunately for Alec, he had mistimed the computer boom by a couple of decades and had not retired a dot-com millionaire, judging by his car. It was a beat-up old wreck, the kind that should have been on Gerry and Louise's front yard, not en route to the Wood Islands ferry landing, where he promised to drop me with the crowds waiting to go to Nova Scotia.

Unfortunately, Alec continued, as the road approached a more scenic seaside route, the island wasn't as accommodating as he had hoped it would be. For one, there was an unspoken gulf between islanders and mainlanders that no amount of time could bridge. Even after five years in a small town on the south side of P.E.I., Alec continued to be called a mainlander—an outsider—and figured he always would be.

"They often reject something because it's never been done that way here," he said of his neighbours. "That's not unique to P.E.I. or the Maritimes. I have brothers and sisters who live around Cornwall, you know, in eastern Ontario. They've been there thirty years and are still considered newcomers. I think small-town Canada is very clannish. It doesn't like to change."

In a nation that was once rooted in small towns, this sort of static was not insignificant, but it was losing its relevance, along with the provinces and regions and economic pursuits that once were essential to Confederation. We used to be people of the land, nurtured in places like P.E.I. and rural New Brunswick. Yet by 2000, there were more Canadians living in Scarborough, Toronto's maligned, crime-ridden suburb, than on all the farms across the country.

What was left of our hinterland was fast becoming a tourist zone, filled with golf courses and tractor pulls that starred salary-men and their sons. If the trend continued, if we continued to become a vast nation of urban islands with little more than lobster festivals, shacks and Ripley's Believe It or Not in between, we'd need a serious rethink of our self-image.

Perhaps we were no longer a nation of feuding regions, held together by history, convenience and fear of our large neighbour. Perhaps we had become like Alec, peripatetic and mobile, able to live in any place as long as there was an airport. But perhaps we were also a people so disconnected from our roots that all that held us together were summer vacations and a common taste for American television.

When Alec dropped me at the Wood Islands ferry landing, the first image of a migratory nation was hard to ignore. The approach road was jammed with vehicles from Ontario and every province east, and several American states too, though not Hawaii. With a gentle sea breeze struggling to break the midday heat, crowds of waiting passengers had turned the parking area into a Sunday playground. Between rows of cars waiting to board the ferry, travellers chatted with strangers about where they had come from, and where they were going. On a grassy ridge, circles of young men played hackeysack, leaving enough room for a gaggle of teenaged girls to sunbathe in their shorts and bikini tops. Farther ahead, toward the ferry, a cafeteria was packed with travellers in search of ice cream.

I walked leisurely to the loading zone, where a few walk-on passengers had gathered. We would easily get on the next ferry, which was due to leave for the Nova Scotia mainland in ninety minutes. Those with cars, fighting the weekend traffic, faced waits of three hours—more if they didn't have a reservation. For once, I felt glad to be on foot, even a bit superior to be hitchhiking. The flow of cars coming off the ferry near Pictou promised to be exceptional.

"One ever-lastin' sound of give, give, give"

NOVA SCOTIA

I stood alone on the upper deck, a breeze knotting my hair, as the lowlands of Prince Edward Island bobbed behind us like a kayak, peeking over each crest and then vanishing. Ahead, the highlands of Nova Scotia began to emerge.

As just about every name in the province suggests, Nova Scotia fancies itself as being Scottish, and nowhere more so than on the north shore where the ferry was about to land. Near present-day Pictou, at the head of an inlet where sailboats darted about in the afternoon breeze, the Highland Scots first landed in 1773. When Thomas Haliburton, the nineteenth-century satirist, arrived several decades later, he found nothing to the place but stone—"enough to starve a rabbit," he wrote. But so many Scottish immigrants followed that they soon were able to build a town on the stone, which they called New Glasgow, and started work building ships, mining coal and running blacksmith shops. Between 1770 and 1993, more than a million Scots moved to Canada, and they all seemed to settle in this pocket of the country.

Wisely, Pictou retained most of its seaside charm, with old stone buildings along the waterfront and a colony of shops run by painters, carvers and the Grohmann family, whose century-old knife business has produced some of the province's most celebrated exports. One of their pieces sits in New York's Museum of Modern Art. While I had wanted to stop in Pictou, near the ferry landing, I needed to get to Cape Breton by dark, to spend the next day seeing the one island that represents so much hardship and promise.

Hitching off the ferry, I figured, would be a breeze. I figured drivers would recognize me from the boat. I figured they would see me as a bona fide traveller on my way somewhere. What could be easier?

It was a disaster. One by one, the vehicles rolling off the ferry sailed past me with all the enthusiasm of those little boats on the water. Cars with bikes on their roofs, motorhomes, SUVs with big empty back seats: they all seemed to be in a desperate race up the hill from the ferry landing. Even the friendly Nova Scotia family I had chatted with on the upper deck raced by me like I was a souvenir stand that had closed for the season. Finally, a group of college kids offered me a lift up the hill to the nearest highway—if I didn't mind squeezing in with three of them in the back seat. This was no time to be picky. Theirs was among the last cars off the ferry.

The students dropped me at the "rotary," a roundabout connecting five roads, and pointed to the one leading to Cape Breton. The traffic was astounding, less for its volume than its wealth. After the ferry traffic waned, every other vehicle on the road was in the $30,000 range, with no shortage of fine cars and SUVs that would fetch much more. It wasn't Rosedale or Westmount, but it wasn't a Newfoundland outport either. Obviously, the people of New Glasgow had come a long way from their coal mining days—a long way, that is, if you don't have a visceral distaste for material success, as my next ride did.

After watching enough Lexuses pass for one afternoon, I didn't mind when a small car pulled over, especially when the driver said she was going to Antigonish, forty-five minutes up the highway. I hadn't forgotten all those short hops across P.E.I. A seventy-kilometre ride sounded like a moon shot.

Clearing the front seat of a few books and magazines, the middle-aged driver introduced herself as Anna Panagopoulos, a name that sounded ridiculously out of place in little Scotland. Anna said she felt out of place, too, which helped explain why a single woman would pick up a lone male hitchhiker. She wanted an audience. As she returned to the Trans-Canada, Anna wasted no time launching into a diatribe against consumerist Canada. All it took was an off-hand remark I had made about the shocking presence of big advertisements around New Glasgow, me having just come from the billboard-bashing republic of Prince Edward Island.

"We've been trained to work and buy, work and buy," Anna said, clutching the steering wheel hard enough that her knuckles stretched her skin. She wasn't angry. She just wanted another ciga-rette, judging by the butts piled high in the ashtray.

"People here, through media and consumerism, have been numbed out. They don't feel part of it. They're just part of a big machine. North Americans, what do they do? They work to buy, to keep their companies alive."

"This is really interesting," I said, pulling my notebook out of my raincoat's inside pocket. "Do you mind if I take some notes?"

I was lying, of course. For the first time since I had hit the road, I felt unsafe, and figured the notebook was my best protection. I had decided at the outset to be up front with every driver about my identity and purpose, treating each conversation as an interview. So far, almost every one was startled, and then delighted, to find a pas-senger so interested in their thoughts that he wanted to record them. It was a lonely driver's dream.

What I hadn't expected was how good a shield the notebook could become. For drivers who might have had weird thoughts about me, it said that I wasn't alone, that if they slit my throat and threw me into the Straits of Northumberland, *someone* might notice. But really, I think it was the way a notebook plays to most people's vanity that worked best. Who, least of all a chain-smoking socialist, could resist an interviewer in their front seat?

Anna explained she was a self-employed dressmaker in Antigonish, where she had spent most of her life since moving to

Nova Scotia, with her family, in the 1960s from Athens. Her single mother had decided this was a better spot to raise five children than revolutionary Greece. What young Anna found in friendly Nova Scotia was a bedrock of intolerance. The tough Cape Breton steel town of Sydney, where they first lived, was surprisingly cosmopolitan, perhaps because of the long history it had with shiploads of immigrants working in the local mill and coal mines. But Antigonish, a university town where they later lived, was about as parochial a place as they could have found in Canada.

"I never heard the word 'nigger' until I moved here," Anna said. When one of her brothers opened a restaurant near the campus of St. Francis Xavier University, hooligans smashed the windows and were heard cursing Greeks as they ran off.

Now forty, Anna put it down to the dominant Catholic Scottish culture of Nova Scotia's north coast, where the rising hills ahead of us were the most visible sign of how protected the area was from outside forces. The sandy coast was quickly giving way to sharp, rocky outcrops that bordered the Trans-Canada as it began to traverse a long series of hills extending to Cape Breton. It was easy to see why the early Scots felt at home.

I had to concede to Anna that the return of billboards was an appalling sight. In the middle of abandoned fields were signs for SportChek, Winners and Nike, as well as miniature golf courses and hotels that were at least half an hour away, as if families needed to fill their travelling time with lengthy debates about the merits of playing nine holes of mini-putt or eighteen. The signs were as obnoxious and unnecessary as those election campaign ads that appear a month before voting day, none more so than the most common billboard on the road. Whether on the edge of towns or in the middle of nowhere, there always seemed to be a sign ahead for McLobster.

Anna said the signs were a good indication of how the Maritimes had changed in just two decades. American retail and fast-food chains had formed such a tight ring around every significant town in her province that she had developed a tinge of sympathy for the

Sobeys and Irvings, the barons of Maritime business who, after decades of giddy monopoly power, found themselves up against the likes of Wal-Mart, a chain with more economic power than all of Atlantic Canada. When the richest people in the entire time zone are threatened, you know the change is serious.

"'What can I do?' That's all I hear from people," Anna said, launching into a Maude Barlow of the Maritimes routine. "If you really wanted to do something, you could not buy Nike. People don't know how much power they have. They can break what they've made, but they won't. They're the laziest people I've ever seen. People here are lazy. They're too comfortable. A hundred years ago, when there were only the rich and the peasants, the peasants knew how to revolt. Only in the last sixty years has there been a middle class. As long as you give them a little lifestyle, they won't complain."

Anna's eyes were firmly fixed on the road ahead, as if thoughts were racing like traffic through her mind. "It's a very good strategy," she said.

I found myself eagerly jotting down Anna's comments. Perhaps I was still reeling from the ride with Joe and Judy, but I began to think of Anna less and less as a raving retro-socialist. Her discontent could be heard in small towns as well as big cities, just not in the main arena of national politics. Around Nova Scotia, there were a growing number of citizen groups, trying to wrest control of the issues affecting their lives, just as the people of tiny Pugwash—150 kilometres on the other side of New Glasgow—once launched a movement to bring down nuclear arms.

The Trans-Canada Highway, now numbered 104, had narrowed to two lanes that shot like an arrow through the thick forests of northern Nova Scotia. Just before Antigonish, Anna pulled off 104 and followed the old highway to a roadside spring, where she refilled some jugs with fresh water from a pipe. She didn't like the chlorinated tap water in town.

I was intrigued that a local man had installed a pipe and tap by the roadside and did not object to anyone stopping and taking what they could. This was the sort of public gesture that probably helped the first generations of Scottish immigrants turn these forbidding hills into a thriving and prosperous society, with its own university. Anna said a newer generation was ready to squander what they had inherited. Even at the university, she found the new generation of affluent students—children of baby boomers, for the most part—to be apathetic in the face of what she saw as corporate domination.

"The children here don't look happy," she said, after loading several water jugs into her trunk. "They're totally discontent. They want this. They want that. They're being raised to be consumers. They'll never be happy like this. They need to wake up in this country. I've never seen such dead people in my life."

I was willing to go along with some of Anna's concerns until we reached Antigonish, a nineteenth-century town layered with twentieth-century fast-food joints. The outskirts were all McBigbox. The old main street was lined with small local shops doing a bustling business. There were a few signs for a local theatre festival and the Antigonish Scottish Highland Games, which had just passed. They had been running since 1861, making them North America's oldest, complete with pipe bands, Celtic dancers, kilted golfers and caber-tossers who showed no sign of succumbing to some new monolithic global order.

I wanted to put the point to Anna but we were already at her shop, and I needed to get back to the highway if I was to reach Cape Breton by dinner. As she lit another du Maurier, I didn't get to ask why she so willingly supported the most successful multinational industry going. I suspected she would have blamed the company.

―――   ―――   ―――

Anna reminded me of something else Thomas Haliburton observed about the people of Nova Scotia. They did nothing but talk. "You hear nothin' but politics, politics, politics, one ever-lastin' sound of give, give, give," he wrote in *The Clockmaker*. That was in 1836.

Haliburton should have spent time in Newfoundland, where a simple request for directions can turn into a vigorous hour-long debate about Confederation, and how Newfoundland was ripped off by the whole deal. But when it comes to the gab, Nova Scotia can give her a good run for her money. For starters, they usually blame the rest of Canada for their troubles. If a rural road in the province is cracked, it has to be Ottawa's doing—eleven hundred kilometres away. If the fish disappear, the interior provinces are at fault. If oil prices soar, there is Alberta to bring into question.

No one makes the point better than the Maritimes' designated finger-pointer, economist Donald Savoie, who blames it all on Confederation. "We got a raw deal, an incredibly raw deal, and the deal continues to this day," he wrote in a book that had just been released when I reached the province. "The region is not doing well because of federal government policy. That's not whining. That's fact."

The root of so much resentment in Atlantic Canada can be found less in Confederation than in the subsequent deals that ensured low-income provinces a share of the national wealth. A boondoggle to some, a welfare trap to others, a national linchpin to still more, these so-called equalization payments were as important as the sea air to understanding the Maritime mind, and there was no point in venturing far in the region without some acquaintance with their history.

Even at the start of the twentieth century, the Maritimes was not going places economically, as my grandfather well knew. By the Great Depression, the place was in such trouble that the Rowell–Sirois Commission floated the idea of transfer payments to maintain some balance in the country's economic growth and wealth. In 1939, the region was producing just five per cent of Canada's goods, a gap that continued to grow after the Second World War, when a new era of government investment poured billions of dollars into new state-owned enterprises in Ontario and Quebec. The Maritimes was left to rely on lumber and fish.

A formal program of transfer payments was enacted in 1957 and entrenched in the Constitution in 1982 so that Canadians could have "reasonably comparable levels of public services at reasonably comparable levels of taxation" no matter where they lived. By the end of the century, the four small eastern provinces were receiving $10 billion more a year from Ottawa than they were paying in taxes. The Nova Scotia government relied on federal transfer payments for twenty-eight per cent of its revenue, and the amount had more than doubled since the mid-eighties. Amazingly, half the province's roads remained unpaved.

The equations of economic development, however, were starting to change. The free trade agreement with the United States had opened up a giant corridor to New England, New York and beyond for just about anything Atlantic Canada wanted to produce. According to the Atlantic Provinces Economic Council, the region's international exports after the free trade agreement had grown twice as fast as its exports to the rest of Canada. The beach volleyball players of Saint John could thank that for their jobs. And now there was oil and gas. Every newspaper I had read since arriving in Saint John had carried articles about the huge finds lying off Cape Breton. There was enough wealth under the sea, it was suggested, to turn the region into a new Alberta, a land of untold prosperity. There might even be enough revenue to keep Nova Scotia politicians talking into the twenty-second century.

For all this hope, Canada's great tragedy lay up the road, on Cape Breton Island, where generations of government plans and bailouts were coming to an end. The northern tip of Nova Scotia once epitomized the hopes of development planning. But now, those plans were tarnished beyond repair. After nearly three centuries of operation, Cape Breton's coal mines were about to close. So was the steel mill at Sydney, one of the great all-time siphons of government money. Even the unemployment insurance program, which so many Cape Bretoners relied on, was being whittled away. The islanders were told to use a little more ingenuity and to pray for those big oil and gas finds to come home.

I walked from the quaint core of Antigonish back to the Trans-Canada, hoping to get a ride from a storybook Cape Bretoner, a people whose charm and wit is too great for their island to contain. The gateway to their land, a causeway across the Strait of Canso, was sixty kilometres up the road. Surely the highway would be crowded with lilting roughnecks like Philip Walker.

A few days earlier in New Brunswick, Philip had given me a short ride in his pickup truck. He actually offered to drive me all the way to Sydney, which was where he was heading after a short detour, but I had to decline the offer. I explained that I needed to meet a range of people for my assignment. Besides, I wanted to cut through Prince Edward Island. He looked at me strangely. Rugged Cape Bretoners, I remembered, hold a special contempt for pristine P.E.I.

A big muscular man, even in middle age, Philip represented both the heart and the heartbreak of Cape Breton. He was returning to Sydney, where his wife and three children lived, for a weekend break from his current job at the Irvings' big new refinery project in Saint John. That he had to commute 660 kilometres to work didn't weigh on his mind. His island's economy was so depressed that many of his neighbours travelled back and forth to Alberta. Philip pointed to his odometer; the five-year-old car had 360,000 kilometres on it.

"I spend about twenty-five weeks a year on the road," he said.

Philip was a refractory worker on the Irving project where, by his count, there were 250 men from Cape Breton on the payroll. When the project was done, they'd all move on to another construction job, somewhere in the Maritimes. Or they'd go back to Cape Breton to collect "employment insurance." In Sydney, Philip's wife had one of the few steady jobs there was. She was a social worker.

I asked why they would stay in such a depressed place when other provinces were scouring the world for skilled workers.

"It's be-yooo-tiful," Philip said, as confused by my question as he had been by my desire to see P.E.I. "I love the water. I want my children to grow up around the water. It's a good place for them to grow up."

Would they be able to stay, I asked, when their schooling was done?

Philip shook his head. He knew as well as anyone the island's days of hope were numbered.

I was still thinking of Philip's romantic bond with Cape Breton when a red Dodge Neon pulled over, about fifty metres up the road. Before I could grab my pack and run toward it, I noticed the car's reverse lights were on, zipping back toward me. The driver said he was going to Cape Breton, but his voice was not from these parts. I thought I detected a mild German accent.

Frank Neubeiser was about as good a lift as a hitchhiker could ask for. At twenty-nine, the German man had hitchhiked around Europe and, the previous summer, British Columbia, and was now stealing a few days from his job back in Berlin to see Cape Breton. He had just attended a friend's wedding in Boston.

"Thank God," I thought as Frank's rental car tore back onto the highway. "No more provincial politics."

Frank sped into the fading light as if he were on an autobahn. A transport planner, he couldn't avoid testing every dip and turn in the road with the steering wheel and accelerator. Generally, he said, nodding his head, Canadian roads were quite good. Not like Germany, of course, but better than America's.

Whenever the road began a straight run, Frank rolled down his window, held out his Nikon in the wind and snapped a few pictures. German efficiency, I marvelled. But more than parabolic curves and drive-by scenery, Frank was eager to see the land of Cape Breton music. Back home, it was all the rage. Natalie McMaster, Ashley MacIsaac. Their CDs could be found at most concerts in Berlin, he said.

The German fixation with North American Indians is well known and usually put down to the immensely popular writer Karl

May, who never crossed the Atlantic but managed to sew the Wild West into every German youth's imagination. The fixation with Nova Scotia was less straightforward.

It began in the middle of the eighteenth century, when the British administration was so concerned about the population growth of Roman Catholic Acadians that it arranged to transport twenty-five hundred German Protestants to this new land. Most of them settled around Lunenburg, southwest of Halifax. Later, during the Revolutionary War in America, the British recruited German mercenaries and paid them off with land in Nova Scotia. More than two centuries on, the roots are deep enough to support a German-Canadian Association of Nova Scotia. But that was only half the story. Over the nineties, as the Deutschmark soared against the Canadian dollar, real estate agents caught on to a German desire for open space. They found it in Cape Breton, where the locals were packing up and moving west for jobs. Germans began to flock to the coastline around Sydney, snapping up beachfronts, majestic rocky cliffs and their beloved log cabins—the hallmark of the Wild West—at such an alarming rate that *Stern* magazine sent a travel writer to explore the phenomenon. He came back from Cape Breton converted.

"Who would suspect that in this region with its Scandinavian charm, you could find Caribbean-style beaches?" the writer marvelled in Germany's most influential magazine, to a nation of beach-hunters. He noted the locals moved "in slow motion" and had ample time to chat—a telling attribute to reticent Germans. For those seeking culture, the article also revealed—and this was news to me—that one Nova Scotian held the world's record for potato-chip eating ("which isn't hard to figure out," quipped the writer, "when looking at the local girls").

Of course, a little culture clash was to be expected when the laid-back and loquacious Maritimers met the inscrutable Germans. As the *Globe and Mail* found in 1996, "Nova Scotians, used to hiking across a neighbour's land at will, look askance at the newcomers' propensity to fence in their sprawling properties." Perhaps this sort of communal spirit was what led *Stern* magazine, with Teutonic displeasure, to refer to all of Canada as "a socialist state where you can get by without working too hard."

In the heartland of Canadian socialism, Frank pulled hard around the last curve on Highway 104 before it opened to the Strait of Canso and a causeway stretching fifteen hundred metres in length, made of boulders carved from a cliff on the mainland shore. The denuded hillside, scraped of ten million tons of rock in the 1950s, was the last image Frank photographed before turning to Cape Breton. He didn't mind the eyesore. Being from the Elbe region, he was accustomed to industrial blight.

Frank planned to spend the following day driving the Cabot Trail, the majestic three-hundred-kilometre stretch of highway that traces both the island's rugged northern coast and Cape Breton Highlands National Park. He said I could join him, which was an offer hard to turn down. After four days on the road, I needed a good long ride. I also wanted to revisit the Cabot Trail, which I had last seen as a young child on a family vacation. All I could remember from that trip was throwing up on the roadside, an isolated memory emblazoned so vividly on my mind I could still picture the clothes I was wearing and the bend in the road where my father had to bring the car to a sudden halt.

As luck would have it, when we reached the Tourist Information Centre in Port Hawkesbury, on the other side of the causeway, a helpful official told us that Kim Stockwood was in town and would be playing that evening down by the waterfront. Frank couldn't contain his glee. A live Maritime Canadian musician! That she was a Newfoundlander playing Cape Breton music would be enough to set off a constitutional crisis in some parts, but not with him. It was as if he had crossed the Atlantic just for this.

The young woman at the Tourist Information Centre had some bad news, though. She said every inn, hostel and bed and breakfast in Port Hawkesbury was booked, as was every room up the highway in three directions. The best we could do, she said, would be a patch of grass by the road to Mabou, next to an old schoolhouse that had been turned into a B&B. Frank beamed. He could pitch his tent there, with more than enough sleeping space for two, he added. I should not have been surprised that a German planner came to Canada with a tent, but my North American paranoia quickly kicked in. I imagined good-natured Frank, whose greatest crime was probably photographing scenery while driving at high speeds, pulling out a knife in the middle of the night and ending my journey. I also knew my only option, with twilight descending on us, was to take to the road again and hope someone better would pick me up in the dark. I decided to gamble on Frank.

The park overlooking the Strait of Canso was packed, as a warm-up group of fiddlers played. High above, a half-moon was perched over the water, casting a deep glow on the old mining pit. Frank and I remained at the top of a slope that ran down to the bandshell, so that he could photograph the curious islanders who had come prepared with lawn chairs and coffee warmers. They looked like they were at a country picnic rather than a concert. But then the gorgeous and very leggy Stockwood emerged, and the laid-back audience was suddenly on its feet.

Frank was shocked. The music, he muttered. It was as far from Cape Breton fiddling as he could have imagined. The performance began with a couple of rock numbers that electrified the Canso evening. This was followed by a few Elvis classics and "Crazy," the Patsy Cline number that years earlier had won Stockwood her first record deal. It was like going to a Bach concert and hearing Spandau Ballet. Frank hollered for the fiddlers to return, but he was horribly outnumbered. The locals wanted more Elvis.

In between numbers, Stockwood charmed the crowd with some folksy Maritimer stories. She talked about how hard it had been getting a break in Toronto when she moved to the big city from St. John's, Newfoundland. Everyone nodded appreciatively. "Toronto is an awful place," they seemed to want to chant in unison. At one point, Stockwood continued, she had thought of moving home and taking a job at the local Shoppers Drug Mart. It was a strange story to hear from a voice that had lost its Maritime accent. But a few women in the crowd cheered. Perhaps they too had dreamed of a singing career, only to have landed behind the cash at Shoppers.

When a freight train lumbered by the park, on a single line bordering the water, Stockwood played on. I admired her determination, singing louder and louder as sixty cars, by my count, rumbled past the crowd like a thousand vendors calling for people to buy ice-cold drinks. I was even beginning to take a fancy to her Elvis numbers, but Frank's displeasure was only growing. Had he known this would be a country and rock concert, he would have pushed north to the start of the Cabot Trail. This, he said in a note of disgust, was not Cape Breton music. The last straw was Stockwood's energetic and bitchy song "Jerk," which had made the charts a few years earlier. Frank suggested we leave, an offer which, since he was driving, I could hardly refuse. Behind us, as we walked up the hill to the Neon, I could hear the crowd cheering wildly for an encore. They wanted to hear "Jerk" again.

The next morning, waking up in Frank's tent, I noticed my life was still intact. I also noticed how numbingly grey it was outside, the kind of Maritime morning that, even though it never gets written about in guidebooks, presents itself with great regularity. Like every second day.

We had a coffee and a quick breakfast inside the schoolhouse and headed up the coastal road as it traced a string of charming seaside hamlets before cutting inland through the rolling hills of Inverness county. The interior, lined with babbling streams and rolling meadows, must have given the early Scots the impression they had sailed around the world and arrived home again, except there were thick forests in Cape Breton and very few people. Not much had changed. Along the rural highway, I was surprised to see one abandoned farm after another, as if the whole population had fled an advancing rebel army. Up on hillsides, barns were crumbling into the landscape, poorly protected as they were by fences that had been overrun by grass and thickets.

Cape Breton's industrial decline, especially around Sydney and the northern coal belt, was the stuff of Canadian legend. I didn't expect to see the same abandonment in the pastoral interior. Every community we passed seemed to have a sign identifying a famous son or daughter who, like Philip, the refractory worker, had moved on. "Troy, Home of Natalie McMaster." "Port Hood, Home of Al MacInnes." "Mabou, Home of the Rankin Family." Cape Breton was beginning to feel like a living museum.

Hoping to preserve what they could, the locals around Mabou still spoke Scottish Gaelic and held on to their dancing traditions, the centrepiece of a big picnic every July 1. They even taught the fiddle and bagpipe in school. No Kim Stockwood here.

In Mabou, we continued over a little bridge and were on our way up Highway 19, the Ceilidh Trail, when I noticed a brief reference in my guidebook to North America's only distillery for single-malt Scotch whisky. I mentioned it to Frank, and for the first time since the Kim Stockwood concert he was enthused. He was a whisky aficionado, so much so that he wasn't sure how many dozen bottles of twelve-year-old Scotch he had in his Berlin apartment. Just recently, he had toured Scotland looking for rare Scotches. A distillery in Cape Breton was something he had to see.

The Glenora Inn & Distillery was located, by design, in a highland glen, backed by a ridge of lush forest, granite outcrops and a shimmering stream. MacLennan's Brook provided lifeblood to the distillery, its clear, soft water meant to remind visitors of another highland. The white buildings, with pagoda roofs, were also Gaelic in style, making it perhaps the only Scottish theme resort on the planet.

Built in 1989, and assisted by the Scottish distiller Bowmore, Glenora had already produced whiskies and rums, and was close to releasing its first batch of eight-year-old Scotch, which was aging in oak casks. By definition, whisky can be called Scotch only when it is produced in Scotland. But the people who ran Glenora felt they had found a loophole to this tradition, by importing from Scotland malted barley, the key ingredient to a single-malt. We paid five dollars each for a tour to see how they did it.

Almost from the start, Frank was disappointed. The operation, to him, was contrived. And then there was the product. When we were given tastes of Glenora whisky, Frank nearly spat his out. It didn't matter that thirty students at Cape Breton's Gaelic College of Celtic Arts & Crafts—founded in 1938 and the only one of its kind in North America—had sampled the same eight-year-old whisky in a blind taste test and given it a passing grade, ahead of some twelve-year-old Bowmore. As Frank sipped the drink, which the tour guide distributed with salt crackers, his face crumpled. The others on the tour, by contrast, were thrilled with their little discovery. There was a couple from Austin, Texas, another from Oklahoma and families from Calgary and Gimli, Manitoba. None was willing to contest the company's description of its product as "an aromatic whisky presenting a pleasing golden-yellow colour highlighted with hints of amber and orange." Or perhaps they just liked Glen Breton as "pleasantly fiery, offering a tight combination of butterscotch, heather, honey and ground ginger with elongated, wood-infused undertones." Personally, I think the clincher was the eloquent portrayal of "a noticeable alcohol expression." The Texans wanted to know when they could buy a case of it.

When the tour ended in the gift shop, which I don't believe is an ancient Gaelic tradition, Frank was eager to get back on the road. But before we left, he asked me to explain a sign near the exit listing the government agencies that had helped Glenora become a "whisky economuseum." There were no fewer than seven arms of government with a hand in the distillery's creation. Clearly, Frank had something to learn about Canadian federalism. The methods we had just seen, I explained, were more than a neat little effort to make a North American Scotch; they were part of an ancient heritage of government subsidies. How else did he think this little operation, nestled in a Cape Breton highland glen, would survive? With the patronage of ten visitors on a summer's morning? Frank shuddered. Socialist state indeed.

Once he had purchased a souvenir of Glenora's moonshine—for display, not consumption—Frank returned to the highway at a frantic speed. He wanted to cover the Cabot Trail by dark, which would require his best German driving. After Kim Stockwood and Glenora whisky, he was keen to find something authentic.

The Ceilidh Trail made its way back to the coast at Inverness, where some of Atlantic Canada's best beaches are usually missed by tourists in a hurry to get to the Cabot Trail. Just off the road, warm waters from the Gulf of Saint Lawrence splash against big, rolling white stretches of sand that seem to run for miles without a footprint on them. A little farther north, at Belle Côte, where the Cabot Trail begins, another strange current hits the shore. From this little town to the gate of the national park just after Chéticamp, the coast is crowded with French hamlets built 250 years ago by French Catholic Acadians after they were expelled by the British from mainland Nova Scotia and New Brunswick. Surrounded by the last redoubt of Gaelic culture in North America, this little Acadian outpost was all the more impressive. In front of almost every house, Acadian flags flapped furiously in the sea breeze, usually with Canadian and Nova Scotia flags next to them. The eight Catholic communities along the coast had also managed to preserve their *caisses populaires,* big-steeple churches and French language, which in conservative Nova Scotia was perhaps tougher than preserving Celtic.

Before we reached Chéticamp, the coastal road snaked back and forth so quickly I wasn't sure Frank would make some of the corners. And then, in the distance, I saw a white church, a noble little structure I was sure I had seen before. The closer we got, the more strongly I felt something coming back to me. The thick sea air, gut-wrenching at times, smelled familiar. As Frank peeled around another corner, I felt myself instinctively reaching for the door handle. But then it stopped. This time, I was safe.

—— —— ——

With an ocean for a front yard, and so many tourists passing by, Chéticamp had smartly gained a reputation for food. A government guide, which I picked up at the Tourist Information Centre, boasted of restaurants offering an endless range of lobster, scallops and clams. But crab was the real local specialty, served at one place with square dancing and fiddle music. This made it all the more distressing that the most popular place in town, judging by the traffic at noon, was the last open door before the entrance to Highlands National Park. It was a Tim Hortons.

From the Chéticamp entrance by the sea, the Cabot Trail climbs hard and sharp around Mackenzie Mountain and French Mountain—big hills, really—to a plateau nearly five hundred metres above the ocean, where there are spectacular views of hardwood forests and bogs that top the park. The trail continues this way for much of its 106 kilometres, rising and dipping and veering every which way. Not surprisingly, drivers are advised, upon entering the park, to check their brakes.

As spectacular as the Cabot Trail was, rising from a rugged seascape to a desolate mountainside, it hardly felt human, unless you counted an ice-cream stand perched in a renovated lighthouse where the road reached the sea again. Frank and I decided to take a detour north, out of the park, to some fishing coves that stood out on my map. We followed a side road up Aspy Bay to the spot where John Cabot, the explorer, was believed to have landed in 1497, five years after Christopher Columbus reached America.

The road deteriorated the farther we got from the Cabot Trail, leaving Frank to work the Neon as best he could, fending off stones and chunks of dirt that kicked up at the underside. But his best autobahn skills were no match for the four-by-fours rolling blithely past us. A GMC Jimmy from Florida was first, followed by a camper van from Kentucky, a big Ontario car with two bicycles on the roof, and finally the biggest passenger vehicle I had seen in Nova Scotia: a white Chevy Suburban from King City, the affluent bedroom community north of Toronto, with half a dozen well-groomed women on board.

At first, I wasn't sure what could draw this many outsiders to a hamlet at the far tip of the island, on the top of Cape St. Lawrence. I also worried about the invasion we were joining and how it might affect the hamlet at the end of the road. But my worries faded as we followed a dip and then climbed a ridge that was lined by half a dozen houses and a small welcome centre to Meat Cove, Nova Scotia.

Out front was a sign for C@P, the Community Access Program run by the federal and provincial governments, with money from the Bill and Melinda Gates Foundation, to put computers and Internet connections in remote communities. C@P was one reason Canada ranks among the world's great Web users—third, according to a recent study of thirty-six nations, behind Norway and Denmark. Sixty per cent of Canadian respondents said they used the Internet. Meat Cove was hardly cut off.

We continued up the dirt road, the Neon absorbing flying stones with every turn of its wheels, until we reached the end, and the obvious reason for the rush that had overtaken us. Sitting above a cliff was a campground with perhaps the best view on the island. There, campers could open their tents or motorhome doors to a stunning view of the sea, where sea lions can be seen in spring on ice floes and whales splashing about in summer .

While Frank eagerly took pictures, I walked to a trailer that served as the campground's office and met Marion McLellan, the owner. She was both gruff and cheerful, in the way Cape Bretoners can be, and I feared what the Internet was doing to her kind, seeing as the World Wide Web was not likely to bring much of Meat Cove to the suburban ladies. But perhaps I didn't give Marion enough credit. She was a walking home page, as she told me about her community. The village got its name from travelling fishermen who many generations ago stopped here for their meat supplies. Fifty people still lived there, eking out a living from snow crabs, which, since the cod's demise, was about all they could catch in their waters. In the off-season, every house turned to government assistance. About the only other enterprise around was Marion's campground and store, which in the summer regularly doubled or tripled the size of the community. Her twenty-five camping spots were booked for the night, as they were every night for the rest of the summer.

As spectacular as Meat Cove was, I had my doubts about Marion's claim that it was too beautiful to leave. Isolation was destroying communities all over eastern Canada, driving young people to alcohol or drugs, or simply to leave, as they tried to find meaning in places that no longer could support themselves, at least not in the comfort that people had come to expect.

We were standing outside her little shop, near the top of the cliff that plunges down to the cove, when another visitor arrived. The man introduced himself as Father Duncan MacIsaac, a parish priest. Until recently, Father Duncan had been posted on this coast, but was now assigned to a parish on the other side of the island. He had returned to Meat Cove for the day, to attend the funeral and wake of an eighty-nine-year-old woman.

To Father Duncan, who had grown up in Cape Breton as one of ten children, the island was going through a wrenching change. "I think we've lost the language," he said, his arm perched on a railing in front of Marion's trailer. "Both of my parents spoke Gaelic. I needed English to get a job." He had a Gaelic language instruction tape in his car, for those long journeys between country parishes, but admitted he usually listened to CBC Radio instead. "I know more French than Gaelic," he said.

The loss of language could be felt in the music, Father Duncan went on. Without the Gaelic lyrics, he had noticed songs were less rhythmic, perhaps because they relied on fiddle more than voice.

Since the 1970s, Cape Breton had enjoyed a renaissance in fiddle music, thanks to a network of fiddler associations. But it was not something you heard any more in every house on the road. Kids from Meat Cove, if they wanted to learn to play the fiddle properly, had to drive two hours to Chéticamp for lessons.

Television had also crept into remote fishing communities, just as it had in most rural places around the world. I had noticed on our drive into Meat Cove that every house had a satellite dish on its roof, the kind that brings 999 channels to a place that used to rely on one storyteller. The days of storytelling were gone.

"We don't take the time, because of television," Father Duncan lamented. "I think we've lost some of the values because there was always a moral in the story. There were values in the stories. There is a tremendous love for people in the culture, a sharing of memories and treasures. Out of that came hope for the future. That's eroding, naturally."

While the end of cod fishing in the early nineties was devastating to the coastal communities, villages like Meat Cove were enjoying a snow crab boom. A shortage of the crabs in Alaska's waters had sent prices wildly higher, which Father Duncan feared was another danger. He pointed to a new van driving by with lobster traps on the roof. It belonged to a local fisherman, a man who had collected enough in a season to buy the van and lots more. Yet, in another couple of seasons, when prices inevitably would decline, he would again have nothing, not even enough to keep the van going. All the fishermen would have were the welfare cheques that come as regularly as ice floes in spring.

I could see that Frank, who had been busy photographing the vista, was eager to move on. He had to get to Halifax the next day, to catch his flight back to Berlin. A few campers were already setting up for dinner on picnic tables. On our way out of Meat Cove, a group of boys chased us down the dirt road on their bicycles. Chasing tourists was as exciting as it got on a Monday afternoon in summer. They could go inside and watch a baseball game from Atlanta or surf the Net. They could do the same in Halifax or Toronto. But in those places, they wouldn't have the spectacular views and fresh sea breeze, or the humour, music and folklore. In those places, they wouldn't have Cape Breton.

— — —

The rain started to come down after nightfall, just before we reached the ferry crossing at St. Ann's Bay. Except for a brief stop for seafood chowder at Neils Harbour, a little fishing village, we had driven straight and fast down the east side of the Cabot Trail, which drops from the highlands like an off-ramp from heaven. There had not been enough light to see Smokey Mountain, where islanders ski in winter, or the marvellous beaches at Ingonish. One of the few objects we could make out was a dead moose on the side of the road, which aside from a lynx crossing the highway a day earlier was the only wild animal I had seen in Cape Breton. Those poor Germans seeking the Wild West. All they'd find here were distilleries and ice-cream stands.

As we sat in the car on the barge, crossing St. Ann's Bay to meet up again with the Trans-Canada Highway, Frank and I realized we had another problem. The rain was teeming. I had hoped to hitch-hike north to Sydney, thirty-seven kilometres up the road, to catch the morning ferry to Newfoundland. Frank had hoped to get a good chunk of the way back to Halifax. Neither of us would get far in this weather, and since I preferred dry clothes to a sopping rag, which is what they would become in two minutes on the roadside, I decided to stick with Frank as he searched for a motel after the ferry landing. Every place along the Trans-Canada was booked. We continued south to Beddeck, an old resort town on the north shore of Bras d'Or Lake, which looks more like a chain of lakes sprawling through the middle of Cape Breton than an inland sea. More motels and B&Bs turned us away. An innkeeper suggested we try the KOA.

When Alexander Graham Bell, who kept a summer home at Beddeck, described Cape Breton as the world's greatest example of "simple beauty," I don't think he could have imagined the Kampground of America. On the banks of a small river flowing into Bras d'Or, south of Beddeck, the campground was as crowded as a Wal-Mart parking lot on Saturday morning. In one of those triangular buildings that are KOA's trademark, a lady at the front desk said there were 459 campers booked in for the night. Roughly half were American. She showed us a brochure describing the campground's convenience store, video shop and restaurant, which, she pointed out, had a lobster special for dinner. On a map of the site, there was also marked a swimming pool, a basketball court and a special building for showers. The check-in lady moved her finger across the map to the far corner, near the river, where there were a few unserviced lots, big enough for a car, tent and picnic table. It was all she had left.

A cold rain continued through the night, making sleep nothing but a miserable necessity. Shortly after dawn, though, as the sky cleared, I went for a walk and discovered a new side to highway travel. A section of the KOA was devoted to the kinds of motorhomes I had never seen up close, the kind that seemed big enough to set sail. Many had Florida licence plates, but the one that caught my eye was from Delaware. "Jack & Muriel's Dutch Star" was thirty-six feet long, with a satellite dish on its roof, a motor scooter strapped to its back and, behind that, a Jeep Cherokee in tow. Jack and Muriel looked like they were preparing to cross the Sahara. On the side, there were enough water pumps and electricity wires attached to a utility stand to keep a small African village clean and well lit.

When I found Frank, shrouded in smoke from our neighbours' breakfast fire, he was packing up his tent. The big puddles we had tried to avoid when pitching it in the dark were still there. On the other side of some pine trees, a camper was playing his car radio. The morning news began with an advisory to local residents to clean their septic tanks at least once every five years.

Before dropping me off at the highway, Frank told me he had enjoyed Cape Breton but would not be back soon. There were too many other destinations in the world. He could not contain his disappointment, either. The island's mystique, formed in the past but struggling through the present, had failed his precise German scrutiny. We exchanged e-mail addresses, which is what hitchhikers do nowadays, and headed our separate ways, he in the Neon and me on foot. He had a flight to catch. I had seven provinces and thousands of kilometres to cover, and I had to believe my last great free ride was over.

4

"The land that God gave to Cain"

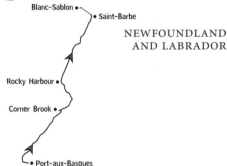

Blanc-Sablon ●
● Saint-Barbe

NEWFOUNDLAND
AND LABRADOR

Rocky Harbour ●

Corner Brook ●

● Port-aux-Basques

The MV *Caribou* prepared to sail for Newfoundland at midday, with a sense of grandeur and legend that only a six-hour crossing can pretend to afford. The super-ferry was more like a small ship. Running the length of two football fields, it had elevators, escalators, a children's nursery and video arcade, forty-nine private sleeping cabins and a hundred and twelve dormitory sleepers, a small movie theatre, a school-sized cafeteria and, this being the bridge from Cape Breton to Newfoundland, a very crowded bar. Okay, so it wasn't the *Titanic*. But for a regular service between two of Canada's poorest provinces, the MV *Caribou* was not a rustbucket either.

I had just spent a couple of hours wandering around North Sydney, having waited an hour for a ride outside the KOA, and just missing the early morning crossing. Most of Main Street was boarded up, and of the shops still in business, the biggest was a buy-and-sell operation called Blue Star Traders Ltd. The area was so depressed that the local real estate office advertised a two-storey house on Main Street, with a large yard, for $44,000. They were asking $18,000 for a smaller starter house, one of the tiny two-bedroom numbers that crowded the hillside of Sydney Mines. Not even German bargain hunters were interested in those.

From the sun deck of the MV *Caribou,* as I watched North Sydney fade from view, it was hard to imagine that in the 1950s this was one of the busier ports on the East Coast. These days, the ferry was the area's biggest employer, along with a provincially owned casino in the main town of Sydney, at the top of the bay. Farther along the main coast, but not quite visible from the ferry, were scattered communities that spoke to a more cheated past, places like Scotchtown and New Waterford that were crowded with big churches, tiny houses and horrible memories of decline.

The Sydney coast was once the Klondike of coal mining. As far back as the seventeenth century, travellers had commented on the black-ink cliffs along the shore where they found enough traces of coal, it was said, to rival Scotland. The French mined the bituminous deposits to fuel their fort at nearby Louisbourg, as did the British when they won control of Cape Breton in 1763, as part of the Treaty of Paris that ended the Seven Years War.

But it wasn't until the late nineteenth century that commercial development took off. The Dominion Iron and Steel Co., which later became the British Empire Steel Co., brought together an avaricious bunch of investors from Toronto, New York and London to finance the biggest new coal mine of their time, a place they imagined would become the Newcastle of the West. The group cut long tunnels under the sea to reach coal deposits that ran all the way to Newfoundland. With a hundred-year lease on land that was once actively used by the Mi'kmaq, they built a township of housing for their workers, stores to sell food and supplies to those workers, and a power plant to service the mine and township. Then, with the help of the new Dominion government, they brought shiploads of workers from Europe, the Caribbean and the Middle East—men with young families who were promised handsome New World wages only to discover they would be shackled to their jobs. Any man who quit or was fired immediately lost his tiny house and access to the shop, the only one around. Any man who was injured on the job was expected to send a son to fill his spot. If he didn't, his family was given three days to vacate their home.

At the peak of operations, twelve thousand men and boys worked in some of the most horrendous conditions known on the continent. Every morning, they were sent through tunnels that stretched, under the seabed, four or five kilometres offshore. The journey to their pillar of coal, in small rail cars, usually took one hour, after which their ten-hour shift formally began. For much of the year they would spend every hour of daylight below the sea, more than a kilometre below my comfortable deck seat on the MV *Caribou*. Some never returned. In the 1920s, an average of one worker a day died at the operation, often when their underground source of light, an open-flame carbide lamp, exploded. Conditions were worse for the miniature ponies bred to haul coal from the narrow shafts under the sea to a main rail line that led to the surface. They spent so many years down there that once, when several were released, the sunlight blinded them instantly.

Between 1901 and 1924, the miners went on strike fifty-eight times, but the coal always surfaced—five million tonnes of it every year. That is, until tensions exploded in 1925, after Besco, as the British Empire Steel Company was known, announced a one-third cut in wages. Union leaders in the region responded by calling for an overthrow of the capitalist system. The company offered a compromise, cutting wages by only twenty per cent. The ensuing strike proved to be the final confrontation, and one of the greatest displays of courage the Canadian labour movement has seen. When the miners walked off their jobs, the company shut off power and water to their houses, as well as to the local hospital and school. The company stores suspended credit. The provincial government, which relied on coal royalties for a third of its revenue, sent in a special police force to pressure the workers, and at one point the federal government added a militia. On June 11, 1925, the militia opened fire on the strikers, killing one of them, William Davis, a father of ten.

Across Nova Scotia, church groups collected money and food packages for the strikers and sent relief convoys to the island. The Jewish merchants of nearby Sydney did their part, giving free credit to the strikers after the company store closed its doors to them. When the company agreed to restore the miners' wages, the settlement was hailed around the world as a victory for organized labour. But within a decade, Besco was dead, a victim of the Great Depression. The mines fell into the hands of one investor after another as oil replaced coal as the industrialized world's preferred fuel. Finally, in 1968, the federal government nationalized the operation so that it could gently wind down the business, a plan that was scuttled when world oil prices went through the roof in the early seventies.

What followed was a glorious boondoggle for anyone connected with the mine, as Ottawa pumped in $1.6 billion just to keep the operations going. As coal regained favour and the federal government saw hope yet, workers were soon making more than $20 an hour, plus medical, dental and vision care benefits. The mines could still not make a go of it. Over the next thirty years, Canadian taxpayers spent the equivalent of $20,000 a year for every miner involved in the elusive dream of Cape Breton mining.

By the 1990s, the patronage machine had run dry. The workforce at the mines was down to 2,700 men. In 2001, when the last mine closed, the payroll was a mere 250. All that remained was a tourist centre run by some veteran miners. After centuries of heroism, hubris and tragedy, the remaining mine workers and their families were given training to work in a call centre, the one enterprise willing to move into the old mining company's offices. They still mark June 11 as Davis Day.

— — —

As the last hints of Cape Breton fell below the horizon, I opted to seek shelter in the Killicks bar lounge. The ferry was already rocking steadily with each swell, and we were barely into the Cabot Strait. A good ninety-six nautical miles lay ahead. If I was going to be sick, I thought alcohol should be involved.

The MV *Caribou* was named for the original SS *Caribou*, which was torpedoed by a German U-boat in 1942 and sank forty kilometres off the coast of Newfoundland. Of the 238 people on the SS *Caribou*'s final voyage, 137 perished. Built in Lauzon, Quebec, in 1986, the new *Caribou* remained the workhorse of the Maritimes. Its enormous lower decks allowed for 77 tractor-trailers and 370 automobiles, making it a durable bridge for the Trans-Canada. It was also under threat. While no one could hope for (or want) a bridge to be built from Sydney to Port-aux-Basques, there were enough people crossing the Cabot Strait to warrant a regular high-speed ferry service. Three times faster, the new catamaran-style boat had cut the crossing time by four hours and raised doubts about the viability of the older super-ferry. It was like that for everything in the Maritimes, as generations of tradition were tossed overboard in the name of efficiency.

When I reached Killicks, on Passenger Deck Five, the bar was already in full swing as the crowd, mostly long-distance truck drivers, tried to make the most of their long stint away from the wheel. I sat down at the bar next to a group of veteran ferry-goers, all of them diehards of the long crossing. "You can't drink enough in two hours," a young wholesaler from St. John's said, dismissing the fast ferry with a swig of beer. He was well into his first pitcher of draft. On the tumultuous catamaran, he wouldn't dare touch the stuff, not when that ferry bounces off waves so easily it had become known as the "Comet and Vomit." The wholesaler said the gentle rocking of the MV *Caribou* kept him sober, even after a pitcher of beer. A truck driver sitting next to him had a different view. "This gives you enough time to get drunk, sleep, cure your hangover and drive home to the local pub," he said.

The trucker had more jokes to share but he was soon overshadowed by "Bread 'n' Butter (Cholesterol Free)," a bar act set to play all the way to Newfoundland. With an electric guitar and squeezebox, the two-man act launched into a repertoire of jigs and crude limericks that seemed to rely heavily on the word "Timbuktu."

I left the truck drivers to their pitchers of beer and roamed the ferry, eventually finding the purser, Elvis Hamlyn, who explained its troubles. This afternoon, he said, there were 126 passengers on board, when there should be five or six hundred. The catamaran was popular among tourists but also among the growing business class that was shuttling back and forth from Newfoundland. "If you're in a hurry, I guess it's okay," Elvis said of the competition. And suddenly a lot of Newfoundlanders were in a hurry.

In a few short years, the one province that was the butt of more Canadian jokes than any other had discovered some economic success. Much of the turnaround came from oil discoveries and a boom in pulp and paper production. The cod fishery, for so long the island's mainstay, remained a memory. But there was also a flurry of new enterprises. If it continued, no one would be able to say that the definition of a Cape Bretoner was "a Newfie who went broke on the way to Toronto." Elvis and I talked a while longer, before I said I had to find a place to write. He was curious about my laptop, which I pulled out of my pack. He looked at me like I was on the wrong boat.

By six o'clock, we had entered the foggy passage to Port-aux-Basques. I took my bag and stole a final glance of Killicks, noticing the wholesaler asleep with a full glass of draft in front of him. Up on the sun deck, a small crowd was braving a fierce damp wind in order to get a better look at the emerging rocky shore. Some clung to the outside wall of the captain's bridge, not wanting to risk the spray coming over the foredeck. But a few ventured to the outer railing, clinging to it as they lapped up the sight of land peeking through the mist. In the distance, I could hear the tinny sounds of a welcome band playing on the wharf. It was wishing us a safe arrival.

As I walked from the ferry terminal up a hill to the main road, an early evening mist hung low, revealing just enough barren rock to suggest that nothing green had ever grown here. Trees were so scarce that it felt like a community north of sixty, not one perched on the same latitude as Seattle. As a first impression, Port-aux-Basques made Newfoundland look like the surface of the moon.

Named for the Basque fishermen who first came here in the sixteenth century, the town had long given up fishing as a mainstay. Like North Sydney, the ferry was pretty much all she had now. Although the hardscrabble hills were dotted with colourful houses, and the cove around Port-aux-Basques was still crowded with rickety wooden docks, the main action was in the motels, takeout shops and filling stations. This ancient community, the site of fishing wars and human sagas, was now little more than a rest stop on the Trans-Canada Highway.

After dropping my pack at a hotel near the port, I went for a walk in hopes of finding a good Newfie pub, the kind where my truck driver friends might be parked. Up another hill and over a ridge, I found Buddy's, a small tavern that was empty but for two men at the bar sipping Black Horse, Newfoundland's own beer. All the cars in the parking lot outside, the bartender said, were for the cinema next door.

Port-aux-Basques's one movie theatre was easy to miss. Built like a small school auditorium, it bore none of the brash, neon hallmarks of an urban multiplex, and on most evenings attracted no more than a few dozen people. But tonight, the eight o'clock show was sold out. All two hundred seats were taken, so I joined the overflow crowd at the back, where some latecomers stood by the door, remarking that they could not remember Port-aux-Basques being this excited about a film. But then, the frustrated fishing community had good cause. The cinema was showing *The Perfect Storm*.

People whooped and cheered like kids at a wrestling match as George Clooney and friends challenged the storm of a lifetime because they had no reasonable choice. If the fishermen didn't get their catch, the story went, they'd lose their boat. But if they didn't beat the storm, they'd lose their lives. At each gut-wrenching burst of nature, the crowd cringed with such anxiety that by the climax I was no longer watching the screen; the women and men who were jammed into the little hilltop theatre were more interesting. It was hard to believe that a crowd of experts like this would so readily accept the preposterous special effects, which to my landlubber's eye looked like a toy boat being filmed in a bathtub. But they did. It was as if the film was made for Newfoundland, where stark choices are as ingrained as the rocky shore.

When the movie was over, I stood by the door and watched the crowd file out to the parking lot. The final scenes, in which the fishermen die and the captain's wife takes over his boat, appeared to have been too much for even the most hardened folk. Several women were still wiping their eyes as they left. The men shook their heads, as if to say, "Glad that wasn't my boat."

"Best since *Titanic*," one woman said to her husband at the door. He nodded in agreement.

A few moviegoers went to Buddy's but most were in a hurry to get home. Within ten minutes, the parking lot was empty.

The next morning, I began to notice that more than movie tastes separated Newfoundland from the rest of Canada. As I walked from my hotel to the side of the Trans-Canada, cars stopped to let me cross the open road. Several times, drivers waved to me, like we were long-lost friends. I wasn't on the roadside a few minutes when a GMC pickup truck pulled over, its driver nodding for me to climb in. Other hitchhikers had told me that Newfoundland would be a cinch, like Alberta was to the Alliance Party, and I was beginning to think they were right.

My first driver on the island, Amos Collier, was a fisherman from Codroy, forty kilometres up the coast. He could have been one of George Clooney's boathands in *The Perfect Storm*. His face and hands were as hard as the rocks jutting out of the roadside. His gravelly brogue, ground by a series of Export A's at eight in the morning, was tougher still. When he smiled, which was often, his mouth was a confusion of stained teeth.

At fifty, Amos had been fishing around these parts for most of his life, except for two years in the 1960s when he worked in Toronto as a carpenter. Toronto has so many tradesmen from Newfoundland that the fastest way to stop the city's sprawl would be to expel all Newfies. Sadly, what little humour the big city has would be lost with them. Amos hated the big city anyway and was back to Codroy by the next fishing season. It wasn't just Toronto. One of his grown sons once spent a year in Halifax before returning to work on the family boat. "You miss this place," Amos said in his steady mumble.

It was easy to see why as the road left the barren coast and wound its way through the thickly wooded hills that form a southern tip for the Long Range Mountains. In the distance, with the morning sun beating back the mist, the higher peaks were ringed by a scattering of clouds, while below, the hillside forests were clear and verdant, the first splash of natural colour I had seen on the island.

Amos played CBC Radio as he drove, softly enough that he would not be distracted from whatever lurked along the roadside. This time of year, there were so many blackflies in the forests that the abundant moose population often sought sanctuary on the open road. The previous summer on this road, he had rammed a Dodge pickup into a calf. The pickup lost most of its front end, with the radiator wedged into the engine. The calf hobbled back into the woods.

Fishing and moose hunting were what Amos had missed most about this place when he was in Toronto. Every summer, he could bag enough game to fill his freezer for a year. These days, he also had cash to spare. The crab boom I had heard about in Meat Cove was greater on this side of the Cabot Strait, where fishermen like Amos were enjoying their best season in years. Not since the collapse of the cod fishery, a decade earlier, had he done so well. With the Alaska fishery in turmoil, his quota for thirty-three thousand pounds of crab was just about filled. Moreover, this season's price of $2.20 a pound was almost double the previous year's, and he had a windfall of lobster and flounder to add to it.

Amos explained that from his gross income he had to pay his son and two other crew, as well as the costs of operating a boat. But he still had enough left over to trade in his damaged Dodge for the new GMC. He also planned to collect unemployment insurance through the winter. "Without that, a lot of people would leave this place," he mumbled. I think it was his longest sentence during the half-hour drive.

Amos dropped me just past an Irving station by his turnoff at Tompkins, assuring me that I would be on my way to Corner Brook in a matter of minutes. He obviously had not hitchhiked before, at least not in August in southwestern Newfoundland. As the blackflies descended, I wanted to wave my fist and curse his name, but his GMC was already out of sight.

The next hour was not the most miserable I had known, but it was close. For the first twenty minutes or so, I stood on the deserted roadside, swatting tiny, ferocious flies, wondering if the highway had been closed. Then came the first bite. It was a tiny painless prick on the scruff of my neck but enough to make my upper body twitch in discomfort. After I rubbed the irritation, I pulled back my right hand to find my fingers smeared with blood. Looking up, I saw a black swarm circling above my head.

And still the sole traffic was a procession of gravel trucks that every few minutes emerged from a side road and dumped their con-tents up the way, at a project site for highway expansion. A sign boasted that the federal government was putting $3.7 million into the project. Why anyone wanted to expand this highway was beyond me. There wasn't a single vehicle in either direction. You could play a set of tennis on the road, doubles if you wished, and not have to think about cars.

But I knew, just as the gravel-truck drivers must have known, that roads here are not about cars. They're about jobs, which are to Newfoundland what rain is to a Prairie farmer. Just that morning a local newspaper had railed against the province's plan to move 257 government jobs from St. John's to outlying communities that, for shame, did not include Port-aux-Basques.

I continued to pace the roadside for another half an hour before surrendering to the Irving station as the hot morning sun tinged my collar with an unpleasant mix of sweat and blood. At least there I could have a blackfly-free coffee and a few moments of peace. The cashier told me I needed to wait just another fifteen minutes for traffic to come from the morning ferry. Of course! An entire boatload of cars and trucks had just rolled off the ferry in Port-aux-Basques and was heading my way.

Feeling I had outsmarted the blackflies, I waited fifteen minutes and then walked briskly back to the roadside, in time to see a long line of vehicles coming over the horizon. The first bunch was a caravan of RVs from Texas that did not offer so much as a polite southern wave. More cars came and went, followed by a dozen trucks that rolled right by me. And then nothing, except a black swarm above my head.

Rather than retreating to the Irving station, I decided to walk up the road, thinking, for some reason that still eludes me, there would be no flies there. I was wrong. There were more blackflies up the road than there would have been in a swamp after a rainy day. There were thousands of them, as if I were the last morsel they could find. And there was no place to take cover. Across the road was an Esso station with a liquor shop and dairy bar attached. They were deserted. The two adjoining storefronts—Doreen's, an army surplus shop that doubled as a Sears catalogue outlet, and a waste disposal office— also looked closed for the season.

I was about to run back to the Irving station when I saw a young man walking toward me from the north. He had a large knapsack on his back, and was improbably happy for someone dressed in shorts and a T-shirt in what was surely the blackfly capital of the world. He also spoke with an English accent, which at first distracted me when he asked how the hitchhiking was. "Just as it looks," I finally cursed, swatting more flies.

The Englishman had little sympathy for someone who had been on the roadside for a mere hour. He was walking across Canada, having already covered the lengths of England and New Zealand. He had set out from St. John's a week before and would take a break for the winter in Digby, at the far end of Nova Scotia, before tackling the rest of the country in the spring. As he described his journey, I could not figure out why he was not swatting the air like I was. But I didn't have time to ask. Turning to the south, the young Englishman said he had to keep moving. He didn't want to break his rhythm.

——— ——— ———

It is difficult to grow up in Canada without being enamoured of the Rock, the one province that enjoys a greater emotional reach than any other. That its population is less than downtown Vancouver's is given no importance. I was taught about her history in elementary school and was made to appreciate her political weight as the years went on. In 1990, this small impoverished island, with Labrador's huge expanse of rock and tundra thrown in, came close to bringing the country down when her goverment rescinded its ratification of the Meech Lake Accord, designed to bring Quebec into the Canadian constitution. What sweet justice it must have been around Codroy, for no other province felt more shafted by Confederation.

I got my first good dose of Newfoundland anger from a middle-aged couple from Stephenville who rescued me from the blackflies outside the Irving station, two hours after Amos had dropped me there. Ken and Emily Gaudet had watched their beloved province lose its hydroelectricity, fish and oil to what they considered the greedy provinces of central and western Canada. And now they had lost their children to the same hotbeds of avarice. One son was a fabricator in Halifax, the other a pipefitter in Edmonton. The Gaudets doubted their boys would ever move back to Stephenville. About a hundred kilometres north of the Codroy turnoff, it did not sound like the happy Newfoundland Amos had painted for me.

The Gaudets and their Honda CRV had crossed from Nova

Scotia on the new catamaran ferry, which Emily said was much better than the MV *Caribou.* They had had enough time for a buffet
breakfast on the top deck and would be home for lunch. "You don't
feel tired like on the other ferry," she said. "You always got off that
one exhausted."

The Gaudets did not seem like "Bread 'n' Butter (Cholesterol
Free)" Newfies anyway. They did not seem like any Newfoundlanders
I had imagined. In the cassette deck, they played a tape of gospel
music with tunes such as "Ask and You Shall Receive" and "God Bless
the U.S.A." But they seemed to have the sort of even keel—stoicism
perhaps—that gave balance to their province.

Ken worked as a pipefitter at a big paper mill in Corner Brook,
fifty kilometres past Stephenville. Owned by Krueger, the American
forestry products giant, it was held up as an example of
Newfoundland's new competitiveness. But he wasn't so sure. Since
the Americans had come in and retooled the plant, the workforce
had been cut by two-thirds. The same was true, Ken said, of the
Abitibi mill in Stephenville. With automatic woodcutters and computerized paper mills, the forest economy was not what it once was.
"They downsize and downsize," he said. "When someone retires or
quits, the job is gone."

He blamed the province for allowing outsiders—Toronto or
Chicago, it didn't matter—to take its resources for a song. Any
Newfoundlander will tell you how Joey Smallwood, the leader who
brought Canada's tenth province into Confederation, signed away
the value of Labrador's massive Churchill Falls hydroelectric project
to Quebec. Joey should have known the mainlanders were out to
cheat Newfoundland, they will tell you.

"The way Newfoundland works is we got lots of resources but
we give it away," Ken said, speaking over the chorus of "God Bless
the U.S.A." "That's just the way it is. Joey Smallwood started it. We
gave our hydro to Quebec. We gave our fish to everyone."

Ken was on a roll. As if reciting the provincial anthem of discontent, he described how Canada had shut down the cod fishery to

please the Europeans, tried to steal the nickel from Voisey Bay in
Labrador and then given Newfoundland a pittance for her offshore
oil and gas. "They just gave it away," he continued. "Look at Alberta.
They built two cities on their oil. What do we have? Nothin'. I think
that was the way it was meant to be."

I noticed a warning sign for moose on the roadside and asked
Ken if he had ever run into one. He looked at me in the rear-view
mirror like I had asked if he had ever shovelled snow. His worst
moose accident, it turned out, was when he and a group of co-
workers in a rented Chevy Celebrity ran into one on the highway.
The animal lay dazed on the road for about thirty seconds before
jumping to its feet and trotting back into the woods. The Chevy
needed a tow truck.

The first humans reached Newfoundland in 2500 B.C. Moose, I
had read, were not introduced to the island until 1904. But the two
stubborn species were determined to fight it out on the province's
highways. Of the estimated twenty thousand moose that inhabited
the island, one a day, on average, was involved in a car collision.
Moose were so abundant that Roddickton, a small town on the
Northern Peninsula, had declared itself moose capital of the world.
The Gaudets and I did not see any moose. In fact, for the rest of the
drive to the Stephenville turnoff, there was nothing on the roadside
but forests, lakes and Irving stations.

Ken continued to talk about Newfoundland's problems. Emily
nodded in agreement. They predicted the exodus would continue,
which left them neither happy nor sad. Just stoic. "It's just the way
it's always been," Ken said.

—— —— ——

The Gaudets left me on the exit ramp of an impressive interchange
outside Stephenville, the kind you might find in a mid-sized city.
Except this cloverleaf looked like some sort of UFO landing pad in
the middle of a forest. What else could explain so much asphalt in
one remote place? At least here, with a steady wind rustling through

the trees, there were no blackflies. There was no other sound, except for the faint humming of a car or truck as it appeared on one horizon, approached, whizzed by and disappeared on the other horizon.

It was already noon, and the prospect of another two-hour wait led me to sit down on the gravel shoulder and pull out an obscure collection of historical documents that I had found in a North Sydney bookstore. I began reading. The arrangement was comfortable. Every few minutes, when I heard the humming of tires, I would jump to my feet and hide the book, just long enough for the vehicle to race by. And then I would get back to reading in the warm midday sun, protected by the wind from blackflies. I was just getting into *The French Regime* when a small car, to my disappointment, pulled over.

"You're lucky, I guess, to get a ride," the driver said, offering me a lift to Corner Brook.

I stared at him blankly.

"You know, that sex offender, he's been on the loose for four, five days now," the man said. "They said he's a young man. They said he's dangerous."

I admitted to not knowing one bit about Richard Ryan, the forty-year-old convicted rapist who had escaped a week earlier in the St. John's area, the same day I left Toronto. Ryan had been visiting his mother, who was dying, when he slipped out a bathroom window and past the lone corrections officer who was accompanying him. Ryan was described as "dangerous and devious," with at least nine victims spread across four provinces. His escape had prompted a province-wide manhunt, with helicopters and tracker dogs aiding federal and provincial police. And there I had been, lounging on the roadside, reading *The French Regime*.

— — —

For the rest of the drive to Corner Brook, we passed little else but forested hills, some of them five hundred million years old but now in the hands of Krueger and Abitibi. The woodlands were all second-generation growth anyway, feeding the mill and its towering plumes of smoke that rose over the next ridge.

I was eager to continue north from the Corner Brook turnoff and get to Gros Morne National Park by evening. Despite the prospect of a serial rapist being on the same road, I would have to leave the Trans-Canada and follow the Viking Trail toward L'-Anse-aux-Meadows, the thousand-year-old settlement thought to have been built by Leif Ericson. Everyone I had met on the island said that it was worth the detour, that Gros Morne was the hidden gem of eastern Canada, a World Heritage Site and landmark to anyone concerned with the planet. Those who knew it well called it a Galapagos of geology.

Situated on the northwestern tip of Newfoundland, where humans have lived for forty-five hundred years, Gros Morne is an ancient collision of rocks and fjords, with subterranean plates jutting above the surface. Deep in the park, in Western Brook Pond, cliffs rise seven hundred metres above a cold fjord. In another spot, you can hike across an ancient seabed. My guidebook said it was like journeying to the bottom of the ocean.

But to get there, I would have to endure a couple of old-timers whose views of Canada sounded like they belonged in a heritage site. My first ride toward the park was with a retired banker from Nicholsville, outside Deer Lake, who, when he heard I was from Ontario, just about threw me out. "Upper Canada!" Curtis said, glaring at me. I knew I would be a fool to say that I worked for the *Globe and Mail.* I knew that in his mind—in the mind of just about everyone who cannot see the CN Tower from their solarium—the *Globe and Mail* was a well-fed mouthpiece of the Upper Canada establishment and had been for 150 years. But I couldn't resist the temptation. I introduced myself and disclosed my employer, and braced for a North Atlantic storm.

Curtis laughed. After all the wrongs suffered by his beloved Newfoundland at the hands of central Canada, he said, this was poetic justice. The barons of Toronto, he pointed out, had robbed, pillaged and deprived his great island of all its visible riches. And now he had the king's messenger trapped in his car for half an hour, which would be just enough time to give a brief summary—on the record, he stressed—of the injustices that my people had brought on his people. The full Newfie rant was about to begin.

"All down through the years, Newfoundland has been screwed," Curtis began by way of an opening argument. "I'm retired. I worked in a bank and I've seen so much of this go on. A lot of people in the federal government don't have a feeling for Newfoundland. They don't know what we produce. It's pretty hard for someone in central Canada who has never seen the ocean to regulate our fishery."

At seventy-one, Curtis had seen his island grow from a British dependency to a Canadian province. He remembered, as a teen in the Second World War, watching the world's greatest air forces flying overhead, as German U-boats slipped enigmatically around his homeland. Had history moved ever so slightly off course, Newfoundland might have been the first piece of North America to fall to the Nazis. Instead, in 1949, with both England and Germany in different stages of ruin, Newfoundland decided to hook its fate to Canada.

Curtis well remembered March 31, 1949, the day Joey Smallwood made what Curtis considered the greatest mistake in the island's history. In his mind Confederation did not propel Newfoundland from backward colony to full-fledged partner in one of the world's greatest countries. Confederation, in his mind, did not give this remote collection of fishing hamlets and foul weather an equal status to the aspiring nation of Quebec or the wealthy provinces of Alberta and Ontario. It did not give half a million people, who had long been neglected by England, the same access to education and health care that every other Canadian enjoyed. The naval protection, the equalization payments, the endless CBC documentaries about obscure outports, the assured seat in every federal cabinet for a mere 550,000 people—these meant little to Curtis. For Newfoundland, he said, Confederation had been nothing but a bum steer.

We were driving through a stunning valley beyond Corner Brook, with high cliffs and thick forests banking the Humber River as it carves its way to Marble Mountain, the only good ski resort between Quebec City and France. Beyond the gorge, the first clear-cut hilltops began to emerge, buzzed of their tree cover by the Krueger mill and recently replanted. Unlike the temperate west coast of British Columbia, Curtis pointed out, these hills would not sprout big trees anytime soon. On such a primeval landscape, everything took a bit longer.

Modern Newfoundland's troubles, he continued, began shortly after Confederation when Smallwood signed the Churchill Falls hydro deal just so he could get the thing built. When Smallwood later spent millions of his province's dollars on technology schemes to ease Newfoundland's dependence on fish, Curtis blamed the foreign promoters for selling the premier a bill of goods. Meantime, Ontario and American paper companies were busy stripping the landscape of trees and then stripping the mills of jobs, he said.

Curtis was not speaking irrationally. He was so fed up with central Canada and the diktats from Ottawa that he had joined the old Reform Party and become its local association president. He felt Reform, and its successor Alliance Party, would give the provinces full control over their resources, which in turn would allow Newfoundland to shape its destiny. As for the benefits of Confederation—free universal health care, for instance—Curtis failed to see them. He was suffering from cancer and Parkinson's disease and was spending $4,000 a year on medical treatment. Only food consumed a greater chunk of his pension.

When we reached the turnoff to Highway 430, the so-called Viking Trail, Curtis said the remaining traffic would be headed to Gros Morne. There was only one glitch, and I didn't notice it until he was driving away. There wasn't any traffic.

I sat down on the deserted roadside and buried my nose in *Historic Newfoundland and Labrador,* a government-produced booklet I had picked up on the MV *Caribou.* Written in 1955 and reprinted thirty years later, it spoke of the province like some sort of lost civilization. The booklet listed the Eskimo (now called Inuit), who arrived on the Labrador coast around 1400 A.D., under "Recent Occupants of Newfoundland and Labrador." From there, the writers fast-forwarded to "Britain's oldest colony, Canada's newest province," which they proudly described as "the cradle of white civilization in North America." Local culture was so old, the Department of Tourism boasted, that you could travel to fishing villages and listen to English "as it was pronounced in Devonshire in the time of Shakespeare."

While not many places are proud of their rapacious colonial heritage, I was surprised to discover that Newfoundland was one. The booklet described various European atrocities with great flourish, like the time in 1001 when Scandinavians overran the island's northwestern corner, which had long been settled by Indians. The murderous Vikings renamed the place Markland, or Land of the Forest, the booklet noted with a degree of celebration. John Cabot was the next to claim discovery of the island, calling it the New Founde Isle in 1497 when he landed at Bonavista on the eastern coast. He claimed the island in the name of King Henry VII. A few decades later, Jacques Cartier combed the west coast and named it Terre Neuve. Then the Portuguese arrived with their fishing fleet, scooping up all they could. They wanted to call the island Tierra dos Bacallaos, or "land of the cod." In a few more decades, however, the British were back in force, with a mission led by Sir Humphrey Gilbert, to restate their claim in the name of Queen Elizabeth I. For centuries, the European powers squabbled over their various claims—actually, it was only the fish they cared about—while the Indian population was slowly driven to extinction. Only in 1904 did France relinquish her right to fish off the west coast of Newfoundland, and that was in return for a strip of land in West Africa.

The booklet went on to revel in the glorious moments of history that were recorded in Newfoundland: the last battle of the Seven Years War, at Signal Hill; the laying of the first transatlantic cable; the receiving of Marconi's first wireless signal from Europe; and the drafting of the Atlantic Charter by Churchill and Roosevelt, in Argentia harbour. There was not a word on Joey Smallwood.

I also noticed there was just a passing reference to Labrador, which covers three times as much territory as the island yet holds about as much value to Newfoundland as Greenland does to Denmark. (In 2002, more than half a century after joining Confederation, the province formally renamed itself Newfoundland and Labrador, in a move that came across like one of those clumsy corporate mergers in which the junior firm gets distinct second billing.) One description said everything I needed to know about the internal relationship of Canada's twinned province. "Labrador is a wild land, ruthless and bare and strong, that seems to have risen overnight from chaos, dripping wet," the official document claimed, quoting directly from the writings of one historian, Lt. Col. William Wood. He went on to identify Labrador as "the only land now left on the face of the earth that actually stood by when Life was born."

Tucked away in the back of the booklet was a discourse on the annihilation of the Beothuk Indians. The original "red" Indians—so nicknamed by European explorers because they dressed their faces with red and ochre paint—the Beothuks lasted five centuries on the island before their last woman died in 1829. The ones who were not killed by fishermen trying to establish settlements along the northern coast had succumbed to the many foreign diseases that the Europeans had brought with them.

The booklet, though, had some helpful Newfoundland hints, which it laid out plainly for the visitor. Did you know, for example, that you can relieve a headache by walking backwards—"around in a circle preferably"? Or cure hemorrhoids with pine tar? Or fight a cough with a mixture of kerosene oil and molasses?

The more I read of the government's take on Newfoundland, the more I grew to like the place. It sure beat the usual bumph of economic growth figures, landscape photography and a welcome letter from the premier. In my time on the roadside, I was able to equip myself with an arsenal of figures of speech, all laid out in the booklet, that surely would serve me well. "Hard as the knockers of Newgate!" I could tell the next driver. Or, given the rain that was starting to come down, "wet as dung." For my long hours on the roadside, I could say that it had been "a noggin to scape." Or "Nofty was forty when he lost the pork," meaning we should never be sure of anything.

I was just getting into the song sheets, fifteen pages of them which the government wanted tourists to have at the ready, when a car pulled over. The driver looked older than Curtis, which I took as a warning for another earful. Given the drizzle, I had little choice.

"We got more resources per capita than any other province," Ted Sheares said within moments of introducing himself. "The federal government has robbed, plundered and wasted it all. We're poorer off today, in a sense, than we were when we joined Confederation."

Ted was eighty years old, and a retired something. I didn't get the chance to ask what he was retired from, because he continued with the diatribe he had started as soon as he heard I was from the *Globe and Mail*—"the *Toronto Globe and Mail,* you mean."

First it was the cod. "While we're not allowed to go out and catch, foreign trawlers are out there scraping the bottom," Ted said.

Then it was Churchill Falls. "Smallwood made a bad deal. I'll agree with that."

And on to offshore oil. "Last year Newfoundland got $10 million while the federal government got $60 million. We should have got the sixty million because we owned the damn stuff and brought it into Confederation. You know who I blame? Trudeau. When Alberta wanted to ship gas and oil to Ontario and Quebec, Mr. Trudeau said,

'Oh, no problem. We'll build you a corridor across the other provinces.' But what did he give us? Nothing."

I wanted to ask Ted if he was related to Curtis, or a neighbour perhaps. Surely they had coordinated this series of rides, just to make sure I got the point. But he wasn't. Ted was on his way home from a visit to the city, driving up Highway 430 alone in his little Dodge to a small town where he had lived most of his life. Up this coast, he said, there were entire villages of old people, abandoned by children who couldn't make ends meet in western Newfoundland.

After his initial outburst, Ted wanted to be conciliatory. The trouble lay with politicians and bureaucrats, not ordinary people like me, he said. Canadians were good. The feds were bad.

"We made the right move to join Canada because Canada is one of the wealthiest countries in the world. But the world has never seen a greater bunch of clowns and thieves than the ones we've seen in Ottawa. There's never been a bigger bunch of rogues in the world than the ones in Ottawa. No country in the world, not even the Communist ones, would treat a province the way Canada treats Newfoundland."

Now this Communist bit was going too far. I had been insulted in every province so far, and could not take it any more. Asking Ted to pull over, I reached under the front seat for his tire wrench and, before he could stop, took the hardest swing I could muster against his windshield. If he wanted to know how Communist countries treated people, I shouted, I'd do the same to his kneecaps.

Actually, I just sat there and agreed with everything he said, nodding politely as he spoke, tsk-tsking when appropriate and feverishly taking notes. It seemed like a good Canadian response. And then I was saved by nature.

We came around a bend that opened to a breathtaking panorama of Gros Morne, unfolding before us in a series of forested valleys and hilltop lakes. The drizzle had passed and the sprawling park, which ran forty kilometres to the coast and another eighty kilometres north, looked like a wonderland of creation. As if to make the point, a sign warned drivers to keep their eyes on the road. In the first seven months of the year, it said, drivers in the park had collided with twenty moose and three caribou.

Ted dropped me by the side of the highway outside Rocky Harbour, a seaside village that serves as a headquarters to the park. I still had a couple of hours of daylight to make my way up the coast, but wanted to see some of Gros Morne. I walked to a bed and breakfast, dropped my knapsack and headed for the closest trail I could find. It was a path that wound its way around a tower-like hill, past a newly posted bear warning and on to a final ascent of wooden stairs.

From the lookout, I could see bogs that would take a century just to fill the impression of a footprint, and the million-year-old Gros Morne Mountain and adjoining ridge that runs like a spine, eight hundred metres high, through the park. Beyond it lay the enchanting fjord of Western Brook Pond, which carves its way through a labyrinth of towering cliffs rising half a kilometre from the chilling water. If the weather held out, I could catch a tourist boat through the pond in the morning and be on the road again by noon.

For all the quirks one can find on the road in Canada, there are more to be found in the nation's bed and breakfasts. They're hospitality's answer to hitchhiking, for no other form of accommodation forces people to share their experiences with strangers. I discovered this at the Evergreen Bed & Breakfast in Rocky Harbour, which I returned to after my hike, hoping I could write my daily report in the living room. From the moment I sat down, I was interrupted with questions from people from Detroit, Halifax and Guelph, Ontario. Somehow, I felt my privacy was being invaded with every query, but clearly I didn't understand the rules. Out on the road, one of the unspoken agreements between hitchhikers and their fleeting patrons is that they will answer each other's questions. It was to be the same here, in the renovated basement of Carson and Sarah

Wentzell's house. If I thought I was entitled to an evening of solitude, I thought wrong.

Cheery conversation with strangers is just one of the universally
accepted rules of a bed and breakfast. Among the others: no
grumpiness in the morning, no underwear in the hallways, no travel
pointer too trivial to share with the other guests. You don't express
strongly felt opinions about political parties or sports teams. You
express interest in how the others slept, even though a day earlier
you probably cut them off on the highway. You indulge the
Americans with their boring stories about sore feet. And if you're
Canadian, you make your bed.

Slowly I was coming to appreciate the B&B as a middle-class cult.
After writing my article for that day, I submitted to the will of the
crowd and watched the end of *Survivor*, listening in commercial
breaks to everyone's experiences of the day. At the end, Detroit and
Guelph said good night. Halifax stayed up to catch the local news.

In the morning, at the exact hour Sarah had urged everyone to
be at the table so she wouldn't have to make pancakes twice, we all
greeted each other like newlyweds. Frankly, I never thought so many
happy people could sit at one breakfast table, at least not outside
Utah. The others, having had a night to sleep on it, still found it baf-
fling that I actually wanted to hitchhike. The man from Halifax
asked why the *Globe and Mail* could not afford to rent me a car. His
wife looked at me sympathetically, like I might be running away
from problems at home. The Americans wondered if I was breaking
the law. I tried again to explain my motives, while tucking a fork
deep into the first mound of pancakes. Eggs, bacon and cereal were
also on the table, and I took a generous helping of each. When
hitchhiking, breakfast is usually the main meal of the day.

"It's a great way to see the country," I said.

The Americans looked unconvinced.

From the living room, Newfoundland Television's morning
program was playing at a loud volume, loud enough that everyone
at the table could hear it forecast a hundred per cent chance of rain

that morning. I assumed Newfoundland Television was a world leader in forecasting rain, but finished my pancakes and said good-bye to the others just the same. I had to see the fjord.

Down the road, as a cold rain drenched Rocky Harbour, I had arranged to catch a ride to Western Brook Pond with the boat crew who travelled there every morning in a minivan. Newfoundlanders all of them, the six young men and women didn't need prompting to talk. They dove into a swirl of simultaneous conversations.

"I am froze!" a young man shouted, as soon as the van doors closed.

"By gosh, look at that guy tailgating," another man exclaimed once we were on the highway. "It's like the 401 on a Friday afternoon."

I was beginning to see that Canadians, far and wide, could describe Highway 401—the lifeline of southern Ontario—better than the Charter of Rights and Freedoms.

"Jeb, is there a pub night tomorrow?" asked a voice from the back of the van.

"Yeah, in my basement," a man responded. I assumed he was Jeb.

When we reached the Western Brook parking lot, the van driver hollered to another driver that he had noticed a couple of hitch-hikers on the road, about a kilometre back, headed in this direction. Would he mind going back and picking them up? Only in Newfoundland, I thought, would a rescue mission be launched for a couple of hitchhikers caught in a rainstorm.

A forty-knot wind was ripping off the Gulf of St. Lawrence, with driving rains hard enough to keep your chin tucked into your chest for hours. "White horses on the bay," they say of a good storm. Our group hiked inland anyway, but did not escape the white horses rolling across the fjord with such intensity that none of the crew was willing to risk it on the water today. The rain wasn't what bothered them, not a group of Newfoundlanders. They were spooked by the inland waves that were big enough to capsize a tour boat.

With so much rain coming down, I was lucky to get back to the road and catch a quick ride north to Cow Head, ten minutes up the highway. Near the park's northern boundary, Cow Head was popular for its summer theatre and the sand dunes at nearby Shallow Bay. But I was taken by its name, whose originality was part of a Newfoundland tradition. The rest of the Maritimes was content with borrowed place names, usually from England. On the mainland, Kings, Queens, Yorks and Kents were so common you'd think New Brunswick was one big Marks and Spencer. But on the Rock, everyone's a poet. They had created the delightfully rhythmic Blow Me Down, Come-by-Chance and Ha Ha Bay, as well as the laconically expressive Confusion Bay, Empty Basket and Misery Point, although I preferred the curiously descriptive Cheese Island, Bacon Cove, Little Cat Arm and Jerry's Nose. So why did they name their capital St. John's? Even that one place name that suggested an empty barrel of creative juice—the northwestern community of Nameless Cove—showed more imagination

More vulgar names sprang to mind as I stood next to the Ultramar station, outside Cow Head, in a torrential rain that drove hard against my rain jacket and pant legs. I stood for just over an hour in the rain and cold wind, losing a degree of hope with each passing minute as my sopping wet clothes became another reason for people not to stop. Most of the drivers were truckers, anyway, who for insurance reasons were usually not allowed to pick up riders.

Between the trucks, there was an occasional RV or camper van, no doubt headed to L'Anse-aux-Meadows, but I had given up on the big daddies of the highway. The drivers, sitting so high off the road, could hardly see me down on the shoulder, except for one camper van. As it roared by me, I made eye contact with a middle-aged woman in the passenger seat. I must have looked genuinely pathetic because fifty metres down the road the camper van pulled over. When I got to the door, the woman was collecting some books and magazines from the single rear passenger seat. She said I need not worry about getting the seat wet. The van was a rental.

Back on the highway, the couple apologized for being so hesitant when they had stopped. They had never picked up a hitchhiker before and had no idea what to expect. "You looked pretty rough," the woman said.

Once I had my wet jacket off, though, she looked relieved, even amused. I spoke in complete sentences, brandished no weapons and resembled no one on last season's *America's Most Wanted*.

Rick and Lee were from British Columbia, on their way to Viking country as part of a three-week driving vacation in Newfoundland. They were also part of a big emerging group of drivers who were changing the shape of North American highways. Handsomely in their fifties, they were semi-retired boomers, with plenty of savings to spend on gas, no shortage of time to take to the road and no serious health problems to hold them down. Back in Abbotsford, British Columbia, Rick had sold his Sears dealership in order to spend more time with his grandchildren, and more time skiing, golfing and hiking. Lee, his second wife, still worked as a special education teacher in an Abbotsford high school, but had an increasing amount of spare time, as well, to spend with her own grandchildren and to travel. That spring, the couple had been to Beijing. Ironically, this was their first trip to the far east of Canada, the first time either had been east of Toronto.

I pointed out that in much of the world people in their position would spend their time watching and raising their grandchildren.

"Grandparents here would rather be out travelling," Lee said, laughing.

"We don't value elders and I don't understand why that is," Rick said sombrely. "Almost everywhere else in the world, it's different. Most cultures respect their elders. They value them."

At the next service station, Rick pulled over. He insisted on buying me a bowl of warm chowder and a slice of blueberry pie. I still looked chilled, he said. Newfoundlanders, I was relieved to find, did not have a monopoly on kindness.

Past Port au Choix, home to an ancient Indian cemetery that was accidentally discovered in 1967, the landscape turned barren again, a prelude to Labrador, which was getting ever closer. The land along the highway was so devoid of green that residents had trucked in topsoil, planted small kitchen gardens and fenced them off from the surrounding bog. The remaining growth consisted of tiny shrubs and struggling seedlings that gave the impression we were approaching the treeline, rather than being eight hundred kilometres south of it in Saint Barbe, the jumping-off point to Blanc-Sablon and the rest of Canada.

When Jacques Cartier sailed through the narrow Strait of Belle Isle in 1534, landing on the mainland at the fishing community of Blanc-Sablon, he expressed the sort of disappointment that explorers rarely share. Usually enthusiastic about the most mundane discoveries, Cartier could not contain his contempt for the shoreline that would become known as Labrador Straits.

"Except at Blanc-Sablon, there is nothing but moss and short, stunted shrub," he wrote during his first voyage into the Gulf of St. Lawrence. He was looking at the oldest rock formation on the planet, as clear an indication as the world could offer of what earth was like before life.

The sheltered coast was also blessed with natural harbours and close to some of the world's great cod stocks, enough to have supported human habitation in this area for eighty-five hundred years before the great explorer's time. Yet Cartier was "rather inclined to believe that this is the land that God gave to Cain." There are only fifteen days a year of sunshine, barely enough to produce the skimpiest of berries on the rocky landscape. "There are people on this coast whose bodies are fairly well formed but they are wild and savage folk," he wrote.

Four hundred and sixty-six years later, I hoped to take a ferry across the same strait to the same remote stretch of Labrador. From what I had read of the place, Labrador Straits was both rooted in its considerable past and changing as fast as any region on the East Coast. Cartier, I dared guess, would not recognize the place.

Rick and Lee dropped me at Saint-Barbe, where the ferry to Labrador docks. Crossing the strait in ninety minutes sounded like the Concorde compared to the MV *Caribou*. I would be in Blanc-Sablon by late afternoon. On the ferry, I found a brochure for a B&B in L'Anse-au-Clair, the first community northeast of Blanc-Sablon, and called ahead to book a room. One of the most surprising discoveries while travelling in remote parts of Canada is the almost universal access to telecommunications. Even the ferries have working telephones and debit card machines. Fashions were also beginning to look universal. On the ferry, a group of teenaged girls returning to Labrador were dressed in bell-bottoms. I noticed a fisherman in Tommy Hilfiger jeans. Another man wore a T-shirt promoting The Rock—the wrestling star, not Newfoundland.

When we landed at Blanc-Sablon, the storm had subsided, leaving only a gentle breeze to rustle a Quebec flag flying over the pier, marking the new province we had just entered. To the southwest, a road leads to four more Quebec communities, followed by a huge stretch of wilderness that divides this region from the rest of the province. Not surprisingly, much of Blanc-Sablon's heart lies to the northeast, on a road that crosses innocuously into Labrador and onward to seven fishing villages.

I had planned to walk through the small francophone community and into Labrador, following the procession of pickup trucks and vans rolling off the ferry, loaded to the brim with packaged foods, garbage cans and building materials. But I was not over the first hill when a woman stopped and offered me a ride. She was the ferry's gift shop operator and had seen me on board. Rhoda notices all the strangers on board. Besides, she asked, what harm could a stranger do? There was a dead end in either direction, and no way out but the ferry.

On the short drive over the ridge to L'Anse-au-Clair, the landscape looked even less hospitable than it had been on the upper reaches of Newfoundland. Nothing but thorn bushes and shrubs emerged from the rocky soil, and this was after a summer of rain and sun. As we drove out of Quebec, I asked Rhoda what people over here did for fun. She was taken aback by the question, thinking for several moments before answering.

"In the summer we go berry pickin'," she said. Blueberries, blackberries and Labrador's cherished cloudberries ran amok on the ridges that otherwise looked bereft of life. But she warned me not to try my hand at picking, unless it was a very windy day. The blackflies, she said, would kill me.

I changed the subject to winter, the common blackfly's worst enemy.

"The men go lookin' fer firewood," Rhoda said without pausing.

And the women?

"I guess we go snowmobilin'."

Before we reached the B&B, Rhoda remembered something else people did for fun around here during their short summers. They prepared for the annual Labrador Straits Bakeapple Folk Festival, which was due to open that night in L'Anse-au-Loup, up the road. If I was lucky, Rhoda said, I would catch a game of chicken-shit betting, which she described as a game of chance in which players bet on the part of a mat where they think a chicken will relieve itself. "You could win two hundred dollars," she promised me.

Fortunately, there was an Ontario couple staying at the B&B, and they were as curious about the bakeapple festival as I was. More importantly, they had a car. When we got to the L'Anse-au-Loup hockey arena, where the festival had been held every year since 1979, the parking lot was full, and a lineup had formed at the door. Inside, the official program was about to begin, starting with stirring renditions of "Ode to Labrador" and "O Canada." There was no suggestion of anyone singing "Ode to Newfoundland."

Everyone bellowed in unison:

Dear Land of Mountains, Wood and Snow,
Labrador our Labrador,
God's noble gift to us below,
Labrador our Labrador,
Thy proud resources waiting still, their splendid task
    will soon fulfill,
Obedient to thy maker's will,
Labrador our Labrador.

"Ode to Labrador" went on to salute stately forests and mighty floods, but I liked the final lines best:

Our snowshoes scar the trackless plain,
We seek no city streets nor lanes,
We are thy sons while life remains,
Labrador our Labrador.

Having declared themselves to be real rural folk, the crowd settled in for an evening of songs and skits. The Ontario couple were not interested in staying much longer, while I wanted to find out what made this place, so far from city streets and lanes, different from the place across the straits. I thanked them for the ride and said I would make my own way back to the B&B.

As more songs began, I worked my way through the surprisingly young crowd, watching them indulge in beer and ice cream, until I came across a woman, Yvonne Jones, who had been introduced to the crowd as their representative in the provincial legislature. I asked her if what I had seen in my first few hours in Labrador was correct, that there was a modest building boom underway. Instead of a series of impoverished fishing villages, which was what I had expected to find, places like L'Anse-au-Loup appeared to be well on the mend after the devastating collapse of their cod fishery in the early 1990s.

Yvonne, the politician, took pride in the resurgence, which she said was the result of the crab boom, as well as a gradual return of the cod. "The stocks are probably better and the fish bigger than even ten years before the fishery closed," she said.

For thousands of years, cod had been a way of life along this coast, until over-fishing took its toll and the federal government was forced to suspend the fishery. The decision threatened to cripple most of Newfoundland, but few places would be hit harder than Labrador Straits. There was nothing else here, other than berries and blackflies.

Yvonne passed me on to Dean Flynn, the local fisheries officer. She had votes to secure and a speech to make, right after a rendition of "Heave Away."

Dean did not look like a fisherman. He wore designer jeans and a crisply ironed shirt, and had the big shoulders and frame of a hockey player, not the lean look of a man who had to spend his summers at sea. He explained that he was part of a new generation on the coast. Twenty years ago, he graduated from high school and left Labrador for college, as did about two-thirds of his high school class. A generation earlier, no one from these parts went to college. Dean lived in Halifax for ten years, but never got used to the way people kept their guard up. Once, when he knocked on a neighbour's door to ask for an egg so that he could bake a cake, "the lady looked at me like I was crazy."

He eventually came home, as did about half his classmates who had left the straits and eventually returned. He had missed being able to leave his house unlocked. He had missed the respect that people around his hometown showed for their elders. Perhaps most of all, he had missed feeling secure about his eight-year-old daughter when he wasn't around.

"She can get on her bike and ride anywhere in town," he said. "If a strange car stopped and talked to her, I know a neighbour would be out right away, asking who she's talkin' to."

Onstage, a group of kids were doing a skit about bakeapples. "My mother says don't eat a lot," one girl said, "or else you'll have to sit on the pot."

This sort of collective spirit, Dean explained, had pulled Labrador Straits through its toughest years. While tens of thousands of young people were leaving Newfoundland, a group of men and women here had decided to fight for their communities. They lobbied the provincial and federal governments for support and got a computer centre and business development centre for the coast. They also started to package the area for tourism, with brochures, guided hunting and fishing tours, and improved air service.

Dean's brother-in-law turned his takeout shop into a restaurant and bakeapple preserve operation that now sold its products to Sobey's, the big Maritimes grocery chain. He was doing a million dollars a year in business. Up in Red Bay, at the end of the road, another family was making outdoor clothing and selling it to shops in Toronto and Montreal. In all, there were 120 registered businesses along the coast—for two thousand people.

"I think five years ago, few young people would have thought about staying," Dean said. "Now a fourteen-year-old sees it as something that can be very lucrative."

The bakeapple skit was followed by Dean's brother-in-law— Uncle Ray to everyone along the straits—doing a Texarkana lip-synch number that wowed the audience.

During the next break, Dean introduced me to one of the evening's stars, Terry Reilly, a children's performer who came here often enough to appreciate the changes. Since he spent his working year travelling around Newfoundland, Terry saw the hardest-hit communities and how they were struggling to stay alive without cod. Many didn't have children any more for him to entertain. In Labrador, by contrast, he found a tradition of neighbours helping neighbours, and generations helping generations. Among adults, there was a passion for community service, which he said explained why eight villages could have 110 volunteer organizations. But Terry saw the greatest hope in the schools, where children clamoured to learn local songs.

"There's a real love and admiration for where they come from," he said. "Sure, they listen to the Backstreet Boys, but they still love

'You Are My Sunshine.' Part of it is the old-timers take time to share the music and traditions. They don't get put away in retirement homes as quickly as in Ottawa or Toronto."

The talent show continued through the evening, with local women doing an exercise routine onstage and more parents lip-synching the Elton John songs of their youth. The evening ended with the entire arena singing "You Are My Sunshine," which must have special meaning in a place that gets only fifteen days of it every year.

Labrador Straits, this little thin stretch of two thousand people laid along the eastern edge of Canada, seemed like some kind of Pleasantville in the bush, where there was no need to write law, order and good government into a constitution. They just happened. Even the first half of the road's postal code—AOK—stressed that great Canadian quest for harmony.

I had just come through the most distraught region of Canada, where entire economies had collapsed and cultures were eroding, so much so that a distinct and essential part of the country was at risk. In many places, those who were willing to stick around were either too old or too derelict to do much to reverse the tide. Yet there were places like Moncton and people like Curtis Baxter who were turning things around. In Labrador Straits, they did it with a bit of local ingenuity, a bit of outside support and a lot of community co-operation, enough to staunch the outflow of youth that was bleeding so much of the Maritimes' last best hopes. If this could be done in the land that God gave to Cain, I wondered, why couldn't it be done everywhere?

As the festival's opening night ended, I followed the crowd to the parking lot and then onto the road, wondering how many homes on the hillside were unlocked. There was no need to worry about getting back to L'Anse-au-Clair. Even though the road was as dark as the Labrador soil, I felt safe in the glare of headlights, holding out my thumb for a ride.

The best way out of Blanc-Sablon was the once-a-week ferry down the St. Lawrence River to Natashquan and the beginning of a highway that ran straight across to Vancouver. Since the next one did not leave until midnight, I decided to spend Friday hitchhiking the other way, up the only road of southern Labrador, to Red Bay. I should have stayed in bed. Despite all the talk about friendly and supportive people here, one car after another drove right by. Where were all those people who had sung "You Are My Sunshine"? Finally, I got a short lift to Forteau and another to L'Anse-au-Loup on a road that jutted and swerved with the coastline.

The unusually sunny day splashed life and colour along the desolate coast. I could see why the entrepreneurs were so excited about tourism. But as I waited for another ride on a ridge overlooking the strait, I felt a nip, then another, and another. When I changed my focus from the road on the horizon to the air above my head, I could see swarms of blackflies. And then they were gone. A burst of wind off the sea had blown them away, as quickly as they had come.

A few minutes later, they were back. The erratic wind had not been enough to do anything more than chase the bugs to shelter and allow them to regroup. When I ran my fingers through the hair on the back of my neck, I felt a string of bumps. Then I felt a nip inside my ear, which I unwisely scratched, pulling out a fingertip of blood. As cars continued to pass with the drivers not so much as waving, I decided to walk briskly back to L'Anse-au-Loup to do something I ought to have done hundreds of kilometres earlier, at the Irving station outside Tompkins. I bought some bug spray.

Safe from the frustrated swarms, I got back to the ridge in time to watch a thick fog roll off the sea and swallow the entire scrubland around me. I couldn't see five metres ahead on the road. The temperature must have dropped five degrees in a quarter of an hour, leaving me suddenly cold. Both the sunny day and the bugs were gone.

I got a couple of short rides but didn't make it beyond Pinware River Provincial Park before worrying that I might not get back to Blanc-Sablon for the midnight ferry. But the thought of a week at the Bakeapple Festival was too much. There was also every chance the sea breeze would fade, and once again I would be devoured by blackflies.

Turning around, I was passed again by a couple of pickup trucks. What did they think? That I was going to pull out a gun and force them to drive to Mexico? Then a Mercedes came around the corner and slowed to a stop. The driver moved his flight bag to the back seat, all the while talking on a cell phone. When the call was finished, a few kilometres down the road, he introduced himself as a stockbroker from the island. We chatted briefly about the market. And then he was back on the phone, talking variously to clients and his wife, all the way to my B&B.

5
René's Children

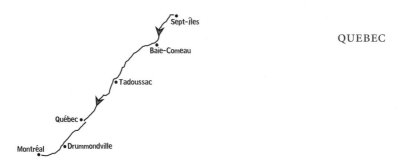

Thereere could not be a worse time, I thought, to load up a ferry and head upriver on a thirty-three-hour journey than midnight on a Friday. The passengers would have all evening to spend in bars near the dock. The first swell would be disastrous to all those with only beer and bakeapple pie in their stomachs. And then the passengers would have to spend the weekend together, recuperating in cramped, undulating quarters. The MV *Relais Nordik* does it anyway, heading into the gulf and up the St. Lawrence every Friday in summer at midnight.

I discovered the hard way how wrong I was, that I was possibly the only novice on board. As soon as I was off the gangplank and searching for a seat, I saw that a few stiff ones were in fact the best way to ensure sleep on a crowded ferry. Every chair, bench and available patch of floor was already claimed by someone who, judging by the heavy snores that collectively drowned out the ferry's engine, had come on board prepared. I would have to content myself wandering the ferry, studying its load, until we were in motion. At the rear, on an open cargo deck, were vehicles, mostly SUVs with Quebec plates, bearing rooftop cases, bicycles, kayaks—the telltale signs of affluent vacation travel. Up front, the passengers were given three indoor decks, including a cafeteria with a menu built around poutine and a video lounge that had started playing an Arnold Schwarzenegger movie when I made my way inside.

Only after I found a narrow interior stairway leading to another deck did I find a place to crash, in the appropriately named Red Room. In the dark, I spotted three adjoining seats that were empty, a miraculous combination that would allow me, in the fashion of a truly fortunate economy-class traveller, to curl up for the night, with my rib cage nestled into a protruding seat-belt clip. As we hit the first swell, I felt a jab and looked at my watch. There were six hours left till sunrise. The deep, rhythmic snoring in the next row went on, undisturbed. And there was nowhere to get a drink.

——— ——— ———

When daylight finally came, the ferry felt no different bouncing along the lower north shore of the St. Lawrence than it had the night before in Blanc-Sablon harbour. Arnie was still on the video screens, in a different movie, killing someone else in a war somewhere else. And in the cafeteria, poutine was still on offer, as a breakfast special, though thankfully the cook had also put out a tray of baked goods.

I took a coffee and muffin and headed to the outside deck, where people were already trying to sun themselves, so their bones could recover from the chilled August night. Watching the Quebec shore roll by, some of the passengers pulled out binoculars and searched for wildlife along the unforgiving rocky coast where little razorbill penguins and Atlantic puffins squabbled over patches of golden lichen-coated rock. One man unfolded his telescope and was busy describing bird life, in French, to his wife.

There was not much else to do, as we chugged leisurely upriver, and not much else to see. As formidable as it sounded in the journals of early explorers, the gateway to central Canada was singularly boring. On one side of us, there was the lower north shore, which was little more than a long scattering of barren islets spread out like an ancient minefield. The tiny islands, thousands of them, consisted of rock and lichen, and nothing more, as did the coastline behind them that gives rise to the Laurentian Shield. On the other side, there was the Gulf of St. Lawrence, a sea big enough to swallow England, Scotland and Wales. The exception to this drab landscape was the small fishing communities that popped up every hundred kilometres or so, each built on the shifting currents of the gulf's fishery and the generosity of very faraway governments. They were the forgotten outposts of far-eastern Quebec.

The ferry's first stop of any duration was at Tête-à-la-Baleine, named for a "whale's head" figure ascribed to a rocky islet nearby. Most of the passengers were content to sit on the pier and nurse their hangovers, but seeing as the ferry would be docked for at least an hour, to unload supplies for the town, I signed up for a Tête-à-la-Baleine tour run by an enterprising local youth.

Davis Marcoux drove a group of us in his family's van along a twelve-kilometre stretch of gravel road and small bridges that stitched one islet to the next, connecting the deep-water harbour to town. The little stretch of dirt and gravel was marked Highway 138, the same road that connects Quebec City and Montreal. The inlets around Tête-à-la-Baleine were first developed, as was much of the lower north shore, as a sanctuary for schooners, Davis explained to the ten of us crowded into the back of his van. In its time, just twenty years ago, the community was home to five hundred people. Davis's grandfather fished all summer for cod and snow crab, and spent the winter on pogey, while trapping and hunting seal. But that was another age. The cod and seal were almost gone. The factory for melting seal fat, the one industry the village had known, was closed. There were 240 people left.

Young people like Davis saw no future here because, realistically, there wasn't one. Like every kid in Tête-à-la-Baleine, he had to leave the village after Grade 10, to continue schooling in Blanc-Sablon and then in Sept-Îles, twenty-four hours upriver by ferry. As remote as his home was, Davis could make work for himself in the summer, guiding tourists around his outport. He doubted he could do the same year-round, at least not enough to allow him to move back to the lower north shore, where his grandfather had shown him every nook on the land and every wrinkle on the sea. The only young people who were betting their future on this place, he explained, were the local Montagnais Indians, who lived in their own community nearby.

We continued along the modest causeway as it crossed more islets. On the larger ones, there were small rowboats as well as several new motorboats beached on the ebb of a low tide—evidence of money that people were earning outside and bringing home, in small doses, on summer vacations. Davis pointed to his favourite fishing streams and the trails that he and his buddies used to follow, in winter, by snowmobile. Just to get a good game of hockey going, they had to drive four hours across snow and ice to the next hamlet. In Sept-Îles, he could walk down the street to an arena.

The routine Davis described sounded similar to the isolated lifestyle that stretches from the Labrador coast up to the Arctic—until we entered Tête-à-la-Baleine. The village was positively Quebec. In the centre of the community was a Roman Catholic church and a *caisse populaire,* the twin pillars of rural Quebec. The school, École Gabriel Dionne, flew just one flag, the province's fleur-de-lys. Only the distinctly sterile architecture of a remote community—square bungalows wrapped in aluminum siding—separated the place in spirit from the heartland of Quebec's independence movement, up the river. It was hard to believe we were still as far from Quebec City as Quebec City was from Windsor, Ontario.

Inside the school, Davis took us to a crafts bazaar set up for an hour whenever a ferry was in port. The local ladies sold a variety of sealskin products. They knew this was no way to keep a community alive. They didn't know what could. Several residents talked about ecotourism, that great chimera of remote communities in decline. But Davis admitted it was a long way to come for a canoe trip.

Having been in the city for a couple of years, he had adopted some affectations of urban life. He wore a No Fear ball cap and T-shirt, and was just enough pounds overweight to look like he hadn't spent much time in the bush lately. But that wasn't Sept-Îles's doing. The whole village was growing soft. I asked Davis what he watched on television when he was out here for the summer. He had two answers: *Survivor* and *Jerry Springer*. He liked to watch Springer with his grandfather. The old fisherman loved the fight scenes, although it was not his favourite program on daytime television. In season or not, the old guy never missed *The Price Is Right*.

If Jerry Springer and Bob Barker could carve their way into the psyche of Tête-à-la-Baleine—as distinct a place as one could find in North America—I wondered what hope might lie ahead for Quebec. Surely if the lower north shore was going American, what chance was there for the Saguenay, with roads and airports built and ready for a cultural invasion?

"For me, Quebec *libre* is not a primary concern," Davis explained as our group piled back into the van. "My primary concern is a career. Canada or Quebec, it's the same to me."

The MV *Relais Nordik* was set to sail when Davis got us there, an indication of how down pat he had the routine. On board, I found the purser's office and studied his navigation map, to see our course for the day. The next port of call, only thirty-seven kilometres away, sounded like a redoubt for the province's last anglophone hope, the sort of place that René Lévesque forgot. Just the fact that it had kept its name was scandalously inviting.

Harrington Harbour was built on a hillside of rock and bog so poorly drained that instead of roads the community had wooden walkways. From house to store to school, people drove four-wheel all-terrain vehicles on the maze of walkways. Even the driveways to the big wooden houses (big at least by lower north shore standards) were designed for ATVs. When we docked, I followed the board-walks up the hill, noticing how in every way this outport was differ-ent from the last. The only church was Anglican. Every flag in sight was Canadian. And almost all the signs were in English. "Rowsell

Welding and Repairs," for example—a dangerous combination of nouns and a conjunction that would be illegal, perhaps treasonous, elsewhere in the province.

At the top of a hill overlooking Harrington Harbour, I found a more curious fixture still, a nursing home. It bore a Quebec flag, the only one I could find in the village, and a plaque to Donald Gordon Hodd, a doctor who joined the Grenfell Mission in 1928 and set up a hospital there, which he ran until 1970. He died eight years later, at the age of eighty, having planted the roots of an anglo community that even the Parti Québécois could not chase away.

On my way back from the nursing home, I stopped at Amy's Bed & Breakfast (plus meals) & Craft Shop to see if I could find a quick explanation of this cultural outpost. Amy Evans was the ideal person to provide it. Middle-aged, she still spoke with a splash of the Newfoundland lilt she took from her grandfather. Like a lot of Harrington residents, he had moved here from the island to fish, and stayed. The local harbour was safe for schooners, and the Gulf of St. Lawrence back then was brimming with cod. "We feel we have more in common with Newfoundland than Quebec," Amy said.

The local fishermen and their families never bothered to learn French. They figured they'd never have to, not as long as the currents took them eastward. They found a way around the province's education law to keep their school English-medium. As for Quebec's sign laws, Harrington Harbour was one of a small number of communities that was allowed to protect its native language. No one had bothered to check anyway, Amy explained, sitting in her cozy shop filled with local carvings and sealskins.

Unlike Tête-à-la-Baleine, Harrington Harbour was not in terminal decline. The village's population of three hundred was stable, thanks in part to a fish plant owned by a local co-operative. It employed up to fifty people at any given time. A local sawmill was kept busy providing two-by-fours to the boardwalk industry.

The retirement home was another matter. When the province took over the Grenfell Mission hospital in the 1970s, it converted the institution into a retirement home, serving the lower north shore. Because of the province's language laws, though, all jobs had to go to French-speakers, which pretty much ruled out the local workforce. As for the Quebec flag, no one really minded. Harrington Harbour had no pretensions to secession. "There hasn't been a lot of hostility," Amy said, although someone in the crafts business tends not to be on the front lines of hostility.

What she really wanted was funding for a museum, but she couldn't write an application to the provincial government, at least not in her province's official language. And no one in the federal government had the slightest interest in this little fishing cove, way down the St. Lawrence. Amy shrugged. She would get on with it, as people in Harrington Harbour do.

I had not reached the figurative mainland of Quebec, but the old language divide was hardly tearing the province apart. Here, not far from each other on the lower north shore, were two very distinct communities—one French, one English—with similar challenges. How they would keep going was by no means a certainty. Harrington Harbour was more secure in its fate, but not for the right reasons. Its young people, schooled in English, could not move to Sept-Îles for college or a job. Newfoundland had little to offer them either. They'd have to move to Ontario for a better living, if that's what they wanted.

Back on the ferry, the moon was rising on one side of the gulf, and the sun setting on the other. Through another evening of action films and deep-fried food, we would make our way south and west toward the Jacques-Cartier Strait, running between the mainland and Île d'Anticosti, the huge natural wildlife reserve that is bigger than Prince Edward Island. Protected by cliffs, the island reserve was home to 120,000 white-tailed deer and three hundred people. By early morning, we would be docking in Natashquan, the western gate to the lower north shore, where the MV *Relais Nordik* met up with the real Highway 138. It was the end of the line, and the beginning.

I sat on the upper deck, under the stars, and looked at my road atlas. From Natashquan to the next break in the road, in North Vancouver, was fifty-seven hundred kilometres. I hoped to cover the distance in two weeks, although it had taken nine days just to cover the Maritimes. Canada, once again, was looking very big.

—— —— ——

Ever since the highway was extended to Natashquan three years ear-lier, the town had become the MV *Relais Nordik*'s main hopping-off point, even though the ferry continued 120 kilometres upriver to a much bigger port at Havre-St-Pierre. As vehicles queued to dis-embark, I could place my fate with either the slow boat or the fast road. I decided to jump ship, and got a ride with one of the first cars headed into town. The driver said he would drop me at the turnoff. That way, I could avoid other drivers who might be headed into Natashquan—perhaps they wanted to see the birthplace of singer Gilles Vigneault, who knows?—and focus my pleading eyes on the ones headed west.

What a mistake! For the next thirty minutes, I stood by the road, watching one vehicle after another—camper vans, minivans, SUVs, compacts, motorcycles—race by without even a gesture. People I had chatted with on the ferry looked right through me. A couple from the Tête-à-la-Baleine sightseeing tour shrugged, as if to say, "Too bad." Even a honeymooning couple, with kayaks, who had sat next to me through *T2*, acted like I was a stranger. I guess they had an excuse, but the others I wasn't so sure about.

I had to recalculate my decision, quickly. The ferry was leaving in twenty minutes and would reach Havre-St-Pierre in four hours, just after lunch. A good ride could get me there in ninety minutes. But at this rate, I could be stuck here all day, perhaps all week until the next ferry came through. I was leaning toward the ferry when a mid-sized sedan pulled over. A Natashquan man was headed for the next town of Aguanish. He assured me the rides would be better from there.

Almost from the moment I agreed to the short hop, I realized my error. All the traffic leaving Aguanish (if a car passing every ten minutes could be considered traffic) would be local, people who lived a day's drive from the nearest big city. They were sure to be isolated and paranoid about strangers.

When we reached Aguanish and I took to a new roadside, despondency set in—the easiest syndrome to hit a hitchhiker. I began to miss the awkward benches and greasy food of the MV *Relais Nordik.* Forty-five minutes passed. The cars and vans I had seen going from the ferry into Natashquan, perhaps to pick up supplies and a late breakfast, were now zipping by, giving me nothing more than a shrug. I was so glum about my prospects that I don't think I noticed the Dodge camper van passing, until, swinging around in boredom, I saw it two hundred metres down the way, reversing toward me.

The camper van looked like something out of the 1970s, as did the driver, a cigarette-smoking man with thinning Guy Lafleur hair. He told me to hop in. Although he rarely picked up hitchhikers, he said, he had seen me on the road at Natashquan and feared I would be devoured by mosquitoes. The blackflies of Labrador must have hardened my skin because I hadn't noticed any bugs here, but I thanked him anyway as we pulled onto the deserted highway and headed through the marshlands and bog beyond Aguanish.

Bernard Morency gave me his business card as soon as I introduced myself. He was headed home to Havre-St-Pierre, after a long sales trip down the lower north shore. He had been on the ferry, in the smoking lounge mainly, after visiting his customers along the coast and taking orders for pretty much anything they wanted. He ran a trading company and piled all the samples he could in the van, which was where he slept when he was not on the ferry.

Bernard had grown up along the Labrador coast and could explain its history as well as anyone. At least that's what he said when, after I explained the purpose of my trip, he started to tell me his life story. It was the driver's prerogative. Now forty-eight, Bernard was born in Blanc-Sablon to a Newfoundland fisherman who was always away, and a Quebec mother who, for the most part, had to raise thirteen children by herself. They ate what their father caught and what he could dry and salt for winter. Their mother made all their clothing. "That was life. We were poor. We had nothing, and we were happy," he said. "We knew nothing of the outside world."

He lit up another Matinée and continued, unmindful that he was not wearing a seat belt. Like most children in the region, he was sent away at twelve to a residential school near Lac Saint-Jean, a million miles from his roots on the Labrador Straits. Although he spoke little French, and his English was spiced with a Newfoundland accent, he went through high school in the crucible of Quebec nationalism. He managed. He went on to college, earned a teacher's certificate and taught French and English—both as second languages.

He quit teaching after he and his wife divorced and took up trading, to support their young daughter. Most of his business came from the lower north shore, especially La Romaine, about halfway between Harrington Harbour and Natashquan. Bernard figured sixty per cent of the town's people were on some form of social assistance, which was a small-time trader's dream. The Indians around there were also good customers, he explained, as long as he treated them on their terms. "They are calm, close to nature, never on time and indecisive," he said. "They don't know what time is. And when they say no, they probably mean yes. It's understandable. They only came out of their tents fifty years ago."

Bernard complained more about the ferry service, which he felt had tried to squeeze more people on board ever since it was taken over by a foreign company. "You can't get a good night's sleep on it any more," he said.

His trading days were almost over anyway. Ever since a friend had died of lung cancer a year earlier, he had been winding down his business. He wanted to enjoy his money. His daughter was in university in Montreal and would soon be out in the corporate world. She, the granddaughter of a subsistence fisherman, had become so bourgeois, Bernard said, laughing, that she refused to go deer hunting with him, not even to watch. If he could sell his business by the end of the year, he hoped to move to Costa Rica, which he had come to fancy during a vacation the previous winter. The weather was good, and the taxes were low—about as different from Quebec as he could find.

The camper van rattled and swerved at the slightest gust of wind as we blew our way through a hundred kilometres of unpopulated bush before reaching the flat marshland around Havre-St-Pierre. The local climate and geography were ideal for berry crops. The bog was also so thick it could swallow a picker. The previous week, Bernard said, a fourteen-year-old was rescued in the mire, stuck up to his chest in the marshland's answer to quicksand. He wasn't joking.

The town appeared by the mouth of the St. Lawrence, but my eyes were fixed on land. The houses—I gasped—they were huge. And in most driveways there were snowmobiles, jet skis and kayaks. A shopping mall that seemed to jump out at us was so big it seemed to cover a city block. I jotted in my notebook that Havre-St-Pierre had to be the back door to North America's leisure society, which was not far from the truth. Although the town once earned a living from a nearby titanium mine, it was increasingly driven by the service economy. Fittingly, the old Hudson's Bay Company store had given way to a local history museum.

Bernard drove me to the edge of town, near a couple of drive-throughs where, he said, I would have little trouble getting a ride. To my shock, he was right. Within a few minutes, a vacationing family from Quebec City pulled over and offered to take me swimming. The couple, with two preteen boys, were on their way to a river by Mingan, thirty kilometres down the road. The St. Lawrence, they said, was too cold.

While I appreciated the ride, I could not understand why the driver had interrupted his family's vacation to add a stranger to the back seat, along with his two sons. Perhaps he was bored. His wife remained silent. The boys played with a hand-held computer game, at least when they were not complaining about their father's decision to bring them here. They had been promised warm water.

The driver turned out to be a mid-level official in the provincial government and was genuinely curious about Ontario. As he asked questions, I felt like a foreign traveller describing my exotic home-land, except my answers were about things like stoplights and tax rates. When we reached the river, just short of Mingan, the man suggested I stay with the family and see the waterfalls where they planned to swim. He had heard they were stunning. Another ten minutes down a dirt road, I thought, would not be a problem, until I discovered why the falls were not mentioned in my guidebook. They were little more than a set of rapids. The boys continued to look unimpressed. The wife went for a walk by herself. Clearly, it was left to me to accompany the man to the riverside, where he took pictures of the rapids and praised their beauty. I couldn't wait to get back to the roadside.

Once the family had regrouped, they decided to continue to Mingan, a native town where the father had heard there was a good beach. For his sake, I hoped he was right, and asked if they could drop me at the first intersection. It turned out there was only one. As much as the vacationing family got to be tedious, they did give me a ride. At least they got me thirty kilometres closer to my destination, even if the waterfall detour took an hour out of my day. It beat standing on the roadside, which was what I was now doing in Mingan, thinking about how far it was from the Maritimes. There would be no cool mists here, just a dusty, hot afternoon sun. For the next ninety minutes, the only respite I could take from the heat was a gas station run by the local native band. At least pop was tax-free.

On the roadside, the threat of heat exhaustion was so great that, for a moment, I thought I was hallucinating, because there on the horizon, coming toward me, was a Dodge camper van. It looked like Bernard's. It was Bernard's.

Once I was back in the front passenger seat, Bernard explained that he was going to the next town, ten minutes down the road, to pick up a truck he had to get to Sept-Îles. He would hitch a ride back the next day to pick up the camper van. We were not out of view of Mingan when he suggested the obvious. If I drove the Dodge to Sept-Îles, he would be saved half a day's travel in the morning. It was, I agreed, a hitchhiker's fantasy. Only after we reached Longue-Pointe and drove to a house where a cube van was parked did I realize what I was getting into. I remembered all the times the Dodge engine had stalled on the road to Havre-St-Pierre, and Bernard cursing the ignition as he tried to restart it. As I got into the driver's seat of the same van, I noticed something else: the fuel gauge was on empty, even though Bernard insisted he had just filled the gas tank. I also discovered why he didn't wear a seat belt: there wasn't one for the driver. For all I knew, the van was loaded with drugs, too.

Before I left, Bernard had one other bit of information to share: the van was heavy and rocked easily. He then thought it necessary to warn me about the dangers of driving on a Sunday afternoon in summer. "There are too many tourists," he complained, lighting another cigarette. "They're looking everywhere but the road. They go too slow. You could kill someone, really."

With that, he told me to enjoy the trip. He would be along after a late lunch, and perhaps a sleep. He asked me to leave the van in the parking lot of a Sept-Îles shopping mall, with the keys under the driver's floor mat. There was no need to lock the door, he added. The locks didn't work.

My first instinct, once I had the van out on the highway, was to race ahead until I could catch and crush a BMW whose lone driver had waved to me as he left Mingan. But that thought didn't last long. I was hardly out of Longue-Point, trying to get the van to a hundred, when it began shaking wildly. This, I assumed, was what Bernard meant by the '79 Dodge being heavy. It swayed so much on turns that I resorted to straddling the highway's centre line, grateful there were no cars coming or going for the next few kilometres.

Once I had control of the Dodge, I looked around the dashboard and noticed Bernard had left two Greatest Hits music tapes.
One was Bryan Adams. The other was Whitney Houston. I put in
Bryan Adams, figuring a tinny bass stood a better chance than a
shrill soprano of getting the van up the next hill. The van lurched
and crawled, its speedometer dropping to zero just as I pulled over
the top. I had never been in a vehicle that had no momentum at the
top of a hill, to go either forward or backward, but the Dodge
stopped dead cold. I thought this would be the end of my journey,
stranded on a hilltop in eastern Quebec, where the police would
eventually find me—an anglophone no less—with a great haul of
narcotics from Costa Rica.

It was nothing that half a minute of pumping and revving
couldn't solve. Moving again, I noticed above the dashboard a
happy-face air freshener that did not seem to work. In fact, I had
started to notice a foul smell in the van and wondered if it was me.
Two nights sleeping on the ferry, followed by a day on the roadside,
could explain the odour. I had gone ten days without laundry, wash-
ing my underwear and socks at night wherever I was staying.

There must be something contagious on Quebec roads because
as soon as I was comfortable in the van, I had it up to 110 on corners, although every few minutes, invariably, another vehicle would
appear in the side-view mirror and then zoom past me. As the
highway hugged the St. Lawrence's north shore and climbed over
rocky outcrops to provide stunning vistas of the rolling coast, I
even tried Frank the German's technique of snapping pictures with
a camera held out the window. Pictures through the windshield
were not an option anyway, caked as it was with dead bugs. The
wipers didn't work.

When the highway was not peeping over the St. Lawrence, it was
cutting through thick forests and over the bountiful rivers that
made this part of Quebec an industrialist's dream. At one rest stop,
just beyond the Manitou River, the thunderous noise of a waterfall
was so loud I decided to risk turning off the engine and leaving

Bernard's unlocked van by the road. A forest trail led from the roadside deep into a gorge to the awesome sight of a cascading waterfall whose current crashed into the canyon and then turned a hard right, leaving water and spray swirling in every direction. I sat alone on a rock on the riverbank, watching two men with reels and nets work the furious current for what, judging by their pail, appeared to be a teeming stock of fish. The scene made the rapids by Mingan look like a country brook, and for a moment I thought of driving back to fetch the bureaucrat and his discontented family.

Back up the side of the gorge, it was 134 steps to the road, where Bernard's van sat untouched. I wrestled again with the ignition, before getting it back on the highway, my hands shaking on the steering wheel as if it were a jackhammer. Soon, the Dodge was rolling along comfortably again at 110, heading toward a glorious sunset over the St. Lawrence with Bryan Adams singing "Reckless," just loud enough to be heard across the water, on the Gaspé Peninsula.

—— —— ——

To enter Sept-Îles from the east is to encounter one of the most discouraging sights in Quebec. From the rugged forests and coastlines of the lower north shore emerges an industrial complex that looks like something out of the Soviet Union. A sprawling mill sits at the head of a rail line, bordered by slag heaps the size of small ski hills and piles of rust in every direction. This is the railhead for the great iron pits of Labrador, which send through enough ore every year to make Sept-Îles's port the country's second busiest, measured by tonnage. No wonder Newfoundlanders feel gypped.

Beyond the mill, it was easy to see why Bernard struggled to get ahead as a small trader here. The city's main road was lined by the likes of Canadian Tire, Wal-Mart, Provigo and Pro-Deco-Habitat, which had crushed the old Quebec shopkeeper. Anyone along the north shore with a car had to do their bulk shopping here, I figured, steering the van into a parking lot.

I had expected this to be the beginning of separatist country. In the 1995 referendum aimed at opening the door to sovereignty, 62.78 per cent of the local constituency of Duplessis voted *oui*. Instead, it looked like the beginning of Pax Americana. Next to the big-box stores were the predictable assortment of restaurants—McDonald's, KFC—that lent the streetscape an air of suburban Ohio, not hinterland Quebec. About the only restaurant franchise that sounded Canadian was Tim Hortons—named for a Toronto Maple Leaf player, no less, and now owned by an American company.

I continued by foot to an international hostel, the one place my guidebook recommended in Sept-Îles. It was close to the rejuvenated waterfront, which was written up as the best reflection of Sept-Îles's identity as a sports town—what else are mill workers' kids supposed to do?—with a boardwalk, bike trail and crisp view of the seven islands that shelter its harbour.

After claiming a bunk and taking a shower at the hostel, I headed for the waterfront, discovering along the way that Sept-Îles had new playgrounds everywhere. In its centre, where one might expect to find a fountain and a few statues of obscure municipal figures, there were two adjoining hockey arenas. More striking still was the number of Canadian flags. From Natashquan to Sept-Îles, I had spotted one Canadian flag, three Acadian flags and more Quebec flags than I could count. But here in Sept-Îles, there were actually a handful of flags for the country we were in. A federal government building, one of the biggest in town, flew one, of course. A few brave shopkeepers and homeowners also displayed them. But the biggest number could be found above a single shop on the main street. Staring down the separatists with a long row of red-and-white Maple Leafs was that great standard-bearer of federalism: Wal-Mart.

There was so much Americana in Sept-Îles that I decided to leave the next morning, walking first to a Tim Hortons—one of three on the main street—where at seven in the morning I joined an improbably long lineup. Mill workers, men in suits, emergency crews, truck drivers and two nurses: the francophone crowd was quite egalitarian in its simple desire for coffee and Timbits. I stood quietly behind them to place my order, realizing that here in Sept-Îles, in the heartland of the movement to destroy Canada, this was what we had become: a Timbit nation.

From a modest beginning, Tim Hortons had taken on the biggest fast-food chains America could throw at it and emerged ahead. It was close to overtaking McDonald's as the number one restaurant chain in Canada. Tim Hortons succeeded because, like Canada, it believed in the fresh and genuine and was pragmatic, focusing on the necessities of a highway society. Donuts and coffee. Soup. Sandwiches. No supersizing here. But what had always impressed me about Tim Hortons was how it looked to America for purpose, and then carved from America a separate identity. It was an American who invented the donut. It was a Canadian chain that used the hole to create its hallmark product. Two inventions made from the same batter, with very different purposes in the world, and two countries just the same: the United States and the anti-donut.

Interestingly, Tim Horton died in 1974 while driving drunk, a fact that Canadians, in our forgiving manner, buried with him. His name today is as much a synonym for goodness and charity as it is for coffee and donuts, linked to the country's most famous summer camp for kids. But there is a greater irony to the success of his name. His former partner, a one-time cop named Ron Joyce, bought out Horton's widow for $1 million in the 1970s and sold the chain twenty years later for $540 million. The buyer was Wendy's International Inc., the American fast-food giant. The Canadian creation had become part of an all-American portfolio. What could say more about Canada's new continental status? Well, this: once again, Canada had developed an idea, sold it to the Americans and moved on.

I ate my breakfast at a table, thinking a coffee cup on the roadside would make me look a bit too complacent, and still managed to get to what I thought was the west side of Sept-Îles by eight o'clock. I would be in time for people heading on long hauls to Baie-Comeau or Quebec City. I knew that standing by a traffic light was useless. In Quebec, a red light is merely a suggestion. So I kept walk-ing westward, hoping to find a better spot around the next curve, or the next one, except a better spot never came. After half an hour of walking, a suburb of Sept-Îles emerged, a new subdivision of pre-fabricated homes and long bungalows stretching back from the road like old seigneurial plots stemming from the St. Lawrence. Finally, a place to wait.

I had started to sense that most of my rides came from older cars and vans, usually with no other passengers—odd since most people cite danger as the main reason not to pick up hitchhikers. Usually, the driver was bored and wanted conversation. And they had no voice of reason beside them, no one to look up from the pas-senger seat and say, "Honey, don't you think he looks like that guy shown last night on the eleven o'clock news?"

Initially, I had thought that being clean-shaven and neatly dressed would help my cause, but by the end of the first week I had begun to feel ambivalent about my personal appearance. On some mornings, I'm sure I looked like I had been at a week-long frat party, and got just as many encouraging looks, and evil glares, as I did on those days when I looked ready for a job interview. A stranger realization was this: I was beginning to feel hostile toward drivers. They expected a bit too much, I thought, from us hitch-hikers, as if we were supposed to stand on the roadside in our Sunday best, holding up resumés (with references), and then amuse them for an hour or two.

It was all part of that unspoken deal I had discovered while try-ing to read books on long roadside waits. In the beginning, I figured an insouciant, coffee-house look would help. Maybe a driver passing by would recognize the book and want to discuss it, like some sort of random book club on wheels. But they didn't. Drivers, I was con-vinced, wanted hitchhikers who looked helpless and in need of their charity. Or maybe they just feared I would get into their car and continue to read. For the lonely or bored driver, a book-reading pas-senger represents the nightmare scenario. So I stood and stared.

After an hour of this, at a quarter after ten, a car pulled out of the Sept-Îles subdivision and stopped. It was a factory manager heading to Port-Cartier, a town famous for the federal penitentiary that former prime minister Brian Mulroney gave to it when he was the area's Member of Parliament. The lush land of patronage was about to unfold. At first, we followed the St. Lawrence through a stark landscape as the sandy soil of the lower north shore gave way to the great rocky shield of central Canada. It would be like this, I figured, for another twenty-five hundred kilometres: rock faces spiking upward, trees struggling to spread their roots, crops splashing the landscape in river valleys and then fading to scrub on the upper reaches of a hill. Siberia and the Sahara excluded, there could be no landscape as long and consistently forbidding as the Canadian Shield. Which makes it all the more remarkable that Canadians, in a couple of centuries, have done so much with it.

The Canadian dream was not exactly what sprang to mind, though, as we entered Port-Cartier and were presented with a sight that was far grimmer than the railhead at Sept-Îles. A vast, hideous mill sat on the heights ahead, towering over the town's bleak landscape of junkyards, truck depots, supply shops, welding yards and sawmills. I suppose the kids from Tête-à-la-Baleine had to work somewhere, but this hardly looked like the new Quebec. This did not look like a province leaping confidently into a new century. The industrial blight looked like a very old Quebec, the one that had stripped its forests, rocks and soil, and shipped them south to the United States with a brief processing stop at one of a dozen towns along the St. Lawrence, each powered by a massive hydro dam on one of the mighty rivers stretching north.

On the western edge of town, where the factory manager dropped me outside another Tim Hortons, I noticed how many more trucks there were on the highway than I had seen east of here, or in the Maritimes for that matter. Flatbeds carrying racks of lumber. Big semis with who knows what inside. More rigs pulling heavy equipment. Eighteen-wheelers returning with goods for all those

big-box stores. This was the start of central Canada's industrial corridor, the economic spine that stretches to Windsor, Ontario. It is
the corridor that produces more wealth and creates more jobs than
any other part of Canada, and its roads were crowded with trucks,
buses, plant workers in their four-by-fours and manager bees zipping back and forth in air-conditioned comfort. Everyone in a
hurry. Everyone with a destination and deadline. I figured it would
be hell to get a ride.

I took up my position just beyond the Tim Hortons, hoping to
catch a sated donut eater pulling out at a slow speed, when the
biggest threat known to a male hitchhiker unfolded before my eyes.
Walking out of Tim's was a young backpacking couple in shorts and
T-shirts—a man who was inconsequential to my interests, and a
woman who was very much a direct challenge, dressed as she was in
volleyball shorts that accented her long, tanned, athletic legs. They
stopped to say hello and mentioned they were on their way to
Montreal. I felt like one of those southern European hockey teams
that shows up at the Olympics. There was no way I could compete
with this.

The young man smiled, cracking a joke about their comparative
advantage, before heading by foot down the road. At least they
respected my patch of gravel. I began to think about lunch at the
donut shop, followed by dinner, when a new white Toyota coupe
stopped by my side, just minutes after the young couple had been in
the same spot. The seats were leather. The air conditioning was on.
A jazz CD was playing. As the driver sped back onto the highway,
I waved to the volleyball kids. With no shade in sight, they looked
very hot, very tired and not at all attractive.

Noel was on his way to Baie-Comeau, to catch a ferry across the
river to Matane, his hometown on the Gaspé Peninsula. He worked
in Sept-Îles, as an engine man on the famous Wabush train, the one
that hauls ore down from Labrador. With a car like this, I said delicately, engine men must get paid a lot more than they used to. Noel
smiled. The local economy, he said, was doing very well.

The highway ahead turned to hills, rising and dropping sharply with each cut of Shield hugging the road. When it reached down to the river's edge, there were more villages, picture-book Quebec with silver-spired churches as their centrepiece and schools that flew only the province's flag. Between villages there were more and more cottages, on the river or facing the lakes that had replaced the thick forests to the east. The tranquillity of cottage country—the one antidote to central Canada's commercial frenzy—seemed to be taking hold, until we climbed the last steep hill to the east of Baie-Comeau and saw before us something that looked like a spaceship. It was so large, so mechanical and so alien that it could not be from here, I thought. Noel shrugged. It was the Reynolds aluminum smelter, Baie-Comeau's greatest temple, built appropriately atop a hill overlooking town and fed by Hydro-Québec wires running up to its side.

For more than a century, Brian Mulroney's hometown has epitomized the subservient nature of Canada's hinterland. The biggest player in town was an American company. The provincial government played the role of understudy. But the picture of some little mill town run by robber barons and government dupes was not what I saw on the main street. Away from the mill, a new Baie-Comeau was emerging. There was the highly visible and equally unattractive service economy, to be sure, with big malls, motels, gas stations and donut shops. There was also a sprawling new subdivision, with its own golf course, parks, playgrounds, schools and yet another shopping mall with a multi-screen movie theatre showing Hollywood releases. It looked as if this service economy kept feeding on itself, growing because it was growing, regardless of what was happening over at the Reynolds plant. In reality, Baie-Comeau had been transformed from resource town to suburb as it merged with the Great Lakes megalopolis that sprawls up the St. Lawrence, through Ontario to Michigan. The tracts of forest and farmland between populated centres were little more than green space.

This growing and powerful urban corridor had done more than reshape the Canadian political map, as it transcended provincial (and perhaps national) borders. It had made hitchhiking more challenging. Standing at a corner in Baie-Comeau, where Highway 138 turned right, I felt like I was thumbing for a ride in the middle of a Montreal suburb. Cars were coming out of gas stations and going into drive-throughs like schoolchildren heading out for recess. It was mayhem. No one would stop for a stranger.

I stood there, with my thumb out, for an hour. I went for lunch at a gas station. I tried my luck farther up the road, where three lanes merged to two, figuring cars would have to slow down. They didn't. I watched another hitchhiker take my old spot at the intersection. Ten minutes later, he had a ride. "My ride!" I cursed. Finally, nearly three hours from the time Noel dropped me there, I got a lift with a member of a local rock group. He had taken pity on my location and said he would run me up the road to a better spot where I might get a late ride to Quebec City. He too had noticed the fading light.

Baie-Comeau was built on a series of hills, and I did not appreciate how far it sprawled. The guitar player, himself a veteran hitchhiker, took me past another subdivision, another golf course, another cinema complex and another shopping mall, each making the place look like it really was a Montreal suburb. But within a few minutes, he was able to drop me by the open highway. I could tell it was the city limits because I was standing next to a Wal-Mart, the universal sign in North America that says you are at the city limits.

In no more than five minutes I had another ride, with someone who was going just five kilometres up the road. That was fine by me. I was willing to take anything but another three-hour wait. Climbing into his pickup, I noticed two things: the driver was drinking a bottle of Bud, and his truck smelled new. A welder at the Reynolds plant, he said the pickup was one of the upsides of a booming economy. He was putting in sixty-hour weeks, earning enough in overtime in the last year to pay for the vehicle. The downside was this: the only time he could enjoy a beer was on his way home from work.

There was not so much as a gas station to slow cars down at the rural turnoff where the welder dropped me, but my fortunes had to be improving because within a few minutes a small red Neon pulled over. The driver, a college student, was going all the way to Quebec City to see his girlfriend. At this hour, on this patch of empty road, I felt like I had escaped a close encounter with an alien spaceship.

—— —— ——

Johann St. Pierre had worked his way through a series of jobs after high school, most recently as a security agent, before saving enough for a one-year college course to become a paramedic. He wasn't really sure why he wanted to be a paramedic, just that he had heard the money was good. That was why he was in Baie-Comeau for a year, studying at one of its schools to join the service economy.

We spoke in broken French, and then in English, the great frustration of Québécois. If they want to speak to the rest of Canada, they have to speak in English. I asked Johann where he learned his second language. "From TV and music," he said, bluntly.

Ever since the 1970s, when the province had moved the first year of English instruction to Grade 4 from Grade 1, the quality of spoken English in the province had declined. Johann remembered hours of lessons in how to say things like "Paul, go to school." Whatever he picked up in the classroom would not carry a conversation.

The same was true across this region. We were entering the heartland of sovereignty, the constituency of Saguenay, which in 1995 voted overwhelmingly against Canada. The *oui* side here got 73.33 per cent. But Johann let me know right away that if this was the citadel of Quebec nationalism, its ramparts were crumbling in every family room, cinema and strip mall we passed. His favourite TV show was *Friends*, which surprised me less than his admission that he preferred the originals to French dubbing. It was the same with American pop music, which he preferred on English-language CDs. He and his separatist buddies even chose to listen to Céline Dion in English. This was one reason Johann was keen to get back to Quebec City, where radio stations played much more English music than in Baie-Comeau. Government regulations forced stations to devote sixty per cent of their daytime programming to French music, but after midnight it was all English, Johann said.

A couple of decades ago, when he was born, the infiltration of English was seen as such a grave threat that it was banned from public places, airwaves and primary schools, except in enclaves like Harrington Harbour. But now, a far more confident generation of Québécois saw bilingualism as essential to its survival. Young people like Johann knew they needed English to get ahead in the workplace and to enjoy the movies and music they liked best. They also did not have an ounce of doubt about their commitment to French. "The French can survive. It's not an assimilation to speak English," Johann said.

We were driving through a golden twilight, over the first rolling hills of Quebec's farm country, the pastoral heartland where the roots of Quebec's sovereignty movement ran deepest. The rivers, I noticed, were much wider and calmer than the wild, raging torrents to the east. The houses were much bigger, too. This stretch of Quebec, between the provincial capital and Baie-Comeau, was where Johann had spent most of his life. He said it was the same for most of his friends. He didn't like Montreal because it was too big and "very individualistic." He had been out of the province only once, on a day trip in high school to Ottawa. He was afraid to visit Ontario again because, as he put it, a gas station attendant might not understand his English and would refuse him service. I told him most gas jockeys in Ontario were recent immigrants and spoke far worse English than he did. Unfortunately, this did not make much of an impression on Johann. The very notion of immigration seemed foreign to him.

The isolationism fostered by decades of Parti Québécois policies had created a kind of paranoia among its supporters. They were not at all like Bernard Morency, the crazy Dodge van driver who wanted to see the world and forget about little Quebec. Among Johann's friends, a cult-like psychology had developed that said you were either with the separatists or you should leave.

"The PQ is just French, French, French, French," he explained. He was drinking a 7-Eleven Big Slurpee as he drove. "Their thinking is very, very popular because it's . . . because it's like Nike shoes. 'Oh, Nike, Nike, Nike.'" (Here, he imitated someone fawning over a pair of new shoes.) "No one then likes Reebok. Some people are afraid to say they like the Liberals. 'You're out of the gang,' someone will tell them. But if they say PQ, 'Oh, you're a good guy.'"

Some of his friends had gone to work in Alberta and British Columbia and come home with stories about being teased for speaking French or taunted for supporting Quebec nationalism. One of them began to salute the Canadian flag, whenever he saw one, with his middle finger.

I told Johann that Torontonians get taunted in Alberta too. It's just the way the country is. Toronto, he said, must be an odd place. He too had heard only bad things about the city, until his girlfriend went to visit. She liked it. She was surprised by how many people in Toronto spoke French. She was surprised how many people spoke other languages too. She was surprised that people were nice to her. And she was surprised, really surprised, that the nightlife was good. Ontario was not supposed to have good nightlife.

Johann offered to show me some of the better nightclubs in Quebec City, if I wanted to stay along for the ride, but I declined. I wanted to see more of Quebec by day and meet more people. I also wanted to see some of Tadoussac, at the mouth of the Saguenay River. The famous little town made its living as a hub for beluga whale-watching tours and boat trips up the breathtaking Saguenay fjord, where Cartier once thought he had found a trove of gold and diamonds only to discover later it was worthless pyrite and quartz.

When Johann let me out by the river, it was dusk. I followed some back streets to a boardwalk that ran along a ridge above the St. Lawrence in front of the Tadoussac Hotel, built in 1941 for the rich and powerful who would drive up here from Boston and Montreal. A full moon was rising over the river, and with it came the crimson glow of a late summer sun that had just set. The air was warm. Sounds of laughter came from the hotel lawn.

I continued to walk, searching for a bench on which to rest and watch the moon's glow devour the river, but they were all taken by young couples. The town was overflowing with tourists. The only bed I could find was an upper bunk in the youth hostel's dormitory. For five dollars, it wasn't bad. Most of my dorm mates were outside anyway, sitting by a campfire behind the hostel with backpackers from around the world. They were sharing songs from their homelands. I found a spot on a log and listened as a group of Québécois staff kept the program going—in French and English, but mostly in English.

— — —

In the morning, I rose before the others in the dorm and headed with my pack into the forest behind Tadoussac, along a trail that started at a government-run fish hatchery and wound its way to the top of a cliff overlooking the Saguenay River. After two kilometres in the woods, a clifftop opening unveiled the majestic fjord that had lured and enchanted so many early explorers. And that was my indulgence for the day. Another two kilometres down the wooded trail, and I was on the roadside again with my thumb out. It was eight o'clock.

Tadoussac and the twin town of Baie-Sainte-Catherine must be among the few places in the world that refuse a bridge across the river that divides them. There are technical constraints, such as shifting tides, active sea life and a narrow gorge, but nothing a brilliant engineer could not overcome. Regardless, I was stuck with a choice: hitch on the eastern side of the short ferry crossing, or try my luck on the off-ramp. I opted for the latter route, figuring drivers approaching the river would have other things on their mind than a hitchhiker. It was a horrible decision. The off-ramp led directly to a steep hill that climbed the western side of the gorge before making a sharp right turn to avoid the St. Lawrence. Any driver in command of his or her faculties had just one thing in mind as they left the ferry, and that was to gun it up the hill. I must have looked like an inflated Ronald McDonald, standing there with my arms flapping, noticed only by little children in the back seats of minivans.

"Of course there was a man on the road, dear," I could hear the parents saying. "And did you wave back to him?"

Two ferry loads came and went, mostly filled with vacationing families, who were a lost cause for me at the best of times and locations. (Unless they were fighting.) So I walked to the top of the hill, where at least the drivers might be able to look at me for a moment. The family vans kept passing at impressive clips, but the first truck to reach the top, an eighteen-wheeler, pulled over, just beyond where I was standing. Gilles, the driver, was headed for Sainte-Foy, a suburb of Quebec City, and was in a disagreeable mood because of the ferry crossing. Every time he took this route, the crossing cost him half an hour, or more if there was traffic.

Around the bend, Gilles followed a long hill through Baie-Sainte-Catherine and into the Charlevoix Valley, furiously working his gears and brakes to avoid crushing a compact car in front of us. I could barely pick up what he was saying, so loud was his engine and the crackling of his CB radio. The scenery was consuming all my attention anyway. For the next half-hour, the road climbed the Charlevoix's bucolic ridges and dipped into its rich valleys, the drama made more thrilling by the fact that Gilles's forty-foot truck would grind close to a halt on inclines and then barrel downhill like a mad roller-coaster car.

For more than a century, the charming beauty of Charlevoix was celebrated by the wealthy and powerful of eastern North America. In Pointe-au-Pic, a village on the St. Lawrence, the vacation home of William Howard Taft, the former American president, still stands. The 1928 Manoir Richelieu, built in the age of Gatsby, also thrives, although now as a casino catering to low-rent crowds bussed in nightly from Quebec City.

On both sides of the road, big fat cows munched lazily on what looked like an endless supply of grain, making this one of North America's best dairy lands. The barns all had red roofs, speaking to their tradition, while the houses, even the new ones, were made of stone, the first ones I had seen in eastern Canada. But there were also signs of new wealth. Handsome equestrian farms dotted the roadside. Several lakes we passed were bordered by mansions, too, although they looked like they had nothing to do with farming.

I was starting to enjoy the unique perspective of a trucker, peeking from on high over hedges and fences, when Gilles announced he wanted to stop for breakfast. It was ten-thirty but who was I to complain? At this rate, I would be in Quebec City by lunch. Gilles had another bit of news. He had to rest for one hour, according to his logbook. He suggested I continue hitchhiking on the roadside ahead. If I didn't have a ride by the time he got behind the wheel again, he would pick me up.

We were at a small country restaurant and gas bar, which by my estimation was nowhere near any town on the map. There was no hope of getting another ride here. Cars raced by at one-twenty, or faster. And those who stopped for gas or a meal must have wondered why I was hitchhiking in the middle of nowhere, far from any turnoff, village or farmhouse. Perhaps I had offended a driver by eating a huge meal during a rest stop and sticking him with the bill. I probably looked like I didn't care anyway, which I didn't, not with a guaranteed ride on its way.

When Gilles emerged from the restaurant, I waved from the roadside to get his attention. He waved back and then folded his hands next to his face and pointed to the truck's cab. It was time for a snooze, I assumed. Since Gilles had another thirty minutes to go to complete his rest stop, I decided to take a quick pee break. I feared if I went into the restaurant, Gilles might believe I had gone and leave without me. I slipped instead behind a row of trucks, relieved myself in a gully and, before he could miss me, started back toward the road, where, to my astonishment, a truck was rolling out of the parking lot. It was Gilles. I shouted and ran after it, reaching the rear wheels on the passenger's side as the rig pulled onto the highway. I was sure my eyes met Gilles's in the side-view mirror, and I was sure there was no stopping him. I dropped my bag and threw my hands up in disbelief. From down the road, he pulled his air horn and kept rolling.

If not for an old Hyundai Excel that did a U-turn to pick me up, I might still be outside that restaurant. The driver, who introduced himself as Alex, said that when he first passed me, he realized I stood pretty much no chance of getting a ride. Taking pity, he had come back for me, and was offering a good ride to boot. He was going to Drummondville, on the south shore between Quebec City and Montreal.

Alex was quickly back to one-twenty on the winding road, telling me more about his life than I think I cared to know. Since his car radio was broken, he also smoked more cigarettes than normal, lighting one Export A after another to pass the time. He was dressed in shorts and a singlet, wore a tattoo on his right arm and had his hair cut in a buzz pattern, with long orange-dyed strands flowing from the top. In one eye, he wore a blue contact lens, to correct his vision from when he was hit in the head, during a fight, with a baseball bat. He said he was eighteen when that happened. The same year, he was jailed for six months for beating someone senseless in another bar where he worked as a waiter and DJ. He remembered the evening well. Someone had pinched his girlfriend's bum, and when he threatened to throw the guy out, the young man struck Alex with a beer bottle. Alex struck back with a chair, breaking the young man's arm. Unfortunately, the young man was the mayor's son.

This was not your usual conversation starter, but Alex was not your usual driver. He was a fifth-generation cook, the son of a French father and Italian mother who both immigrated to Canada in their youth. Although his father introduced him young to Continental cuisine, he said he never wanted to be a traditional

French cook. As a teenager, he preferred Oriental. He liked the meticulous presentation of Asian food. He also knew it was a way to rebel against his father, which was why he took a job at a hotel in Forestville, east of Tadoussac, preparing the daily Chinese buffet.

Now twenty-three, Alex was firmly part of Quebec's lost generation, the children of Lévesque who saw little hope in independence because they saw little hope in the old men who kept telling them it would be good for Quebec. "I'm not proud of Canada. I'm not proud of Quebec," Alex said. He explained what it meant to be a rebel in modern Quebec. He left home when he was fourteen and had been working forty hours a week ever since. This was his first day off in two weeks.

After the Charlevoix, the road skirted around the ski resort at Sainte-Anne and entered the St. Lawrence flood plains, where the river visibly narrowed. I had noticed that in every village we passed there was a massive old church, usually erected on the highest point in the community and in the same design, as if they came from a nineteenth-century catalogue of prefab drawings. More often than not, the church was the biggest structure in town, and yet no one I had met was interested in their local church.

Alex said he had returned to church only briefly, because of "tradition." He had not lost his faith casually. He did not simply turn the channel. As a boy, in a school run by priests, he had been forced to copy passages from the Bible as punishment for misbehaviour. One of the passages said Jesus had dark skin and hair like black sheep's wool, which was not at all like the portrait of Christ in his classroom. That Jesus had fair skin and blue eyes. "I thought, 'If they lie about this, what else do they lie about?'"

Curiously, he and his wife were married in a Roman Catholic church when she got pregnant. They were teenagers. They had their son Bobbie baptized too, and planned to send him to a Catholic school. They wanted to expose him to the Bible and let him decide on spirituality for himself. "We don't believe in anything," Alex said. "Me, I think it's important to believe in yourself first and then, if you have some time to lose, believe in something else."

In his Quebec, Alex's biggest concern was to find a school that could teach Bobbie in English, which was the language of the boy's favourite TV shows, *Sesame Street* and *Pokemon*. In a province so heavily dependent on the United States, Alex thought an exclusively French education was unthinkable.

Quebec's economic landscape changed dramatically after Highway 138 broke onto the plains southwest of Mont-Sainte-Anne and headed toward the provincial capital, the very beacon of nationalism. The road was now a lifeline of commerce, as bland and anonymous as any in North America. We could see Quebec City's Citadelle towering over its realm and river, as it had for centuries. But outside the ancient walled city, following an eight-lane expressway past sprawling parking lots and factory outlets shrouded with neon, we could just as easily have been in Saskatoon or San Jose. We passed a new Cineplex complex featuring six American films. A big new Loblaws, a bastion of Toronto commerce, sat next to it.

One of the oldest settlements in North America, Quebec City was created in 1608 as a small fort by Samuel de Champlain, who four years later became the first governor of New France. Since he was having little luck in his search for gold or a route to the Far East, he figured he best settle down here at the narrow, where at least he would have better access to the fur trading routes. The Europeans had been disappointed ever since. They never did come across Canada's great mineral wealth or a profitable passage to the Orient. Those all came much later, and elsewhere.

With a string of bad press back in Paris, where the phrase "false as a diamond in Canada" became popular, Champlain scaled down his ambitions, fretting about nothing more than beaver pelts and good government. Over the next two decades, he established the most centralized administration the continent has known. Supported by monopolistic industries and a powerful Church, the regime carried Quebec well into the twentieth century. Some would say Champlain's legacy of protector and paternalist lingers on, at least in the decline that it has forced on a troubled province.

In his lifetime, Alex had seen his sheltered province fall well behind Ontario in economic wealth, political clout in Ottawa and even cultural creativity. By the late 1990s, his province was home to thirty-five per cent of Canada's unemployed. Many of his friends had moved to Toronto, a city that once was Montreal's poor cousin. He had been lucky enough to find a decent job in Forestville, where the tourist trade paid $15 an hour. In Drummondville, the best he could do was $9.

"I have a question," Alex said bluntly, as we rounded the old city and passed through Sainte-Foy. I did not see Gilles or his truck. "Is it true that clubs in Toronto are open only till one A.M.?"

No, I said. The province had extended last call until two. He laughed. "In Quebec, it's three or four. No one pays much attention to details."

I had thought of jumping out at Quebec City and following the north shore to Montreal, but Alex was such an intriguing character I asked if I could stay on to Drummondville. We crossed the river on a dual-carriage, four-lane expressway that lifted us right out of Quebec and into the stratosphere of superhighway driving. Alex sped up to one-forty, confident the police would not be patrolling today. If they were, they would have to ticket every vehicle on the road.

Pulling into the fast lane, Alex changed the CD to something called Rave-olution, a work produced by one of his Drummondville friends, and drove on with the dashboard pulsating to a techno-beat. As best as I could tell, all the words were in English.

From where Alex dropped me, at the first of five exits to Drummondville, it took two long waits and two short rides to get to Saint-Hyacinthe, on the edge of greater Montreal. It was one of those faceless homes to the auto industry, and appropriately so.

I sensed I was entering a more frenetic land, the realm of the big city, where even a fast-food order was faster.

I crossed the manic divide, from rural to urban Canada, on the Saint-Hyacinthe on-ramp, climbing into a van marked with the name of a Montreal air-conditioning company. The driver did not look at me as he sped onto the highway, immersed as he was in a conversation on his cell phone. Only after hanging up—and here we were ten kilometres up the road—did he ask where I was going. I guess he had assumed Montreal all along. "This will be a good ride for you," he said. He too was going to Montreal.

The driver introduced himself as Daniel and then took another call on his cell phone. For the rest of the half-hour drive, he continued talking, putting one call on hold for another, and then that one for another. The calls seemed to merge together, like the cornfields beside the road that became car parts factories and then subdivisions and then one long blur of concrete until we were in a tunnel heading to the island of Montreal.

The tunnel heightened Daniel's anxiety, as it instantly cut off his cell service. For a good two minutes, he could do nothing but fidget with the steering wheel as he drove. When we saw daylight, the phone rang again and Daniel was occupied until we came to a Métro station. I motioned to stop. Daniel wished me well. He was still on the phone.

Standing on a Métro platform in Anjou, an eastern suburb, I felt like a wide-eyed country boy coming to the city for the first time. The crush of people was intimidating, and their skin colours made me feel like I had drifted ashore in a far-off land. After two weeks in rural eastern Canada, the ethnic diversity of a big Canadian city—and there are only three—was breathtaking. On board the crowded subway train, the range of languages and accents was equally so. Looking back at the three thousand kilometres I had covered, I recalled seeing only one black face, in Prince Edward Island, and the man had looked like a tourist. Here, rattling into downtown Montreal on the Métro, I was the visible minority.

Quebec's open-door policy to French-speaking immigrants was one of the great ironies of modern Canada. Faced with a staggering decline in the province's birth rate, the government figured it could help matters by encouraging immigration from the French-speaking world, from Haiti, North and West Africa, Indo-China and, not least of all, France. What the separatists failed to consider was that all these newcomers were not just coming to Quebec. They were coming to Canada. And during the 1995 referendum, they voted overwhelmingly for Canada.

All these new faces and voices were just as fundamental to the revival of Montreal. In the eighties and nineties, Canada's first great city was in serious decline. Smart young people were moving to Ontario and the United States in big numbers. The Canadian Football League franchise collapsed. The Expos of baseball and Canadiens of hockey were in trouble. But as I got off the Métro and walked along rue Sainte-Catherine to the only bed and breakfast I could find with a vacancy, Montreal was a city transformed. A tennis tournament and comedy festival had packed the city. It felt like a little New York. The good New York, that is. Pre-Giuliani, before Manhattan became a two-hundred-block film set.

For one, men and women carried themselves with a singular mix of care and ease. They looked like they had been born beautiful. For another, they dressed beautiful. Rue Sainte-Catherine, and every other major downtown street, resembled a Milan catwalk. Police might not ticket drivers for going through stop signs, but I feared they would tag me for wearing something from The Gap.

Montrealers, though, old and young, are unfazed by whatever the city presents. Uptight—that great Toronto sensation, which is also not unknown to New York—has no place there. When I turned onto rue Sherbrooke, I noticed a silver Jaguar and a BMW convertible, with its roof down, parked outside a homeless shelter. In restaurants, I began to count the number of smokers who, rather than being banished as they would be anywhere else in Canada, enjoyed the best tables. And everywhere couples were holding hands and kissing, as indiscreetly as possible.

After dropping my bag at the B&B, I hopped back on the Métro to boulevard Saint-Laurent, an avenue of upscale restaurants and bars, where at ten o'clock on a Tuesday night every place was packed. Quebec had always been that way, as exuberant as Ontario was restrained. In 1744, after touring France's possessions in North America, the great Jesuit Pierre François-Xavier de Charlevoix—immortalized by the district of rolling cow pastures—found in Quebec a "pleasant society" that made much with little. "One does not see in this country people who are rich, and this is unfortunate, for they like to display, and almost no one amuses himself by hoarding," Charlevoix wrote in his *Histoire de la Nouvelle France.* "They set a good table if they are able . . . ; if not, then they retrench on food so as to be able to be well dressed."

Charlevoix marvelled at the healthful climate, the lack of disease and the vast forests of Quebec—"surely the largest in the Universe," he wrote—that served a mere forty thousand people, Indians not included. But he also wrote home to warn about the colonials' "imprudence, aversion to assiduous work, lack of discipline, and spirit of independence." In short, the makings of a great city.

Unlike Quebec, which was forcefully carved into the landscape by a determined administrator, Montreal grew organically. Originally, Mount Royal was meant to be a centre for converting Indians to Christianity, as envisioned by a secret society of Counter-Reformation zealots who in 1639 created an agency to colonize the island. Three years later, Sieur de Maisonneuve opened the Ville-Marie mission. For the proselytizers, the chief problem lay in the fact that the island was gaining popularity among fur traders—not surprising given its access to the Ottawa and St. Lawrence rivers. A tension arose between Church and market and never really went away. But the power of commerce drew more and more immigrants. New France, at the time, was desperate for people—not unlike the new Quebec of today. In 1681, the census of Canada enumerated a mere fifty-six carpenters, thirty masons, twenty-six shoemakers, thirteen surgeons, six locksmiths, two land surveyors and one lonely carpet-weaver. The word went out across France that able-bodied youths would enjoy a handsome future in the colonies, and the French navy would do all it could to get them there.

That New France's pernickety administrators were downriver in Quebec City, and the Jesuits were off in the bush converting Indians, were not insignificant factors to those who set out to make Montreal a real city. As newcomers poured in, the island saw a boom in the cabaret business. It also became a serious entrepôt for booze, as fur traders discovered that alcohol could win them an unlimited supply of pelts from the natives upriver.

The Church managed to reclaim some hold on the wild new city when priests retreated from the hinterland to tend to the fast-growing population. For a time, in 1710, the government even managed to limit the sale of liquor. According to an edict that year, Frenchmen could buy alcohol in only nineteen cabaret-hotels, and only then until nine o'clock at night. (Indians were to be restricted to beer, at nine cabaret-hotels.) But the days of paternalism were numbered, starting in 1714 when the Treaty of Utrecht ended another European war and greatly reduced France's possessions in North America. Cut off from the French military base on Cape Breton, Quebec was no longer able to count on France for any sort of defence against the English, or to underwrite its projects, through either Church or State. It would have to foster its own economy and learn to tax it. Montreal could not remain a mystical island or iniquitous outpost. It had to become the engine for New France.

Nearly three hundred years later, little of this spirit had changed. On Saint-Laurent, the rich and poor, old and young, white and black continued to meld as priest and trader once did, unmindful of what the others were doing and unrepentant about themselves. In nearby Square Saint-Louis, where I wandered after dinner, I came across a group of punks wearing dog collars around their necks, drinking beer. Sitting opposite them was an elderly couple watching their dog splash around in a fountain. A sweet aromatic current of marijuana wafted by. Two policemen patrolling the park did not so much as glance in its direction.

It would be hard to refute that Montreal, whether in the seventeenth century or the twenty-first, was one of the continent's great meeting places. What baffled me was a reference in a local newspaper to its casino becoming the city's biggest attraction. In a place with four thousand restaurants and perhaps more bars and clubs, the fact that a darkened room of slot machines was drawing people at all hours of the night did not seem possible. I had to check it out.

At eleven o'clock at night, the Métro to Île Sainte-Hélène was as crowded as a downtown train during rush hour. Dozens of people poured into each waiting bus to cross to Île Nôtre-Dame. On a series of small islands in the St. Lawrence, the casino and a huge amusement park had filled the space and buildings left by the 1967 World's Fair. The casino had operated around the clock since it opened in 1993 and probably has not known a moment of peace. On my bus were the usual blue-rinse set, but also a fascinating potpourri of Vietnamese gamblers, Haitian couples, blue-collar workers, a few people dressed to the nines, one couple on in-line skates and a pack of young men coming from an AC/DC concert downtown. Small wonder gambling was about to overtake all sin taxes combined, from liquor and tobacco, in their contribution to provincial government revenue.

As our bus crossed the bridge from one island to the next, Montreal's six-level casino burst into view, glowing with a blanket of lights draped down each side, as bright as the full moon hanging over the river. The city bus had barely come to a halt when the crowd, in-line skaters included, rushed through the doors into the former convention centre, past a sign declaring the biggest slot machine score—$50,000—so far that day. As in many buildings designed in the sixties, there was no way of knowing which way was up. Small corridors and rooms jutted off in every direction. In the middle, an open interior was connected by central escalators, which were cleverly routed so that gamblers had to walk half the circumference of each floor to get to a connecting way up or down.

I wandered the open floors, looking for the big-stakes tables (to watch, not to play), but for the first half-hour could find only pocket-change amusements. A table with toy racehorses drew a crowd, although none of the bettors expressed the faintest enthusiasm for their choice, as if they felt a need to maintain poker faces in a game of chance. After a few races, I followed a hospitality trolley into the next room, where slot machine addicts fetched free coffee and juice and went back to their lucky arms. The only way to get something harder to drink was to find a small bar carved into one of the building's many nooks.

Perhaps it was the lack of free alcohol, or maybe even the building's warped aesthetics, but I could find no one in the casino who was having fun, or at least allowing others to see it. The place could not be more opposite to boulevard Saint-Laurent. I rode the escalators up and down, searching for a smiling face or, better yet, a laugh or a yelp, and came across nothing. The greatest excitement seemed to come from the lighting of a cigarette. The casino attracted so many smokers that eleven of its sixteen blackjack tables were set aside for them. And so, drone-like, the casino's customers sat at their chosen machine or table, smoking and plotting. If they were also dreaming of a jackpot, they did not let on. On my last walk through the upper levels, I found a members-only table where bets started at a thousand dollars. At midnight, every seat was taken by a francophone, judging by their exchanges with the dealer. And they were all Asian. The zealots who came to this island four hundred years earlier had to be spinning in their graves.

——— ——— ———

The last time I tried to hitchhike out of Montreal had been in 1982, when I walked from a friend's downtown apartment to the nearest expressway on-ramp. It took me ten hours to get back to university in Kingston, Ontario, just two hundred kilometres away. This time, an overnight thunderstorm had cooled Montreal to a late autumn temperature, and there was no sign of the rain letting up. Since little else can do more damage to a hitchhiker's chances than looking wet, I decided to get a head start by taking an early morning commuter train to Deux-Montagnes, a cozy bedroom community on a river northeast of Montreal.

After passing through the tranquil riverside suburb, where people could boast of a two-car garage and a dock, the train ended its run at a small station that felt like something out of the English countryside. The impression did not last. Away from the station, I was soon lost in a suburban maze of monster homes, with their big yards and pools, driveways wide enough for three SUVs parked side by side, bicycle trails, tree-lined meridians and curlicue roads. I wandered around and around, not knowing if, like in *The Truman Show,* there was any way out. But at least the rain had stopped. It was better to be lost and dry, I thought hopefully, than lost and wet.

After a while, I swallowed my pride and returned to the station for directions. The attendant was baffled. Why, she asked, would I want to walk to a highway? Why, she asked again, would I want to hitchhike when I could take the train or bus?

"Follow the street next to the station," she said, pointing to a map before I could answer, "until it reaches an end, turn left and walk to the Canadian Tire. The highway is there."

If there is one truism in our world, it is that everything everywhere looks smaller on a map, and nowhere more so than in suburbia. I've crossed Himalayan passes that were more straightforward than the route from Deux-Montagnes rail station to Highway 148. From the depot, I walked for what felt like an hour just to reach the end of the street. I turned left and continued on to the Canadian Tire. What I didn't realize, until I got to the Canadian Tire, was that the road I was following *was* Highway 148. Except that at this point it wasn't a highway, despite the big, thick red line on the map the station lady had given me. It was a suburban artery.

I continued on foot, past a strip mall, a hospital, several car dealerships and a cluster of theme restaurants named for people I had never heard of. At every set of lights, I held out my thumb. I felt about as confident as one of those men on the subway platform predicting the Second Coming of Christ. No one was listening. They weren't even looking at me.

I walked another kilometre, past a Superstore, hoping beyond hope to see a Wal-Mart and with it, surely, an adjoining cornfield. Instead, I found another subdivision, more shopping plazas and cars turning in every direction but mine. Slowly, I began to realize there would be no Wal-Mart in wherever it was I was. Saint-Eustache, I think. But ahead, there was something just as divine: a construction crew laying down sewers. I had reached the end of civilization, and the beginning of hitchhiking country. I picked up the pace, past the construction crew, past one last Nissan dealership and past the first cornfield northeast of Montreal, until I reached a spot where I could begin my day. It was one o'clock.

— — —

It took two short rides, and another hour, just to reach Mirabel, home to Montreal's international airport. The rain had started again. Standing next to some rolling hills of corn and cow pastures, with big jets roaring overhead, I tried as best I could to look dry, which became less easy with each passing car that sprayed me. At last, a small blue pickup truck pulled over, with a passenger seat that looked like it had nothing to lose.

Christian Bigras was a private contractor, on his way home from a renovation job in a Montreal suburb. As we headed into the rain, he asked if I would mind a detour in Lachute, the main town up ahead, to pick up some lumber. After an hour in the rain, I said, the extended drive would be welcome.

Lachute was a pleasant farming town, divided by a river. Christian said half the population was comfortable, thanks in part to government subsidies for the local dairy industry. The other half struggled on welfare. There was little incentive to work in Quebec, he said, not when taxes were so high and red tape so thick. He ran through a litany of government insurance rates, licence fees and basic deductions that he would not face were he in Ontario, across the Ottawa River from his home in Grenville. Quebec's unions didn't make matters easier, forcing employers to guarantee him nine hundred hours of work before he could get a labour card. It seemed fitting that Lachute's biggest industry was a weekly flea market—that great emblem of the informal economy—which every Tuesday attracted up to ten thousand people to buy and sell clothing, food, books, building materials, even airplane parts diverted from Mirabel.

At the lumberyard, Christian strapped some two-by-fours into the back of the pickup and continued on 148 to Grenville. The rain had stopped. "Everything in Quebec costs money," he said, complaining about how difficult it was to run one's life under the table. Often for his renovation work, Christian said, he drove across the bridge to Hawkesbury, Ontario, to buy cheaper materials. He sometimes took his teenaged son to the hospital there, too, rather than waiting four or five hours for a doctor on the Quebec side. "I would not want to have my own business here," he said. "Nothing but a headache." I noticed there were a lot more Canadian flags around Grenville than I had seen elsewhere in Quebec—and a lot fewer fleurs-de-lys.

———

I stood by the roadside food shack where Christian dropped me and had a late lunch of a Pogo and poutine. I feared it would be my last meal in Quebec. The highway in front of the food stop was a narrow two lanes, or about the width of a Deux-Montagnes driveway, but that did not slow down any drivers, who raced by me at a hundred or more. It felt like it could be as bad as my morning in Saint-Eustache, until I caught a man's eye in an old blue K-car. A minute later, I noticed him coming back in the other direction, turning around and pulling onto the shoulder in front of me.

These were the sorts of rides I feared most, but the driver assured me I was safe. He introduced himself as Jean, a drug dealer for the Hells Angels in Montreal. He said he was out for a drive to clear his mind.

"I need to get out of the city," Jean continued, looking at the large riverside homes more than the road. I had simply asked what brought him to Grenville. "I'm heavily into drugs. Basically, I'm a dealer. I was in really bad shape a few months ago. This is where I come to chill. I come here for a few days and don't do anything. No drugs. No booze."

I asked if he minded if I took notes. He said he didn't.

Jean dealt mainly in cocaine. There was a good market in Montreal, he said, and the Hells kept it stable. Anyone who tried to disrupt the market was taken care of accordingly. The lawyers had also been helpful. Because of civil rights decisions, he claimed, the police found it much harder to search his car when they pulled him over. "It's a good time to be a con man," he said, laughing.

It sounded like the kind of paternalism that Champlain would have admired. Stable, orderly, structured—nothing like the new Quebec, which, aside from its anachronistic separatist movement, was changing beyond public credulity. Its political order was unstable. Its economic progress was disorderly. And its society was as unstructured now as at any time since Montreal's indulgent days in the 1690s. If the Hells Angels were able to hold sway over the province, it was partly because there was no legitimate authority to challenge them. This vacuum was allowing urban Quebec to burst with life, but also was drawing in perilous forces that could lead again to its decline. I had only to think of Bernard Morency's complaints about corruption, crime and patronage.

Of course, I didn't say that to Jean. I wanted to get to Ottawa, and a new province, with my life in hand.

6

Colonization Avenue

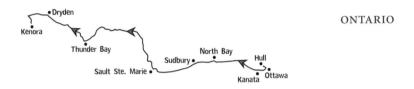

Getting to the western edge of Ottawa was easier than I had expected. Jean the coke dealer had dropped me outside Montebello, the resort town on the Ottawa River, where he was staying in a large riverside house that had a curious number of luxury cars in the driveway. A federal bureaucrat drove me the rest of the way to Hull, half an hour up the road, where after 3,400 kilometres of highway I stood in a parking lot, staring at a shopping centre in one direction and the Peace Tower, across the river, in the other. I was no longer sure which was the greater symbol of Canada, but I opted for the mall. I needed a pay phone.

With my feet still wet from the Saint-Eustache disaster, I called a friend in Ottawa to say hello. She knew it was a call for help. Anne drove across the bridge to pick me up, took me home for dinner and with her husband and another friend walked me through an episode of *Survivor*, which I had discovered a week earlier in Rocky Harbour, Newfoundland. This wasn't just any episode, they explained. It was the last episode of the season, and the three of them were glued to the television. In the morning, Anne said during a commercial, she would drive me to a place where I was guaranteed to get a ride.

The next morning, the traffic following the Queensway from central Ottawa to the adjoining town of Kanata was impressive, all

the more so because there were more cars leaving the city than
entering it. And this was Thursday, too early for even the wiliest
politicians to be sneaking home for the weekend. The capital region
was no longer a one-horse town. It was now an old grey mare and a
thoroughbred. The inbound lanes, carrying cars of assistant associ-
ate deputy ministers and their kind, looked like the parking lot of a
bowling alley. The outbound lanes, full of entrepreneurs and engi-
neers who had survived the tech meltdown, were all country club.
Every third car heading for Kanata was a black Explorer, Mercedes-
Benz SUV, Jag or run-of-the-mill BMW.

"This looks like a gold mine," I said to Anne, who was driving
an old compact.

She didn't warn me the luxury fleet was headed no farther than
the high-tech fields of Kanata—Silicon Valley North, they call it—
where the average dot-com loser was still richer than all of Prince
Edward Island. She didn't need to. There was already a long queue
of cars at the Queensway exit where she planned to drop me.

I didn't mind. On the other side of the overpass, the westbound
on-ramp had it all: good sightlines for drivers to see me well in
advance, steady traffic and a nice slow approach from a big shopping mall and entertainment complex that already was doing a brisk
business at nine in the morning. The Kanata Centrum was one of
those suburban malls that looks as mass produced as its merchan-
dise, with a big Loblaws inside, and next to it a twenty-four-screen
movie theatre, a dozen theme restaurants and a Wal-Mart, indicating we were indeed at the city limits. Best of all, there was nothing
behind me but countryside—no subdivisions or malls to divert traffic, no more Wal-Marts to siphon country shoppers. Anyone leaving
here would be bulked up and hitting the road.

Once Anne was gone, I stood next to the on-ramp to Arnprior
and beyond, amazed at the very size of the Durangos and extended
Expeditions coming out of the Centrum, each large enough to dwarf
an ordinary Jeep. They were big enough to match the monstrous
homes I could see being built behind the mall, homes that would

probably house four people but had the same amount of floor space as the MV *Relais Nordik*.

For the next hour, I continued to believe Kanata, the most affluent city in Canada, would be a good place to hitchhike. I thought in an area that was more car-friendly than any I had come across, drivers would be eager to help. For them, it would be like giving something back, a kind of thank-you for all these beautiful roads leading to and from the Centrum. But as one hour turned to two, I realized I was wrong. Kanata was hitchhiking hell. By my count, every vehicle that passed me had between three and seven empty seats. None of them stopped. None of them slowed down. I stood away from the pavement, and then stood with one foot on the pavement. The response was the same. This gold mine, I thought, contained nothing but pyrite.

Watching the facial expressions of each passing driver, I tried to understand what made them not want to stop. In case it was a question of inconvenience, I tried standing by a traffic light at the top of the on-ramp. A willing driver would lose no more than thirty seconds from his or her trip by picking me up. More people looked to be driven by fear, though. I could see it: they would look right past me, both hands gripped on the steering wheel, as if I was going to leap from the roadside onto their windshield. Even large men driving big SUVs with frivolous vanity plates—4LOU and CRZZ ME— had timid looks on their faces. The night before, they were probably watching *Survivor*, imagining themselves in the jungle.

In a very polite Canadian way, those with legitimate excuses tried to explain their reasons for not stopping, in a simple sign language that did not require them to slow down. Those going a short distance, say to the next interchange, held up a thumb and forefinger, a couple of inches apart, in a "this close" gesture. Others pointed to the front passenger seat, to suggest it was already occupied with Wal-Mart bags. Still others pointed to the left or the right, like a cyclist indicating the direction they wanted to turn, way up ahead. And then there were the few who tried to express contempt. One man gave me the finger. I was intrigued by drivers who gave hitch-hikers the finger. It was like mouthing an f-off to a teacher behind his or her back. What was the point?

So I gave him the finger back. That may have seemed as point-less, but I felt good. Perhaps we both felt good and could get on with our day.

Another irritated driver mouthed something at me. I'm sure his lips said, "Get a job."

"This is my job," I shouted back.

As the third hour passed, with hundreds more cars and SUVs going by, my anger turned to boredom. I was tired of watching bull-dozers at work up the hill, and seeing people come out of Flavour Coffee who had gone in an hour earlier. I was cold, too, shivering in a late August wind blowing straight across the farm fields to the north. The new subdivision had cleared all the tree cover to make way for access roads. Figuring I had nothing to lose but my spot, I walked to the top of the on-ramp, to a Country Style Donuts. It was drive-through only. No feet allowed. The Centrum, across a four-lane road, was the only alternative, and it too seemed approachable only by motorized vehicle. I made a dash for it.

The closer I got to the mall, the more I learned about Canadian urban geography. First of all, the name, Kanata Centrum, gave the impression that it was in the middle of something, like an old farmer's market or a town square, when it was actually in the middle of nowhere. The Centrum was built next to a highway so you could drive to it from all parts. You could park your car, shop, dine at Alice Fazooli's or Jack Astor's, watch a movie and then drive back to wher-ever you came from. The mall was no longer a chore. You went there to relax, to unwind, perhaps to drop by Alice's, whoever she was. And you could do it without talking to another human being, other than a waiter or cashier. That was the calculation behind the Centrum, behind suburban culture really. Destinations were invented, packaged and placed somewhere close to an expressway. Hitchhikers were not part of the deal.

I stopped at the Flavour Coffee, figuring a break might bring me some luck. This was no Tim Hortons. It had exotic blends and fancy muffins, which said something about the affluence of suburbia. It was also as far from a drive-through as a coffee shop could get. The franchise had doors and tables, and was doing a brisk business because of it, mostly with salesmen holding quick meetings and seniors on their morning outing. At the table next to where I sat down, a group of older men were laughing over their lattes about the adolescent humour of a beer commercial in which a man tries to pour a Heineken while looking at a beautiful woman. Pretty quickly, his mug froths over. "Premature pour," one of the old guys laughed, quoting the ad slogan. The others chortled so loudly I thought for a second I'd have to call 911. But then they got back to their medical conditions and a long list of treatments that each had to tell the others about—in far more detail than a coffee shop should allow.

I walked back to the on-ramp facing a stronger wind than before, and was wondering what to do if I didn't get a ride all day, when an elderly man in an old Pontiac pulled over. He was going to the next interchange, but at least I was moving. Four hours and twenty minutes after Anne had dropped me in Kanata, I was moving. Within minutes, at the next interchange, I got another short hop with an insurance agent who had once hitchhiked across Canada, and then I caught a ride that would take me up the Ottawa Valley and wipe out any bad memories of the morning. It was the kind of ride hitchhikers talk about on the roadside. It was in a piano van.

John Chard and Willy Thibadeau had been moving pianos for a good chunk of their adult lives—forty-year-old John for twenty years and thirty-nine-year-old Willy for five. When they picked me up on the side of Highway 17, they had already moved one piano that morning from the Toronto suburb of Scarborough to Ottawa, five hours away by road, and picked up another, which they were carting to Pembroke, an hour up the road in another direction. From there, they would head back to Toronto for an early morning delivery to northern Ontario. It was backbreaking work for short bursts of time, followed by hours of long, boring drives around southern Ontario, which I think was why they picked me up. They seemed like an old married couple who couldn't stand the thought of another fifty kilometres together, especially since the next fifty kilometres looked as mundane as anything I had seen on my trip. There was nothing in any direction but flat farmland.

The men were driving an '85 GMC cube van that had no radio, no air conditioning and no middle seat. By John's count, it was on its fourth engine. He suggested I sit on a drinks cooler wedged between the driver's bucket seat, where Willy sat, and the front passenger's seat, which he had hopped out of to let me in. John was a big brick of a man, six feet two inches tall, and well over two hundred pounds. He was the backstop of the pair, the one who usually stood on the lower steps when they had to move a piano up a staircase. He was also something of a streetwise philosopher who liked to stroke his buzz cut and offer what he considered sage words on just about every subject that came up. That's what comes, he said, from growing up in downtown Toronto's violent Regent Park housing project, raised by a single mother.

Willy was the taciturn one. He was shorter than John, with a goatee, but looked every bit as strong, judging by his forearms working the wheel. Each was the size of a bull's leg. He warned me that he had a short fuse and, although he deferred to John's experience, had more clout than his partner on at least one front: his girlfriend owned the company.

As we traced the Ottawa River northwest, past a string of kayaking and rafting centres, Willy and John tried to make up for the lack of a radio in the van by telling piano stories. John was once chased down a flight of stairs by an eight-hundred-pound piano when another partner lost his grip. He had to jump over a banister to escape. Another time, he was stuck in a broken elevator for three hours with a baby grand. And then there was the cottage move, when John and Willy had to haul a piano to an island by barge, before lugging it by hand up a rocky slope. Two months ago, they had had to move a twelve-hundred-pound Heintzman down a fire escape.

Lately, they had also been called to a lot of homes where pianos were stuck in rooms or basements that had been renovated. In one house, they had to call in a roofer to open a hole so the piano could be lifted out by crane. This was what they liked best about piano moving: solving the puzzle of how best to get half a ton of furniture down a narrow stairway, around a tight corner or through a single door frame. It was why both men said they would never consider moving ordinary furniture for a living.

"We're special," John said. "We really are. We have a saying: Furniture movers are piano movers with their brains punched in."

"A piano is like a woman," Willy chimed in. "If they're not upright, they're grand."

"It takes more than muscle," John said. "You've got to have brains. You've got to have patience. A lot of people think you're moving a newspaper."

I had never equated moving a piano with moving a newspaper, not even the Sunday *New York Times,* but they went on to explain their art.

"It's a special breed," said Willy. "You need patience and common sense."

"And a carefree attitude," his partner added.

The two men, who looked big enough to play pro football, broke into the theme song from *Laverne and Shirley,* looking at each other as they sang, "Give us any job, we'll do it." They lasted one verse before stopping to light a couple of du Mauriers.

Amazingly, on nine hundred dollars a week in the city of Toronto, John was able to support eight children, including two sets of twins, and two grandchildren. He came by it honestly. Growing up in Regent Park, he watched his mother raise eight children after his father died. She made $124 a month working part-time at a local mission, and in the 1960s that was it. "She paid for the rent, our food and our clothes with that, and we never wanted for anything," John said. With his size and strong arms, he became the star quarterback of his high school football team, even though he had failed every year from Grade 6 on. After high school, he was invited to the Toronto Argonauts training camp and promptly broke his ankle in a scrimmage. It was the end of his football career.

He moved back to Regent Park, married and had a baby, and then got out. He could see the insanity of a housing project. Most of his childhood friends were dead or in jail. It was the parents' fault, he said, for not teaching their children to respect order. And it was society's fault, he continued, for allowing children to get away with what they did. "Kids today are a lot different than what we knew. First of all, they can't get a kick in the ass because the parents would go to jail. Imagine the kick in the ass those kids'll get in jail 'cause they didn't get kicked in the ass earlier. When I tried to kick my kids in the ass, one of my own sons said he was going to call Children's Aid. I said, 'Come here and I'll punch you out. Then you'll have a reason to call Children's Aid.'"

One problem with hitchhiking is that promising conversations come to an abrupt end as soon as a destination appears. No driver ever suggests going for coffee to finish a chat. And so I didn't get to ask John to expand on his observation that Chinese immigration was fuelling a new demand for pianos, or how long his body would hold up. He was complaining of a calf injury when he stepped down from the van to allow me to get out.

We were just outside Pembroke, where their next appointment was waiting, and I was back to the land of short hops. An Ottawa man who was taking his young son on a canoe trip in Algonquin Park took me fifteen kilometres up the road. He had picked me up for nostalgia's sake. In 1967, he said, he had hitchhiked from Ontario to Vancouver. A local butcher took me another fifteen kilometres. And then a Chinese-born nuclear scientist took me from Chalk River, home of one of Canada's greatest atomic energy facilities, to

Deep River, where he and some of the brains behind Canada's nuclear program lived. In the Cold War, a hitchhiker riding with a Chinese-born nuclear scientist around Chalk River would have been very suspicious indeed. But my next ride would assure me that such fears were misplaced, that this was not a danger zone, above the rapids of the Ottawa River. This was the birthplace of a safer, cleaner world.

— — —

I stood at the western edge of Deep River, fearing the late summer sun would set faster than I had anticipated. The traffic from Ottawa to North Bay was already drying up, as the shadows of trees along the roadside crept eastward, like some strange animation of an aboriginal myth. I watched as they swallowed each hash mark in the road, before darkening my spot and moving on. There was so little traffic that I could pace back and forth across the Trans-Canada, pitching pebbles at trees on either side.

When the occasional car appeared from the east, the driver was usually so distracted by the dropping sun behind me—flipping visors into position, fiddling for sunglasses, looking to the pavement instead of ahead—I don't think any of them noticed me. By five o'clock, I was so resigned to the prospect of a night in Deep River, barely 170 kilometres from the day's starting point, that when a car pulled over I thought it was part of the animation. The driver apparently thought the same of me. A plump-faced young man who looked barely out of high school, he was more nervous than I was. Before I could even get to my seat belt, he asked, "You're not going to do anything weird, are you?"

I think I fuelled his fear by not responding immediately. What did he expect me to say? If I was going to do something weird, would I announce it? And would I announce it before fastening my seat belt?

Finally, I said my only weird intention was to interview him. He laughed, saying I was the first hitchhiker he had ever picked up. He was still unsure why he had stopped. Perhaps it was the blinding light.

Kyle Haygarth was twenty-two years old and on top of the world. A physics major at the University of Waterloo in southwestern Ontario, he was nearing the end of an eight-month co-op placement with Atomic Energy of Canada Ltd., the Crown corporation that dominated Canada's nuclear program and pretty much owned Deep River. Living there and working down the Ottawa in Chalk River, Kyle got to sit with some of his industry's brightest minds as he spent his summer writing computer codes. It also put him close to canoe country, which was where he was headed for a long weekend. By nightfall, he hoped to be at South River, half an hour beyond North Bay, setting up camp with some friends.

We sped along the northern route of the Trans-Canada in Kyle's ten-year-old Plymouth Sundance, having the two lanes to ourselves for the first fifty kilometres beyond Deep River. Occasionally, the Ottawa River would pop into view, its waters glistening in the late sun, but then it was back to forest.

The Sundance aside, Kyle led a charmed life. His parents were baby boomers, and they gave him everything he could want and saved enough so that he would never be in need. When university tuition skyrocketed in the 1990s, his parents did not balk at the cost of $2,700 a term. He said the same was true for most of his friends. But there were downsides. Kyle said his generation had an attitude.

Thinking back to John the piano mover and his kick-ass upbringing in Regent Park, I asked Kyle if he felt the same way about his age group, that it was able to get away with anything. Of course his upbringing in a comfortable suburb, as the only child with two working parents, could hardly compare to that of John's family, surviving on an hourly wage. But he surprised me by repeating John's line. Rich or poor, he said, the kids of his generation were troublemakers. And of all the children in the world, they had perhaps the least cause to make trouble.

"I think my generation are goons," Kyle said. "They think they have something to prove. People shooting up high schools. There was a high school in Kitchener where a jock—another kid was bugging him—jumped over a table and stabbed him. I don't know why. People blame video games or TV or movies. I think it mostly has to do with parents. My parents raised me well. I had Nintendo. Everyone did. I don't play it that much. You have to know the difference between reality and a game. Blaming video games is just a cop-out for parents to get out of putting in more time with their kids. One of my friends was a Nintendo junkie. Now he's going to med school. He's perfectly normal. I've got a job. I've never done anything violent."

As the light in the wooded areas along the road began to fade, Kyle continued to talk about his generation and how it created its aggrieved sense. All the good jobs were taken by baby boomers, Kyle explained. He knew he would have to wait for them to retire, which in Canada made him feel doubly shortchanged. As a prospective computer engineer, his talent and that of his classmates were eagerly sought in the United States, where they would be paid handsomely, taxed less and showered with research funds. Coming to Chalk River for a work term had already opened Kyle's eyes to the growing gap in research and opportunities between Canada and the United States, especially in the hard sciences. He was shocked at how old the AECL buildings were, not at all like the new American facilities he had seen in pictures. It felt like he was walking into the 1960s, and in some ways he was. As a result of government cutbacks, the local population was on the decline for the first time in forty years. There was talk of the whole place shutting down.

Having watched some of Chalk River's best scientists head south, the question of leaving Canada remained a sore point for Kyle. He had grown up in Canada and gone to a Canadian university. He did not want to abandon his country or be seen to be abandoning his country. Yet he had a more continental view than his parents' generation, a more global view, really. In his mind, he could be as Canadian living in Dallas as in Deep River.

"Most of my friends are patriotic," he explained. "Patriotism doesn't mean having to give up something or give up opportunities."

I had not heard this before. Kyle viewed Canada as an ethnic group as much as a nation, a land that did more than receive people. It originated them. This did not follow the most commonly accepted definition of ethnicity, based on a common heritage, distinct language, original culture and occasionally a shared physical trait. None of those could be claimed by Canada. But ethnicities also come with their own state of mind—their own values, world views, customs and traditions—and Canadians had plenty of those. Kyle felt he could go anywhere in the world, for any length of time, and would remain Canadian: a Canadian-Texan, a Canadian-Briton, a Canadian-Singaporean. Even if he were a citizen of the world, his Canadian blood would flow through him. It was an intriguing thought, for a nation of immigrants and aboriginals.

The road began to rise and dip like an ocean swell as we entered a more hardened northern landscape. Then, as we came around a bend in the road, a strange silhouette appeared before us. It was someone hitchhiking, though all we could see through the glare of a setting sun was the person's shape on the roadside. We zipped by, without Kyle so much as letting up on the gas. I saw the shape of a toque, long hair and nothing else. I never was sure if it was a man or woman. Neither was Kyle. I jotted in my notebook: Do not hitchhike with a setting sun at your back.

At Mattawa, the highway cut away from the Ottawa River, turning west and never really looking back. This was a gateway to northern Ontario's lake country, the wondrous collection that runs as tiny as Tim, on the eastern edge of Algonquin Park, and as great as Superior, dwarfing continental Europe in size, beauty and romance. Even at 120 kilometres an hour, the passing scene of the first northern lake, softened by twilight, was impossible not to embrace: wooded shorelines, boats docked comfortably for the night, shrieking children jumping from a dock for an after-dinner swim.

I asked Kyle if he thought he could get this in the United States, or anywhere else. He believed he could, just as he figured he could find great health care, a safe neighbourhood and excellent schools.

There was nothing in Canada, he said, that he could not find south of the border, except Canadians. And he figured he could always root them out.

—— —— ——

From the perspective of anyone who lives in the North, North Bay, at a latitude of forty-six degrees, is very far south. In Ontario, it lies only one-third of the way from the province's southern tip to its northern extreme. In fact, it's closer to New York City than to Thunder Bay, and about the same distance from Miami as from the Arctic Circle. On a map, it is Canada's most southern northern city. While North Bay's name comes from its position on Lake Nipissing, opposite South Bay, it also illustrates the great depths of Canada's North. Just as the United States has varying degrees of southernness, so too do we have varying degrees of northernness. There's North, the near North, the Far North and the really far North. But unlike the United States, very few Canadians ever get to the North. From southern Ontario, where one in six Canadians lives, just making the four-hour hike to North Bay is considered an effort. Going beyond is nothing short of an adventure.

The town itself has long been one of Canada's great crossroads, where fur traders paddled to the Great Lakes or portaged to the Mattawa River and on to the Ottawa and St. Lawrence. Today, it is where the Trans-Canada from the east and west meets Highway 11, the extension of Yonge Street, Toronto's main artery, from the south. Yet for all its importance to travellers, North Bay is eminently forgettable, like one of those highway interchanges I had been stranded on in New Brunswick. It may be home to a major North American air base for patrolling the Arctic skies, with its own command structure housed in an underground village, but what lies above-ground is far less interesting. The best North Bay can offer a visitor is the Dionne Homestead Museum—the log farmhouse in which the famous quintuplets were born in 1934— and even that was borrowed. The homestead had to be moved up the road from Callander, the girls' hometown, to make it more accessible to tourists.

In the morning, I took a pass on the museum and walked to the western fringe of North Bay, where the last strip mall gave way to the Precambrian Shield that stoically carries the landscape from here to beyond the edge of Superior. I could only wonder what kind of derelict vehicle would pull over. Run-down sedans, compacts and the rusting floors of vans had become so much of my lot on the road that I no longer wasted my thumb on a Mercedes. I was ready to give up on Volvos, Buicks and Oldsmobiles too, when an Olds stopped on the gravel behind me. It looked like a godsend. There was even a priest at the wheel.

Father Norm Clement did nothing to disguise his identity. He wore his white collar, kept a crucifix on the dashboard and stowed a bottle of holy water on the floor next to the gas pedal. He said he was on his way to Sudbury to fill in for another Roman Catholic priest for the weekend and was well used to this road, having moved to North Bay from the big mining town thirty-two years earlier. We cruised along the Trans-Canada, with the soft voices of a CBC Radio program playing in the background. I had started to notice that northern and remote communities tended to have two choices on the radio: CBC and E-Z Rock. What was left of a Canadian identity was packaged into the first. What was left of country music was packaged into the second, along with the great oxymoron of pop music, "soft rock," and pre-recorded filler from stateless DJs working somewhere, by the hint of their accents, in southern Illinois. A restless driver could only wait for the next big town and a third inevitable option of a Classic Rock station, that other franchised outlet of the airwaves.

Father Norm paid little attention to the radio anyway. He usually had a hitchhiker along for the ride. Highway 17 was a good route, he said, to pick up the weak, the weary and the despondent—his stock in trade. At this time of year, there was usually a string of Maritimers heading to the mining camps north of

Superior or the oilfields to the west. Once, he picked up a Russian man outside North Bay who was dressed in a business suit and carrying only a briefcase. The man said he was on his way to Alaska.

The priest's favourite passengers were the local Ojibwe who lived along the north shore of Lake Nipissing, the "Little Waters" that flowed down the French River to the Great Lakes. "Honest to God," Father Norm said, remembering one rider who was carrying a bag of freshly killed fowl back to his reserve. "I pick up some of these Indians hitchhiking and you'd swear they are from another time."

Just as I had left the great river valleys for the land of lakes, this was also the beginning of Indian country, the great swath of northern woodlands where aboriginal communities still held influence and were poised to reassert some control over their lives. For much of my journey so far, any hints of native life had been on the margins. In the Maritimes, Indian communities were still small ghettos next to the bigger fishing towns of New Brunswick and Nova Scotia. In Newfoundland, they had been wiped out centuries ago, and they appeared headed for the same, slow fate on Quebec's north shore. In North Bay, by contrast, Father Norm had seen the town's population struggle to replace itself over his thirty-two years there, increasing from forty-five thousand to a mere fifty-two thousand. But at least there was one group adding to the area, in numbers and clout: the original inhabitants, the culturally and linguistically diverse Anishinabe nation that stretches from the Ottawa Valley to Manitoba.

Along the highway, Father Norm pointed to the small signs of progress for the natives of northern Ontario. An Anishinabe police cruiser was able to pull over motorists exceeding the speed limit and ticket them. In Sturgeon Falls, a roadside town near the Garden Village reserve, a slew of shops and fast-food restaurants gave some indication of growing wealth in the area. And there were plenty of new houses in view, most of them owned, he said, by natives benefiting from federal housing money.

We were halfway to Sudbury, between the breeze-through towns of Warren and Hagar, when I noticed something very non-aboriginal on the south side of the road. It was a powder-blue building, a Kingdom Hall, the place of worship for Jehovah's Witnesses. I had seen Kingdom Halls in the strangest of places, like the Quebec north shore, but this spot, on the road to mining country, seemed as odd a place as you could find to await the imminent end of the world, which Jehovah's Witnesses actively do. Or was it?

Father Norm was not surprised by the sect's growth here. He had watched the changing nature of faith in the Ontario North. There used to be a strong sense of order here, but those days were long gone. Entire towns came and went on the whim of a company decision, usually made in a head office in another country, perhaps on another continent. Governments were not much good any more either. With so many votes in the tax-paying South, they scarcely thought about the North.

That pretty much left communities to their own devices, which wasn't much help either, seeing as young people today, he said, worried mostly about themselves. Among his parishioners, the biggest fears involved losing the cottage, boat or van. Kids were the same, worrying before they reached adolescence about how they would afford such luxuries. Father Norm appreciated why these people turned to a sect with firm rules, even one as austere as the Jehovah's Witnesses, with their hope for a theocracy under God's rule. "There's a security in that," he said. "A lot of people will impose rules on others and you'll ask why. They'll say they don't know what it's like to have rules imposed on them."

Before we reached Sudbury, Father Norm urged me to follow another course, one that the Ojibwe knew very well. People without direction, he said, don't need rules. They need silence. "If you want to meet your God and meet yourself, go inside," he said, looking across the front seat with a smile. "You'll find it in silence."

I was not sure if he was rehearsing his sermon for the weekend, but it was hard to imagine people in these parts needing to seek silence. Emptiness surrounded us, and with it silence, save for the CBC and E-Z Rock. In this, one of the world's better stretches of wilderness, it was a bit like prescribing solitude to the Bedouin. But even in these parts, silence was eroding, by choice rather than design. Father Norm had to struggle to persuade teenagers to give up their weekends of television for fishing trips. Most would prefer a weekend in Toronto to both. The big city had become their known world, because it was the world they saw on television and heard about on radio. It was a noisy and busy world, and it had become familiar, while just outside their doors, the world of lakes, rivers, forests and silence, the world of the Canadian wilderness, had become foreign.

The hills of Sudbury were a shock to my eyes. The last time I had been through here, twenty years earlier on a high school trip, the legendary Inco slag heaps were in their prime. They were barren in those days and cast in a hideous black that made them look like death mountains towering over the mining town. People said astronauts once trained here to get a feeling for the moon, this being the one place on earth that was stripped of all life. Today's Sudbury was a place regenerated. The former desert in Coniston, one of the little villages that make up the city, had been remade as a golf course. Other heaps had been reclaimed and planted with enough trees to be reclassified as forested land. And the air—it was as clear as a winter's day.

Like the coal towns of Cape Breton, Sudbury had once known nothing but dirty mining. The city and its huge mines were built on the rim of a crater that through the twentieth century produced much of the world's nickel. Inco, one of Canada's biggest companies, made its greatest fortune here mining and processing the nickel that the Big Three automakers, not far away in Michigan, used in every car they made. But as in many resource-based economies, the good times did not last. The automakers found ways to replace nickel with plastics. New mines started to come on stream in the developing world, where labour was cheaper and environmental standards less strict. And at the end of the Cold War,

Russia began flooding the world market with its own nickel, causing prices to collapse.

With so much working against it, Sudbury had sensed doom from the seventies on, but some remarkable moves may have helped save it. Both the provincial and federal governments transferred several offices here, including the entire Revenue Canada operation for Ontario, which handles the biggest share of the country's income tax returns every spring. A large science centre specializing in minerals and mines, called Science North, also began to draw tourists, as did the opening of mine shafts to the public. Environmentally, Inco installed a superstack to reduce emissions and spread them over a greater area. The stack still spewed close to a tonne a day of sulphur dioxide emissions into the local air, but that was considered benign compared to the past. Since launching an $830-million clean-up program in 1988, the company had cut its metal emissions by close to seventy-five per cent.

Father Norm dropped me on the eastern edge of Sudbury, near the Coniston golf course, where he suggested I follow a bypass around the south of the city, if I hoped to get to the edge of Lake Superior by evening. I discovered he had been away from Sudbury for too long, as I stood on one side of the city for two hours, and then the other side for another couple of hours, with only a short hop in between.

The renaissance of Sudbury, if that's what a tax office and tree-planting program can be called, was noted far and wide, overshadowed in northern Ontario only by the revival of Elliot Lake. It was a much smaller town that relied entirely on the mining of uranium and for years had been celebrated in government studies and media reports as a model of what a tiny, remote one-horse town could do when the horse lay down and died. I had read so much about Elliot Lake that I almost cheered when a former miner pulled over and said he was headed there.

From the moment he started talking, Les Turgeon came across as a moving study in the North's hopes and despair, and I was relieved to listen for as long as possible. With little but villages, bush and Indian reserves between here and Sault Ste. Marie, I needed two or three good shots to cover the next three hundred kilometres, and this was one of them.

Les was on his way to Elliot Lake to drink beer and play golf for the weekend with his buddies and relive some memories of the town where he was born, where his three daughters were born, where his father worked and started to die, and where for fourteen years he had a decent job. The thirty-eight-year-old had been driving his old Escort since morning from the Toronto area, which was the closest place with steady work that he could find. His Elliot Lake buddies had also dispersed, to Sudbury, to mining camps farther north and, of course, to Toronto, the big city that probably had more northern residents than any northern town.

For Les, Elliot Lake was what the North, cruel and compelling, had always been. He spent the first six years of his life in the town where his father, a francophone man, started to work in the Denison mine when it opened in 1954. It was a legendary operation, scraping uranium from the ground at a time when uranium meant life or death to the military prowess of the world's two great powers. For any miner, they were the wretched years, when men like Les's dad and uncle were required to coat their lungs with aluminum dust before entering the mine. Nothing else was available to protect them against uranium.

Although the mine eventually banned this method of dusting lungs, it was too late for Les's father and uncle. The two men died before they were sixty. The mine closed anyway. Les remembered the entire street being boarded up in 1968 as his family moved to Sudbury, where there were still jobs in the nickel and copper mines. Remarkably, by the time he finished high school in 1980, the uranium market was humming again and Elliot Lake was resurrected as a boom town. Les moved back to his birthplace, to a cot in a bunkhouse and a job in the mine. He worked there for the next fourteen years, making the best money of his life. In good years, he cleared $80,000. He and his wife thought they had nothing to worry about for their three young girls. But it was too good to be true. In 1990, the company announced five thousand layoffs, pretty much its entire Elliot Lake payroll.

Les was among the lucky few to be given a job in the last mine to close, which kept him working in the town for a few more years. He tried to get work in Sudbury after that, but Inco and Falconbridge, the two big mine operators, were already cutting back. When his marriage fell apart, his wife took the girls and moved to North Bay. To find a decent job, he had to move to Brampton, a satellite city northwest of Toronto where he lived in a basement apartment and worked in an aeronautics repair shop near Lester B. Pearson International Airport. In a strange twist of fate for someone whose father mined uranium to threaten the Russians, Les worked mostly with a group of Russian immigrants and lived in a house owned by a Russian family. He didn't mind. What bothered him was the sheer length and cost of the drive to any wilderness.

"The North has everything," he explained in a voice that seemed too soft and polite for a guy who grew up among miners. "You can have your snow machine, boat, skiing, the lakes. I used to drive my snow machine right from my driveway. I'd leave the garage and I'd be off. I don't know why people move south. Well, yeah, I do. The jobs."

After the mine shut down again in the nineties, Elliot Lake reinvented itself as a retirement community, which must rank among the boldest and most bizarre moves ever made by a chamber of commerce. Imagine thinking about your golden years in Florida, and then being pitched the idea of moving to a frozen little ghost town, twenty-eight kilometres off the Trans-Canada, where a good many of the world's nuclear weapons got their start. But it worked. Several dozen old folks took up the offer of the great outdoors and a decent provincial health post that stayed with the town. The provincial and federal governments helped by financing the modest Elliot Lake Mining and Nuclear Museum, while someone else added a small academy to help bring artists and painting groups to the stunning scenery of the northern bush. But the real selling point was cheap housing. A bungalow could be had for less than $50,000. Even those moving to Elliot Lake from Sudbury saved enough to fly to Florida every winter, if they wanted.

Well west of Sudbury, we were now driving through one depressed town after another, with little but abandoned farms in between. These were simple places, with street names such as Church Road, Village Road and Ballpark Road. There was no greater effort to give a sense of permanence, other than a few curious Hispanic names like Espanola. According to legend, the names were assigned by French explorers who had come across a local Ojibwe tribe that had learned some Spanish while on an extended raid in the southwestern United States.

At the village of Spanish, Les said there was little more than retired folk left, along with a few truckers and a handful of residents who worked at a pulp and paper mill in Espanola, fifty kilometres away. The town's motel and bowling alley were boarded up. A couple of restaurants and one other motel were all that remained visible of an economy. Other than the mill, he said the area's best hope lay with half a dozen Indian communities at the top of Manitoulin, the great island that divides Georgian Bay from Lake Huron.

Just before the turn to Elliot Lake, Les slowed down to show me one of the things he missed most about the North. Ahead on the road was a small bear cub, perhaps four months old. It scurried back into the woods when it saw the car. "The mother cannot be far," Les said, sounding as awestruck as a child seeing his first bear. He dropped me up at the road, at the deserted turnoff to Elliot Lake. Daylight was fading. In the three directions that the roads followed, there wasn't a sign of human life. In the fourth direction, there was thick forest. One misplaced bear cub, Les said before driving off, and my hopes of reaching the Soo by nightfall would be ruined.

I was too busy watching for bears on the road to have noticed the big red pickup coming around the corner from Elliot Lake. The Ford came to a halt just in front of me. The driver was a middle-aged man dressed in a Ford baseball cap, long tights and a singlet that did nothing to control the beer belly rolling over his waist. His greying beard and raspy voice gave the impression that he once could have played for The Eagles.

Wayne was headed for the Soo, where he stayed with a brother and worked four days a week, running a crane at Algoma Steel as he had done for most of his adult life. On the four days off that followed his rotation, he stayed in Elliot Lake with his wife. The air was cleaner, the housing cheaper and the hunting accessible by foot. He could ride his snowmobile from the garage in winter. His wife could walk to the bingo hall and to Tim Hortons, where she worked. They both could visit relatives who had also moved to Elliot Lake: her parents, one of her daughters and a cousin.

While Wayne boasted about the attractions of Elliot Lake, he admitted another reason for his move. He was keen to save as much money as he could while racing toward retirement as his employer hurtled toward bankruptcy. Algoma Steel, which had been in the hole for three years running, was perpetually on the brink of collapse. The workforce had been cut to forty-five hundred from a high of ten thousand. As part of the latest restructuring, Wayne had agreed to nearly $3 an hour in wage cuts, to about $21 an hour, but he wasn't sure that would be enough to save his job. He could only hope the steel mill would keep going for another seven years, when at the age of fifty-five he was due to retire.

The Soo economy was once strong enough to attract Wayne's grandfather from Quebec. He got a job at the mill, as did Wayne's father. Wayne knew he would get a job there too, although he had to start as a truck operator until a union posting came along. He knew this would not be so for his children. Of the six, one worked in a restaurant, another in a scrapyard, a third in a hair salon, a fourth as a cleaner and one more with a youth services agency. The last one was unemployed, a boy who dropped out of school after Grade 10. "If we go any further, we will be so high-tech it will be hard for anyone to get a labour job," Wayne said, taking a sip from his travelling mug.

If there was a reason for this downward drift, it lay in the inability of schools, and their students, to keep pace with a changing economy. Wayne may have been able to get by with Grade 10. His children couldn't. Just one of the six had studied beyond high school, the daughter who worked for a youth services agency. "What makes this generation different?" Wayne asked. "Lack of responsibility. They didn't have the responsibility placed on them that we had on us. I basically knew I'd have to take care of myself. They figured they'd get handouts."

We had passed the tranquil Mississauga River—"deer country" to the busloads of artists who come here every summer—and were following the St. Marys River, which was dotted with fishing boats searching for salmon in the sunset. In the middle of the river was St. Joseph Island, a large body that straddles the border and where, the previous summer, two young hitchhikers and their puppy were murdered. The young man and woman, both twenty-one years old, were vagabonds, variously street kids and squeegee kids, who had been criss-crossing North America in search of a good time. Before their journey became a nightmare, Shawn Barrett and his girlfriend, Melody Lopez, had caught a dream ride from the edge of Toronto all the way to the outskirts of Sault Ste. Marie. They could not have known that the driver, Robert Armstrong, had by the age of twenty-three earned a long record of criminal offences, from drunk driving to sexual assault. Seemingly affable, he took the hitchhikers to his cabin on the island, just east of the Soo. They partied for a couple of nights. Then something went horribly wrong. Robert and Shawn disagreed over something. Robert shot and killed Shawn. Then he killed Melody and the puppy, burned their corpses and buried the remains. Melody was pregnant.

Robert was later convicted of first- and second-degree murder and sentenced to life in prison. The story, which I had read about, did not sit well with me as we passed Saint Joseph Island and began our final approach to the Soo. How many Robert Armstrongs were out there?

I told Wayne that I had two goals for the next day: to reach Wawa, three hours north of the Soo, and to get out of Wawa. The little town was legendary as the most difficult spot on the continent to hitch a ride. I had heard of hitchhikers being stuck there for days. Or was it weeks? For a hitchhiker, heading to Wawa was a bit like approaching Everest.

Wayne offered nothing but caution. Although he had heard similar stories about Wawa, he said the real challenge would be getting out of the Soo. There had been a spate of roadside murders lately, and everyone was spooked. And with that information, he dropped me at a bus stop on the city's edge. He was headed to his brother's house in a different part of the city. If I was lucky, he said, I might catch the last bus downtown before nightfall. Already, I could see what he meant. It was eight o'clock and the city looked deserted.

——— ——— ———

Although Algoma Steel, its main employer, was on the ropes, Sault Ste. Marie had it better than many communities. Its other big employer, the Saint Mary pulp and paper mill, was thriving. And there was more hope in a new casino. Gamblers would pour across the border from Michigan, it was predicted. Algoma might not even be missed, they said, if the Soo became a Vegas of the North. This, I thought, had to be seen.

Downtown, where the Station Mall advertised itself as "the biggest mall in northeastern Ontario," the most visible sign of nightlife remained the Algoma stacks, silhouetted by smoke spewing against an auburn horizon. Beyond, the international bridge sat like a paperweight straddling the border and the twin cities, with their connecting locks that carried water around the Saint Marys River rapids, a seven-metre drop from Lake Superior to the entrance of Lake Huron.

The casino, when I found it, looked much less exciting. On a weekend no less. At the doors, a sign welcomed visitors "Into the wild!" Below it was the official logo showing a canoe shooting the rapids. On the actual gaming floor was wall-to-wall carpeting coloured with maple leaves. The walls were decorated with cut-outs of forests. A model float plane hung from the ceiling of the casino bar, which could have passed for a nicely decorated Moose Lodge were it not for a band playing Jimmy Buffet tunes. The audience of a dozen people looked like they were struggling to stay awake. It was nine o'clock.

I continued to circle the slot machines and blackjack tables, writing notes about how lifeless the place was, when a young man with an English accent, dark suit and stern look stopped me. He was the floor manager, wondering what I was doing with a pen and paper. Didn't I know, he asked, that casinos strictly forbid the taking of notes?

When I professed my ignorance and gave the floor manager my card, he lightened up, just a titch, and told me about the operation. Since it had opened a few months earlier, as Ontario's first charity casino, it had created 450 jobs and nearly a million dollars a month in local wages. But the "activity," to use a gambling euphemism, was a bit slow. So slow, in fact, that the casino's British managers had to install more nickel slot machines to compensate for the rather inactive quarter, dollar and five-dollar slots.

The quarter-slot fiasco was just about the last thing Sault Ste. Marie needed. Although the city's image was not grand in the first place, it had just endured a decade of bad publicity, in which it was portrayed nationally as a haven of intolerance. The Soo had long been known as a racist outpost. From 1926 to 1929, it had a small but thriving chapter of the Ku Klux Klan, which, given the lack of blacks north of Superior, chose to target the large number of Italian Catholic immigrants who kept the local blue-collar economy going.

The Italians were accused of taking scarce jobs at the steel mill, while their churches were not appreciated by the Protestants, who considered themselves to be the Soo's bedrock.

The Great Depression took care of the Klan, as well as many of those jobs at the steel mill. But the air of bigotry did not drift away. The anti-immigrant views became anti-French, as the federal and provincial governments promoted bilingualism. A group named the Sault Association for the Preservation of English Language Rights flourished in the eighties when Pierre Trudeau and then Brian Mulroney pushed for greater French-language rights. The group was further outraged by the provincial government's decision in 1986, with all-party support, to provide French-language services to the surrounding district of Algoma, where there were several francophone communities. The association got its chance to strike back, just as the controversial Meech Lake Accord was going before the nation.

On January 29, 1990, with Canada hanging in the balance, the Soo city council adopted an English-only resolution. It was a small but symbolic act of defiance, as the city said it would officially resist efforts by the province of Ontario to impose French-language services. A few other small Ontario communities adopted similar resolutions. In the end, they were struck down by the courts and rescinded for good measure by several councils. But the declarations served to convince many Québécois that the rest of Canada didn't want them, or their language. It was the sort of statement that spooked Johann St. Pierre and his friends from ever visiting Ontario.

Like that other casino town, Montreal, which once tried to drive away the English, the Soo had learned the hard way about the consequences of bigotry. It drove away good people, irrespective of background, and left a community to rot. Whether a metropolis or a mill town, there was nothing to be gained from exclusion, and lots to be lost. Montreal, now thriving with diversity, had learned the lesson well. Sault Ste. Marie, struggling to survive, did not seem so sure of itself.

The next morning, I left my downtown hotel for the highway at the same time as a group of tourists, across the road, were climbing aboard the daily train headed for the stunning Agawa Canyon. Judging by the trickle of people around the station, the Soo's efforts to revamp its image, including a national newspaper ad the previous year, were not paying off.

I caught a local bus to the north side, where there was little other than a trading post, forest and signs pointing to Thunder Bay, seven hundred kilometres away. For those going west, this was the beginning of the long-haul drive. I bought a muffin and a bottle of grapefruit juice at the trading post, the last stop for 315 kilometres, and headed for the gravel roadside. I expected to be there for hours, going by Wayne's caution. But before I could think again about what he had said—before I could finish my juice, even—a van pulled to the side of the road, just beyond me.

John Mutch, the driver, was a retired school principal headed back home to Manitouwadge, nearly five hours from here and fifty kilometres off the main highway. He had dropped off his wife the previous night at Sault Ste. Marie airport and wanted some company for the return trip. Apparently, his first effort had flopped. The front passenger seat was occupied by another hitchhiker John had picked up a couple of kilometres back, a scrubby man from New Brunswick who had little to say other than to tell us he was heading to Alberta, to a meat-packing plant where he worked. He had just been home to the East Coast for a vacation, but smelled more like the place he was going.

As soon as I got in the back of the van, I told John I wanted to get out at Wawa. I needed to test the legend that it was the hardest place in North America to get a ride from. Both men in the front laughed. John said the enormous stretch of highway from the Soo to Thunder Bay used to be crowded with hitchhikers going east and west, so many that on some mornings there would be lines of them outside the two cities. He remembered those days well. "Twenty years ago, this stretch, Christ, there were guys all over the place. There were more kids on the road. Personally, I think part of the problem is financial. The other is fear. More kids these days have to work. I used to pick up kids who were taking the summer off, just to see the country. They're more pressed to work these days."

The other hitchhiker piped up for a minute. He knew guys who had been stuck in Wawa for three or four days.

The mist was still rising off the forest north of Sault Ste. Marie when a coyote trotted across the highway in front of us. From there, the Trans-Canada cut through chunks of Shield and then returned to the moody shoreline of Lake Superior, with sandy beaches in one cove and towering rock faces in the next as it unfolded into a tempestuous inland sea. Deeper into Lake Superior Provincial Park are the steep crags and tumultuous rivers that once attracted several artists from the Group of Seven who, in this wilderness, unshackled Canadian art from its long servitude to European schools. But beyond the northeastern shore of Superior, there was little more than forest and history.

"You could drive this stretch in the winter and go for hours, literally, without seeing another car," John said from the front seat.

A century ago, this trail attracted gold diggers from every corner of the planet. The Shield around Hemlo, Marathon and Wawa produced some of the world's better mining fortunes and greater legends still. But those days had passed, with gold prices never quite recovering from the end of the gold standard, and miners turning their eyes to more exotic, and cheaper, locations. Twenty-first-century drifters, people like the hitchhiker in John's front seat, were left to seek their money in the oilfields and livestock farms of Alberta.

When I asked the man why he went all the way to Alberta for a job that paid ten bucks an hour, he said he had been looking for a diversion ever since his wife had died. It was an unpleasant existence on the feedlot farm. For ten to twelve hours a day, he handled some of the 6,500 cattle that were killed in the slaughterhouse each day. At night, he slept in a trailer provided by the company. It was the best job he could find west of New Brunswick.

John had seen the same trend in Manitouwadge, another mining town that was packing it in. He and his wife, both schoolteachers from the South, had moved there in the seventies for a one-year posting. They stayed because even though the weather was harsh—minus thirty-five for much of the winter—the community was solid and the housing cheap. But now, with the mine winding down, Manitouwadge looked liked it would become a ghost town, another Elliot Lake but with colder winters. Houses that were worth $90,000 a few years ago were listed for $40,000, and they weren't selling. At last count, John said, eighty houses were on the market.

John and his wife didn't have to leave just yet. He had his teaching pension, his wife still worked and they never felt isolated. He read *The Globe and Mail* every day on the Internet and chatted with friends all over the country by e-mail. When he'd had a battle with cancer ten years ago, he'd been treated at Thunder Bay and then spent four months recovering at Toronto's Princess Margaret Hospital. Manitouwadge, he said, was a good place to go home to.

The town's youth, on the other hand, were leaving in droves. John figured sixty per cent of his students left and never came back. Among them were his two daughters, one who went to Vancouver, the other to Guelph, in southwestern Ontario. At his old elementary school, enrolment was down to 250 students, from 550 in the early nineties. While the school system was chronically underfunded, it had managed to parcel John into a comfortable retirement at the age of fifty-four. His wife would soon join him, and they too would probably leave Manitouwadge.

John continued to play a tape of bagpipe music that was going when he picked me up. It must have been on automatic rewind, although how would you know? The music sounded like one long drone, not at all like Kilt's take on Kiss. As we left the park and followed the Trans-Canada inland to the Wawa turnoff, there were signs for Dad Lake, Mom Lake and Baby Lake, which should have been my warning of what was to come. Both John and the drifter thought I was a fool to give up another hour's free ride just to see if I could get a lift out of Wawa. John warned me not to stay on the road much after three, because nothing much along the highway stayed open beyond dark. I felt like I was being dropped in the middle of the bush, which, judging by the roadside at Wawa, was not a bad assessment.

The most visible sign that you are close to Wawa is a giant steel goose on the side of the highway, which was erected in 1960 to mark the completion of Highway 17 across the north shore of Superior and another link in the Trans-Canada Highway. The completion of Canada's national railroad is marked by the golden spike in British Columbia and is a legendary story that every Canadian schoolchild must learn. How disheartening, I thought, standing alone outside Wawa, that a milestone in an equally great project should be immortalized by a bird, a creature whose primary interaction with cross-country traffic comes only when it fails to vacate the asphalt fast enough.

The Trans-Canada goose took its legend from Wawa, Ojibwe for "wild goose," which owes its name to the thousands of geese that stop every spring and fall on Lake Wawa during their migrations. After those other lakes named for Dad, Mom and Baby, the Ojibwe word seemed wildly creative, even daring. But the sheer size and ugliness of the roadside goose was less defensible. According to a plaque at the roadside tourist centre, the original bird, made out of plaster, did not survive three winters and had to be replaced by the present, hardier model, which was made from Algoma steel with iron ore mined in Wawa. The bird weighs two thousand kilograms and stands close to ten metres in height.

While the goose was good publicity for Algoma, it said little about modern-day Wawa. The iron ore mine closed in 1998, and the company was rapidly scaling back its presence in the region. Once I reached the town, along a two-lane road that led to the great gold belt stretching from Timmins to northern Quebec, the most active life form I could find was a centre for the Polish Alliance of Canada, followed by the three essentials of small-town life: a Canadian Tire, a bank and a beer store. Down a side street, at the famous lake of wild geese, there was an empty public beach and a few idle pleasure boats moored in the placid waters. Wawa felt like it had been evacuated, which didn't ease my fears about getting a ride out.

Back on the road leaving town, there was only one shop doing any semblance of business. Young's General Store understood the needs of the long-distance driver. In summer, the family that owned the store made and sold close to twenty kilograms of fudge daily, including chocolate-peanut butter and butter pecan. The chocolate fudge was so sweet, the shopkeeper's daughter warned me, that if I had a ten-gram chunk I wouldn't need to eat for the rest of the day. She was right. After trying some and then walking two kilometres back to the highway, I still felt bloated. I couldn't imagine how cross-country drivers, popping into Wawa for a quick fix, managed to keep their seat belts on.

I stopped in once more at the tourist centre to see if there was anything worth seeing between here and Thunder Bay. One of the attendants said that if I got out of Wawa, I should stick with my ride. As a child, he remembered stories of how awful it was to catch a lift from this place. "There'd be hundreds of them out on the highway!" he exclaimed, a little shocked to meet someone still daring to hitchhike. He reluctantly wished me luck, as I headed with some trepidation to the junction of Highway 17 and the road from Wawa. A truck coming from the east blew by me without hesitation, and then a small white Avis rental car came around the bend from town, with two women in the front seat. So rare was it for a woman or the driver of a rental car to stop for a hitchhiker that I decided to put out my thumb only at the last moment, when I noticed a Quebec licence plate. The car stopped. I was out of Wawa in less than sixty seconds.

Heather and Gerry promised to be the drive from heaven. Their Chevy Malibu was air-conditioned and playing a cool mix of fifties and sixties classics. The two women from Montreal did not look like they would be putting on any bagpipe music, either. Moreover, middle-aged Heather and her mother, Gerry, were headed to Vancouver to a family wedding. I could be finished my journey in seventy-two hours, Heather said, telling me to relax and enjoy the ride. And here I was fretting about spending the next three nights in Wawa. The great legend of hitchhiking, I decided, was a myth.

Heather was a typical Quebec driver, hitting one-forty on the open road before I could fasten my seat belt. She almost never picked up hitchhikers, she said, but thought I looked both pathetic and harmless. I also must have looked like a good listener, because she seemed determined to talk the entire way to Vancouver, except for the pauses that her mother used as cues to carry on. The two women gabbed for forty-five minutes, without a break, until White River, a hundred-metre-long hamlet that I feared they would blow right through. The place was written up as the coldest centre in Canada, with a record low temperature, hit in the nineteenth century, of minus seventy-two degrees Celsius. I wanted to stop for another reason: White River was the accepted birthplace of Winnie the Pooh.

Slowing down, Heather turned into a parking lot. "Hey, they have an A&W!" she blurted out, cutting off her mother. "They're moving up in the world."

On August 24, 1914, Lieutenant Harry Colebourn, of the Thirty-Fourth Fort Garry Horse and Canadian Army Veterinary Corps, purchased a black bear cub in White River while en route to the battlefields of Europe. "Winnie," named for Lieutenant Colebourn's hometown of Winnipeg, became the company mascot and stayed with the troops as they awaited deployment in southern England. When the call to battle came, in December 1914, the bear was left in the care of the London Zoo, which kept him permanently after Lieutenant Colebourn's return from France. Winnie became a favourite of a young boy named Christopher who frequented the zoo with his father, A. A. Milne, and soon became the inspiration for Milne's 1926 children's classic.

The White River bear lived for close to twenty years in the London Zoo, but in northern Ontario, like everywhere, was remembered for the character he inspired. On the roadside at White River, the town in 1992 erected a plastic sculpture of Disney's Pooh Bear, honey pot and all, with a sign, "Where it all began." Sure enough, like bees to honey, busloads of Pooh admirers stop every summer to take pictures.

While Heather and Gerry went into a souvenir shop next to the A&W to buy postcards, I watched a crowd of Chinese tourists receive a quick history of Pooh from their guide. The visitors were probably good for White River, fast food and all, but there was no shortage of irony around their fascination with bears. In northern Ontario, it was widely thought there were too many of them. Yet the province had placed a moratorium on the spring bear hunt. Ever since environmental groups and the animal rights lobby won the ban, northern towns said they had faced an influx of bears—cute to children but a menace to any resident with a garbage can. In the local newspaper, on sale at the souvenir stand, the letters page was filled with angry comments from people wanting to bring back the spring hunt. One writer said there were now four thousand bears in the area, which made me feel doubly glad to have secured a ride over the top of Superior.

When we were back on the highway, Heather and Gerry found no shortage of new things to talk about. There was a ribbon flapping in the back of a pickup truck, a crime-watch sign, a slow transport truck, an ordinary van—all worthy of comment.

"He's braking!" Heather snapped when a truck started to slow down in front of us. "There's no logical reason to brake. Why is he braking?"

"I'm not followin' him all the way to Calgary!" Gerry said, noticing the truck's Alberta plates. I didn't know what she was talking about. She wasn't driving.

Closer to Marathon, about halfway around the lake, a series of billboards served as a kind of running teleprompter for the women, who took turns reading the advertising slogans to each other. Heather must have been inspired by the many billboards about food, because she turned off at Marathon in search of a place for lunch. Following a hill down from the highway, she turned into Robin's, a regional donut shop chain that somehow managed to resist the tide of fast-food conglomerates. Heather and her mother aimed to stop every day for lunch at a donut shop, for soup and a biscuit. The one other standard on their road trip was to complete at least a thousand kilometres a day. Gerry, who did only some of the driving, insisted on it.

When we got out of the car, I noticed Heather was wearing a Lear Jet T-shirt. She worked for Bombardier, the huge Montreal company that makes snowmobiles, Sea-Doos, trains and executive jets, and had spent time on its Lear Jet program, which was dominated by Americans. She was the ideal person to ask about the brain drain, that great force that Kyle and I had discussed on the other side of Ontario.

A divorced mother with three grown children, Heather had seen Montreal transformed in one lifetime. Her mother, Gerry, an anglophone with a grade-school command of French, had come of age in a Montreal that was a complacent transportation hub, run by an anglo elite. Heather came of age when it was a struggling backwater in a separatist province. Her three sons, a chef, an actor and a computer technician, enjoyed the city as a thriving multicultural centre that drew people from around the world.

Where Heather worked, her part of Montreal was packed with aeronautics firms. She and her colleagues were the model of the new Quebec. But the province, as much as it had bounced back, was still bent on driving out anyone who thought beyond its parochial boundaries. The separatist government, for instance, would not allow children of anyone but anglophones to be educated in English. Yet in her industry, all the best jobs, training manuals and computer programs demanded English. It was why, she said, so many of her francophone co-workers were sending their children to private English-language schools. The transformation of Montreal as a continental city was rich with irony. Heather knew of an entire local tech team hired by a Washington-state company, that, as part of its recruitment drive, found a French immersion school in Seattle for their children.

As we headed back to the highway and were into a new Tony Bennett tape, the conversation returned to road talk.

"Oh, that was a good one!" Gerry said after we hit the first speed bump leaving Marathon.

The Trans-Canada snaked through a series of provincial parks, passing through thick forests and over hills before kissing the lake and heading back into the woods. Its two lanes curved, climbed and dipped so often over the 180-kilometre run to Nipigon that the road offered few open stretches for passing. To Gerry, sitting up front and minding the tapes, there was no end to the frustration.

"Pass her, girl!" she commanded her daughter when a car in front of us slowed down.

The car's driver was apparently not willing to overtake a motorcycle in front of him.

"Will you just go by!" Heather cursed at the car.

Gerry treated the delay as a sort of intermission and a chance to change tapes in favour of *Phantom of the Opera*. She had already played the two-cassette musical a couple of times since leaving Montreal, but today she had saved it for the late afternoon slot. "I just love that show," she said, not noticing that Heather had found an open stretch and was speeding by the car and motorcycle.

"Thank you there, boy," Heather said to the young man on the motorcycle.

We didn't get much past the motorcycle when Heather had to slow down again for a truck. "Come on, Sleepin' Moses!" her mother exclaimed, apparently convinced that this would be enough to push the truck to a faster speed.

Over the next hill, Heather pulled into the oncoming lane, muttering, "Come on, car!" to the Malibu as she pushed down on the gas pedal and shook the steering wheel to make it go faster. It didn't work, and she dropped back behind the truck. She tried again and again, until finally there was a long, flat, straight stretch of road that allowed her to race past the truck at a hundred and thirty.

The leapfrogging continued through two sides of *Phantom*, which Gerry had turned up so loud there was no hope of conversation, not even about billboards. In the side-view mirror, I could see her pink lips mouthing the lyrics. For the next hour, the only words I heard from her came when she turned around and said, almost in a shout, "Andrew Lloyd Webber, what a mind!"

Beyond Nipigon, as we approached Thunder Bay, the highway opened up, although it was still two lanes. The thick forests of the north shore gave way to fields of granite that rose and fell like giant swells, and soon the twisting road began to feel more like a wild Jackson Pollock journey than a rugged Group of Seven canvas. In places, the highway builders had blasted their way through the rock, forming towering gates of stone that dwarfed even the biggest transport trucks. Above us, as we climbed through these gates, the sky began to look like the lake in the distance, with its clouds taking the place of islands. On the way down, the dark water took on the image of a late afternoon sky.

This last stretch around the lake, before breaking into its long run west across the Prairies, had been renamed the Terry Fox Courage Highway, with regular markers depicting the immortal image of a one-legged man running along the roadside. A generation had passed since 1980, when Terry Fox carried out the greatest act of heroism that modern Canada has known. While dying of cancer, and having already lost a leg, he hobbled and ran from Newfoundland to this point, hoping to reach the Pacific but never getting past Thunder Bay, in his campaign to raise money and awareness for medical research. East of the city, atop a hill, the government had erected a statue, nine feet high, of the great young runner looking west, struggling to unite the country in a common cause. As we approached, Gerry turned down the *Phantom* tape.

The monument enjoys a sweeping view of the head of the lake, and in the distance a land formation known as the Sleeping Giant. The long horizontal rock was a reminder of the mythical Dakota Sioux who betrayed the local Ojibwe and was turned to stone. But the real giant, I thought, reading again about his life at the memorial, must be Terry Fox, who made a commitment and lived by it. "It feels good to give," he told Canadians during his Marathon of Hope, which covered 5,342 kilometres.

The three of us sat silently in the car as we drove away from the monument and into Thunder Bay. It was almost six o'clock, but Heather and Gerry were determined to stick to their thousand-kilometre target for the day. They hoped to make Dryden by nightfall, and Vancouver in a few days. They urged me once more to stay with them for the ride. I knew I wouldn't get a better offer. I was even warming to the Phantom. But I had to say no. Canada was more than the back seat of an air-conditioned Malibu.

We were not yet in the city when a Honda Civic overtook us in the oncoming lane. "Where's he from?" Heather asked. "Quebec?"

The Honda driver was going fast enough to clear a line of cars ahead of us just before the oncoming traffic closed the passing lane, ending any hope of us following him. In front of us, it was difficult to count the number of cars slowing to a crawl behind what looked to be a small white bus.

"Holy Toledo!" Gerry cried. "It's an ice-cream truck!"

We entered Thunder Bay at such a slow speed that Gerry returned to the Phantom, blaring an organ sequence through the rear speakers until we reached the corner of the Trans-Canada and Arthur Street. They let me off at the intersection, near a row of motels, where the highway took a sharp and symbolic turn right. Having cleared the mammoth trail over Superior, the Montrealers headed due west, with only 3,200 kilometres of lake, forest, prairie and mountain between here and the Pacific. I watched the white

Malibu speed off toward the sunset, wondering if Heather and Gerry really would make Vancouver in three days. And whether they'd still be talking.

—— —— ——

After checking into a Best Western, I wanted to see more of Thunder Bay than the Terry Fox memorial and Sleeping Giant. The city is probably best known as the world's largest grain-handling centre, funnelling much of the Prairies' harvest onto Great Lakes freighters and beyond. It is also Canada's crime capital, an ignominy due in part to the 1970 amalgamation of Fort William and Port Arthur, the gutting of their downtown cores, suburban flight and, not least of all, a strong and steady inflow of low-income, socially dysfunctional Indians from reserves across northwestern Ontario.

There was sad justice in this. The original Fort William, built in 1801 by the North West Company, on the meandering banks of the Kaministiquia River, was one of North America's first planned communities. Retail stores, warehouses, repair shops and the fur traders' equivalent of a motel were all clustered around the fort as they would be today around a big-box mall. When it came to convenience and protection, my Best Western had nothing on these guys.

With a bit of daylight left to see this great crossroads of ancient and modern Canada, I headed downtown on a city bus to a startling sight. Near the banks where so much of Canada's bounty had passed, from furs to trees and grain, I found an urban wasteland. At seven o'clock on a Sunday evening, central Victoria Avenue was devoid even of cars. Walking along several downtown blocks, I passed three more people. Two looked to be native. All were drunk. Up ahead, at the end of the street, a small crowd gathered outside a shelter. More drunks wandered by. I followed another street back to Arthur, then continued along several more deserted blocks until I reached a series of strip bars, the first sign of retail life in the core.

With no buses in sight, I grabbed a taxi back to the motel, using the chance to ask the driver why his city looked so rough. He said the big issue before city council was "boobies on Sunday." Ever since council closed strip bars on Sunday, the Fort William side of downtown had looked anemic. But it looked like Thunder Bay needed more than a splash of seedy nightlife. Like so many northern communities, the city's population was in a rut, stuck at about a hundred thousand and aging rapidly. There were two big paper mills, a regional hospital, a university and shopping malls, but prospects looked so poor that Thunder Bay, like every struggling city I had seen, was pinning its hopes on a new casino.

⸺ ⸺ ⸺

I quickly found out what many voyageurs discovered long ago, that Fort William is much easier to enter than it is to leave. It used to be nothing more than storms on the lake, or restive Indians, or a bit of sabotage on the part of the rival Hudson's Bay Company. But today, one had to face the more mercurial moods of a driving population.

With a weather forecast for rain, I got on the road before eight o'clock, thinking I could get to Kenora, maybe even Winnipeg, by the day's end. At the corner of Arthur and the Thunder Bay Expressway, I figured I had the best spot in the country for hitchhiking. It was the all-Canadian equivalent of First and Main, the great divider between neighbourhoods and regions. In one direction, traffic would be seeing the Great Lakes for the first time, knowing it was all gradually downhill from here to the Atlantic. In the other direction, my direction, it was the beginning of an almost straight line from Lake Superior to the Rockies. Trouble was, I quickly discovered, no one stops for hitchhikers at First and Main. Cars were headed to the airport, or Thunder Bay Mall, or a Robin's donut shop. An occasional camper van was obviously going farther, but, with the exception of Rick and Lee in Newfoundland, I had had no luck with camper vans.

After half an hour at the fabled crossroads, I took my bag and walked, first to the mall, then to the airport turnoff, then to a side road that was drawing a lot of local traffic. A couple of hours later,

I was a good five kilometres from my starting point, still without a ride and slowly getting soaked in the morning drizzle, when a pickup truck pulled over. The driver said he could get me as far as Kakabeka Falls, about twenty kilometres up the road. There, at least, I could spend some time hiking around the waters where the Kaministiquia River begins its final, thundering descent to Lake Superior and, according to legend, the place where Greenmantle, daughter of an Ojibwe leader, lured a Dakota war party to its death.

(The Sioux warriors had kidnapped the girl and demanded she lead them to her father. She agreed and led them down the river toward his encampment, but bailed out of her canoe just before the falls, leaving her captors to plunge helplessly over the forty-metre-high crest. According to the Ojibwe, Kakabeka's incessant roar still carries the Dakotas' doomed and angry cries.)

When we reached Kakabeka, there was a lull in the rain, allow-ing me to follow a path around the falls for about ten minutes before a drizzle resumed. I could not hear any cries, Dakota or otherwise, except for my feet. Waiting half an hour in the rain this time, my shoes and socks were soaked when a service van pulled over. It adver-tised fire extinguisher and sprinkler systems on the outside and was decked out inside with comfortable bucket seats and a good music system, the kind of options I had learned were favoured by travel-ling salesmen. The driver was on his way to Dryden, a good three-hundred-kilometre hike through the monotony of northern forests, with few roadside stops, little traffic and no radio frequencies. I had done the drive myself and understood why someone on a sales or service call would want company.

Dion McKenzie was no ordinary northerner. From his home in Thunder Bay, he installed fire protection equipment in a region the size of a small European country. More interesting to me was his Newfoundland accent. It was as thick as they come on the island's western coast. At twenty-nine, Dion had spent most of his adult life in Ontario, but there was little the province could change in his Maritime spirit. We were barely out of Kakabeka, and Dion was telling me about lobster prices in Dryden, the best place to buy cod in Thunder Bay and why a singular lack of good music in these parts drove him to play nothing but CDs on these long journeys. He had just inserted *The Celtic Collection.*

"Lobster in Dryden?" I was incredulous. There must be no town in Canada farther from a sea than Dryden.

"You wouldn't believe how many Newfies are around here. There are 230 working in Dryden," Dion said, casting the smile of a traveller on his way home. "You've not heard of Bill's Newfie Store? It's right there in Dryden. Lobster, screech—he's got it all. I'll take you there."

The usual hesitation I had getting into a car was gone. Dion felt more like an old pal, and we were on our way fishing. I hadn't had this kind of ride since, well, Newfoundland.

Dion was a strapping man with short blond hair and gentle blue eyes. He was dressed in jeans and a T-shirt, and despite the warm rain outside wore a leather jacket as well. He came from Norris Point, near Gros Morne park, where he grew up learning to work both the sea and the federal welfare system. In Norris Point, you learned how to scam the system at about the same age you learned to gut a fish. As a teen, Dion had worked for free, in order to collect enough weeks of employment to qualify for unemployment insurance. Sometimes he paid an employer on a fishing boat to pay him, so that there would be a money trail. And then there was the old trick of getting a fortnightly pay slip printed every week. That allowed him to double his UI take. This was how Dion's father, a carpenter, made ends meet, working nine months of the year and collecting pogey for the other three. But Dion realized when he was barely in his twenties that this was not how he wanted to live, not even in Norris Point. "I'm strong," he said to himself. "I have my Grade 12. I can work. I don't need UI."

It was a noble belief that wouldn't get him far in Newfoundland. So at twenty-two, he accepted an uncle's offer of a job installing sprinkler systems in Brampton, that hideously mundane satellite town outside Toronto where Les Turgeon, the Elliot Lake miner, and too many other young men from the hinterland had sought economic refuge.

Dion lit a Player's Extra Light and went on. He hated Brampton. There wasn't a spot of open water in sight, and what Ontarians called rivers produced fish so small they weren't worth the bait on his hook. Whenever his job took him into Toronto, the city's traffic was usually so thick it would take two hours just to get home. Besides, his big-time paycheques weren't going very far, not in a place where cod sold for seven dollars a pound. He used to get it for thirty-five cents off the boat.

After seven years in the big city, he took a union job in Thunder Bay, where a three-bedroom house in a good neighbourhood went for $150,000. The job paid the same money, at $31 an hour, but allowed him to live closer than half a day's drive to the wilderness. "If I could get this job in Newfoundland, a permanent job, I'd move back right away, even for less money," he said. "I'd go for seventeen, eighteen dollars an hour."

At least in the North, he had some sense of being out East. Living outside Thunder Bay—he left his first home, downtown, because of the crime wave—he felt as safe as he did back in Norris Point. He seldom locked his house or his van. In fact, he had left his keys in the ignition all weekend. "I like northern Ontario," he said. "You can stop and drop your hook in any lake. You can't do that in Brampton. You'd have to skim the green off the lake first and then test the water."

But this was what Dion missed most: in Newfoundland, he was always cooking for people, usually something with the fish he had caught. Even when he went home for a summer holiday from Ontario, he brought back boxes of lobster, halibut and what little cod he could find, which he always cooked up for friends in Dryden and other points along his routes.

(The secret to good lobster, he said, is putting two handfuls of pickling salt in the pot. "Not fine salt!")

We passed a sign marking the start of the Central Time Zone, with Ontario fast fading behind us. In a short while, we passed another sign outside Upsala that said we were entering the Arctic watershed. From here on, all rivers flowed north. As Dion changed the CD to The Fables, another Newfoundland group, I noticed the landscape also appeared to be changing. The trees looked smaller, and the scrub thinner, as if everything here had a harder time of it. Dion said I shouldn't be fooled. The woods were rich with wildlife, and the rivers brimming with fish, though he knew he would never catch a hundred-kilogram halibut here like he once did back home.

At Ignace, the first town of any size that we passed, signs had gone up warning people about a new bear menace near the dump. There were also more and more night watch signs for moose along the highway, and the local trucks all had moose pushers on them, to save their engines from a direct hit.

I asked Dion about hunting. He knew there was as much wildlife here as there was in western Newfoundland, probably more. So he couldn't figure out why the Ontario government would want to make hunting so difficult for everyone but the local Indians. Coming from the only province without an official native population, Dion was still adjusting to the discrepancies of aboriginal rights. In Brampton, he had befriended an Indian and discovered the joys of his treaty card, which he often borrowed for its tax-exempt status when he went shopping. But here, in northwestern Ontario, he was in the middle of Indian country, where frictions were as old as they were deep.

I asked him if his impressions had changed since moving north. He surprised me. He said his views had hardened. "I don't think a native has any more of a right to shoot a moose than I do," he said, his soft eyes showing a bit of steel.

In his travels, Dion had come across Indians who shot moose for fun, taking home only the best chunks of the rear and leaving the rest of the carcass in the bush. In Newfoundland, he had been taught to put every bit of the animal to use, from the skin and ribs to the innards for moose sausage.

The aspect of native rights that bothered him the most was the tax treatment. Now that he was in a top income bracket, and part of Canada's biggest tax-paying province, he resented the fact that so many natives paid no income tax. He didn't mind the fact that so much welfare went to Newfoundland. That was the glue that held the country together, in communities, he argued, that would be decimated without federal support. But he wasn't sure why natives in a rich province like Ontario needed a special deal.

I sensed something in the new Canadian tribalism, in the belief that what was good for one's own group—be it a town, province, region or ethnicity—was good for the nation. This didn't bode well for natives. In a 1999 poll commissioned by the CBC and *Maclean's* magazine to measure how Canadians saw themselves, sixty-three per cent of respondents felt aboriginal peoples were an important part of what makes us Canadian. Among national symbols, that put natives in eleventh place, just behind hockey and well back of the flag, climate and our health care system. They were like the carcass left in the bush.

I was trying to think of a polite way of putting this to Dion when he lit another cigarette and, fortunately, changed subjects.

"The best Newfie jokes come from back home," he said.

I don't know what prompted this, but he felt the need to share the one about a Newfie buying a car in Toronto.

"'I'm sorry, sir,' the car dealer says, 'this model doesn't have reverse.'

"'That's okay,' the Newfie says, 'I'm not planning on coming back.'"

I could tell we were nearing Dryden by the growing number of logging trucks on the road and by the lakes, each funnelling as much wood or water as the town's huge paper mill could devour. Even before we reached the sign welcoming us to the "Forest Capital of Canada"—after the sign welcoming us to the birthplace of hockey star

Chris Pronger but before the intersection of Colonization Avenue and Government Street—the Dryden mill was visible on the horizon, with its huge smokestack towering over the community.

More striking than the mill were all the new four-by-fours on the road. All along the Canadian Shield, one-horse mining towns were hurting, but here in the woodlands, where roots do not have to fight monstrous slabs of granite for space, there was nothing but prosperity. At a new Wal-Mart on the eastern side of town, the parking lot looked like an SUV dealership. There were three of those up ahead. Farther along, there were new hotels and restaurants, and a rail yard crowded with freight trains headed south. A decade-long economic boom in the United States had created an insatiable demand for paper. Americans couldn't get enough of it to print their e-mails and flow charts. Clearly, the paperless office had flopped.

Dion followed a line of eighteen-wheelers into town, each carrying a couple of containers of wood chips that would have been ground up at a mill in the bush. He promised to show me an awesome sight, crossing the Wabigoon River and driving around back of the mill. We were just in time to see a truck drive onto a ramp and be tipped back to an eighty-five-degree angle, as its contents flowed into a vast bin. Next to the mill, the eighteen-wheeler looked like a child's toy.

Back on the main street, Dion dropped me at Bill's Newfie Store, the only shop in Dryden, perhaps in the entire Arctic watershed, to sport a row of Canadian and Newfoundland flags on its roof. Dion wanted to show me around the store himself, but he had a service call to make. He apologized for that and I apologized for taking him out of his way. For a moment, we both must have forgotten we were in Ontario.

─── ─── ───

Bill's had two live lobster tanks, cases of frozen shrimp and crab, and racks of Newfoundland souvenirs—fishing boat models, lobster traps, CDs, books, yellow Newfie hats and screech bottles among them. Near the cash register, one book of Newfoundland sayings declared on its cover, "When I get too old to laugh, shoot me."

Unfortunately, Bill was out of town. I was more interested in seeing the paper mill anyway. Its scale was breathtaking, but more intriguing was its place on the economic landscape. Following the introduction of a continental free trade agreement and a sharp devaluation of the Canadian dollar, the 1990s had brought on a historic sale of Canadian assets to foreigners, largely Americans. Entire industries that were once considered foundation stones of the country were now in foreign hands. In 1998, Weyerhaeuser Co., a $15-billion-a-year company based in Federal Way, Washington, purchased the Dryden mill along with two local sawmills and timber licences to 1.8 million hectares of land. Overnight, it became Canada's largest forest products company, with eleven thousand employees. It also had become the dominant economic force in the region, the kind not seen since the naming of Government Street and Colonization Avenue.

This sort of centralized power, especially in foreign hands, was slowly beginning to spook Canadians. In the CBC–*Maclean's* poll, people named Canadian ownership of businesses operating in Canada as the seventh most important aspect of our identity, ahead of bilingualism. Moreover, eighty-three per cent of Canadians believed growing foreign ownership was a serious threat to our identity and sovereignty.

In a little over one decade, $800 billion of Canadian assets had been sold to American buyers, while the U.S. market had come to account for eighty-five per cent of Canada's exports. "Aside from tiny Luxembourg," a CBC report on the poll noted, "Canada now controls a smaller proportion of its national productive wealth than any other industrial country in the world, and . . . faces the very real possibility of becoming an economic colony of the United States."

If the Dryden mill was one of the citadels to fall in this last great war of commerce, I wanted to see inside. I walked back to the mill in time for a mid-afternoon tour, which I had seen advertised at Bill's. Paper mills everywhere were keen to give the public a glimpse of their operations, I guess because they had come to be seen as environmental scourges.

After crossing a small bridge over the Wabigoon River, I was allowed through the front gate with ten others who had signed up for the tour. The only other Canadians were a local woman and her daughter who was home from university for the summer, and a couple from Sydney, Nova Scotia. The rest were on holidays from Pennsylvania, Ohio, England and Australia. We had to leave our bags at the guardhouse and promise not to use our cameras inside. Other than that, we were at the mercy of a couple of university kids whose summer jobs were to buff Weyerhaeuser's image.

The visit began with an upbeat video that showed local kids having lots of clean, wholesome fun: water-skiing on Wabigoon Lake, splashing in the water at Dryden's main beach and skiing on nearby fields in winter. I was impressed how each shot was framed without any evidence of the big smokestack that was visible from almost every corner of Dryden. The recreation scenes cut to shots of happy, paper-consuming customers somewhere in North America and then returned to Dryden, Canada's happyville. "The fish are almost always biting in nearby rivers and lakes," the announcer proclaimed. I was sure it was the same voice I had heard in grade school on a film reel promoting nuclear energy.

After the video, we were led to a part of the plant that was as big as a semi-pro hockey arena. Enormous rolls of paper, the size of trees, came out of the mill to be handled by a dryer that was three storeys tall and connected to ducts big enough to swallow small cars. Below, giant rollers squeezed any remaining water out of the two-tonne rolls before pushing them onto a machine that sliced and bound them in a plastic wrap and shipped them out the door to waiting trucks and trains.

The handful of humans who looked to be involved in the process were sitting in a control room or working forklifts to get more rolls into the waiting containers. But somewhere, the mill was using lots of people. In one decade, the tour guide said, employment had increased by more than fifty per cent, to thirteen hundred people from fewer than eight hundred. The extra jobs, she added on our way out, were due to the American market.

— — —

After the mill tour, I walked to the edge of Dryden in time to see the daily parade of Dodge Rams and Ford F-250s—$40,000 vehicles that said it was five o'clock and the day shift was over. About a million dollars' worth of fancy pickup trucks, the new vehicle of the working class, blew by me in the span of a few minutes. I continued to walk past a new subdivision until I reached the first hayfield I had seen since eastern Ontario. At last I felt I was over the hump, beyond the mighty Shield and into the West.

Up a hill and beyond another subdivision, I continued on foot past Dryden's edge to a place where there was nothing but woods ahead, a place where, surely, someone headed for Manitoba would want to stop. The sun was starting to fade when a beat-up old pickup pulled over. It had no fancy seats, or stereo, or push-button gadgets that every unionized mill worker seemed to want and could now afford. Tom Halverston's truck looked like pickups should look when they're used for getting around logging camps rather than for running to the corner store for milk. As I tried to get my door to click shut, without complete success, I told Tom I had waited two hours for a ride. He said I was lucky to get a ride at all. He once waited in this spot for ten and a half hours.

Tom had been to Dryden and was on his way home to Ear Falls, a logging town an hour north of the next turnoff, in bear country. That summer, he pointed out by way of a warning, the bear problem had become a full-blown menace. That very morning, provincial officers shot two bears that had ventured into Ear Falls. "I've seen more bears this year than in the last ten years," he said.

Tom knew his bears. He worked in the woods outside Ear Falls, on one of the big concessions controlled by Weyerhaeuser where he ran his own grappler, moving felled trees to a portable chipper, the kind of work my grandfather once did by hand in New Brunswick. When he started to work in the woods twenty years ago, Tom also used his hands, aided by nothing more than a chainsaw. But with his modern grappler—air-conditioned in summer, heated in winter, stereo year-round—he was able to work in any condition, in any season.

Because his mother was Ojibwe, Tom was eligible for cutting contracts and an array of government financing reserved for aboriginals. His paternal white ancestry was seen as immaterial. He also gained from his mother a spirituality that included reverence for the divine spirit of nature, trees included. He didn't like the idea of cutting trees for a living, but knew of no other work in these parts that paid so well. "I like nature. I don't like to see a tree killed. I do it for the money, to put beer on my table," he said. The money had become so good that he planned to fly to Toronto the next weekend for a friend's birthday party.

We reached Vermilion Bay, and Tom's turnoff to Ear Falls, in less than half an hour. The sun was still high enough to sparkle some light on the lake next to the highway. I decided to make a stab for Kenora, but it was hopeless. I stood on the road next to a motel for ninety minutes, until the sun was well and truly gone. All that remained visible on the lake was the crimson glow of twilight, the sort of scene that draws lovers and artists, and does nothing for hitchhikers.

After checking into the motel, I wrote in my logbook: twelve hours, three rides, three hundred and seventy-nine kilometres. Since leaving the corner of Arthur and the Thunder Bay Expressway, I had spent more time standing on the roadside than sitting in cars and trucks. The only day worse had begun in Kanata, on the other side of Ontario. My own province, I thought. How heartless.

——— ——— ———

After eating dinner at a chip truck parked across the highway from my motel, I was keen come morning to get out of Vermilion Bay as fast as I could. The thought of another day on this stretch of road inspired me anew to look more appealing to northern drivers. I ruffled my hair, untucked my shirt and, for good measure, kicked a bit of roadside gravel against my pack. Within a few minutes, a pickup truck pulled over.

Kevin Gill-Cash was a woodsman like Tom and looked the part, with a baseball cap and long hair, scraggly beard and Player's cigarettes on the dash. He too worked in a camp outside Ear Falls, and was going to Kenora, forty-five minutes up the road, for the day with his dog Blue, who was riding in the back.

When I said my ride into Vermilion Bay had been with a logger like him, only native, Kevin let me know the score in these parts. His mother was not native, and he did not feel kindly about natives these days. "None of them work. They all say they work for the band," he said. "They got it made and they don't know it. No, I don't feel sorry for them at all."

Blue watched us eagerly through the back window as the husky's owner continued to talk. Kevin had worked these woods for twenty years, ever since he moved here from Moncton. He came to the North chasing a girl, got married, then divorced, bought a Camaro race car, then lost it to the bank, bought another one and lost it, too. That's the thing about working in the bush: it gives you the money and the time to dream big, and the cockiness to lose bigger still.

Up where he lived, he thought the local Indians fished, hunted and chopped trees with abandon. Around Red Lake, beyond Ear Falls, he had watched men hunt from the side of their super-cab trucks. "You could go there and sell firewood like a bastard," he said. "You'd think they'd chop their own wood, but no. They give it to outsiders to cut, and then take a share of the money."

Whether he liked it or not, a lot more was coming down the road for natives. Weyerhaeuser was building a big new mill in Kenora and vowing to buy as much wood as possible from local bands. In the North, the foreign-owned mills had found that little else did more for government relations than good aboriginal relations. Because of this preferential treatment, small-time operators like Kevin were unable to get more concessions. At forty-three,

Kevin was on a bit of a downswing anyway. The environmentalists had made his life rougher than he thought need be, calling for logging moratoriums even as forest fires raged. "The environmental people, instead of bitching about us cutting wood, should lobby for more water bombers," he said. "I don't know, maybe you're like this, but I met people who would rather see a tree burn than someone cut it down. A fire can wipe out twenty-five years of growth. I've cut hundred-and-thirty-year-old trees that were rotten inside. Who's doing anything about that? Even a jack pine dies and falls after eighty years. There's no such thing as a virgin forest."

We drove by a palette of Shield and lakes, and then a large stretch of forest that had burned to a char in 1980. Except for a patch of stubs on a distant hill, the regenerated woods looked as old as ever. This was something well-meaning southerners didn't understand, Kevin said. "There are places I worked twenty years ago and you can't even tell. It's all back again."

I assured him I worked for a newspaper. Felled trees were our manna. But he looked at me with some doubt. He knew I was from Toronto.

When we reached Kenora, I stayed with Kevin and Blue, who were heading downtown, rather than get out at the bypass to Winnipeg. I wanted to see the town that I had heard described as an Alabama of the North, a redoubt of racism that was purportedly worse than the Soo. But as we made our way to the downtown docks on Lake of the Woods, Kenora did not seem like a haven for the Klan. There were a few clusters of drunks, wandering the sidewalks or sitting in the park off Water Street. They looked to be aboriginal, as well as harmless and unharassed. Kevin said there were occasional gang fights involving natives and non-natives. A sensational murder trial, involving the alleged killing of an Indian by a white man, had to be moved to Thunder Bay for fears of racial incitement. But a new mayor and city council were determined to heal the divide. They realized that Kenora's future, like much of northwestern Ontario's, lay in the hands of aboriginal peoples. Big companies would not come here without native consent.

This was the quiet revolution of central Canada, the emergence of corporations as the dominant force in public affairs. Whether it was aboriginal hiring practices in Kenora or the location of bypasses in Kanata, private interests were mingling with public goods at an extraordinary rate. It would be an exaggeration to say governments no longer played a role. Elliot Lake was saved by public action, when a private investor walked away from the community. The greening of Sudbury also owed its origins to public regulation as much as it did to Inco's benevolence. But no government could do for Sault Ste. Marie or Thunder Bay what Weyerhaeuser had done for Dryden with that titanic new mill. In the roaring economy of Ontario, young Kyle Haygarth expressed this new *Zeitgeist* best. "Patriotism doesn't mean having to give up something or give up opportunities," he had said on that long drive up the Ottawa River at dusk.

In Kenora, opportunities were abounding on a cool summer's morning. As the retail hub for Lake of the Woods, where the population doubles in summer, the city had learned to build its economy around the boat. The Canadian Tire, laundromat, liquor store, Best Western and Lake of the Woods district hospital were all accessible by water. For a community built along the lake, the downside was that no one paid much attention to the land. And so Kenora, while beautifully designed for boaters, was nothing but a stormy sea for the simple pedestrian.

After Kevin and Blue dropped me at the waterfront, I had hoped to walk to an open patch of road to begin my next leg, to Winnipeg. But I had failed to appreciate how Kenora sprawled over several islands and peninsulas, each with a little community. I followed Lakeview Drive from the harbourfront to Tunnel Island and then to Norman, Cameron Bay and Keewatin before I could be sure there was not another coffee shop around the corner. It took four bridges and five kilometres of road to get out of Kenora, and on my way out of the province. But finally the last Ontario gas stand was behind me, with nothing but highway and bush ahead.

7

Forks in the Road

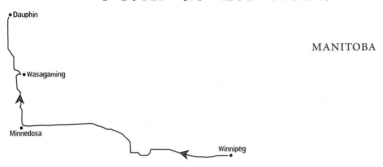

MANITOBA

Outside Kenora, it took only a few minutes for one of those designer pickup trucks to pull over. On the door was the name of a mill supplies company. Glancing at the back seat of the extended Silver El Dorado cab, I spotted a set of golf clubs and a few shirts strewn about. Next to the clubs was a stack of binders. In the front seat, there was an assorted mess of coffee cups, candy wrappers and an overflowing ashtray. The driver, a big-shouldered young man who looked fresh out of college, moved a box of cassette tapes to the floor and welcomed me to his travelling office. The floor beneath my feet was cluttered with business cards, brochures, cigarette ashes, donut bits, cassettes, a cell phone and several other candy wrappers. He had to be another salesman.

It was my lucky day, the driver said, gunning toward Manitoba at a hundred and forty. He was headed all the way to Edmonton. But not long after we reached a cruising speed, the driver gave me his business card, with the name Scott Sutherland on it, and said there was something else he needed to tell me.

Scott sold computerized saws and other mill equipment across the Prairies and into northwestern Ontario. He spent most of his working life in the three-hundred-horsepower El Dorado, driving from his home in Edmonton to Kenora and up to The Pas and back across northern Saskatchewan. The transformation of the forest economy was fuelling his business, but Scott faced other pressures, too. Wherever he was, he said, he always had to find a branch of Alcoholics Anonymous. The cassettes on the floor were AA tapes. Even back in Edmonton, with his girlfriend and their expected baby, he needed that daily shot of support.

"I am an alcoholic," he said.

At twenty-seven, with sports sunglasses nestled in his neatly cut hair and forearms still big from his days as an arm-wrestling champion, Scott looked too young, and too fresh, to be carrying such a burden. But no sooner had he made his confession than he wanted to give me a detailed explanation. He had grown up in Castlegar, in the interior of British Columbia, supported by his mother, who was single. Although he was gifted in many sports, his mother could not afford to keep him on Castlegar's best teams, where he belonged. He could not play hockey because the equipment was too expensive. On the ski hill, he had strap bindings, paid for from his paper route, when everyone else had moved to the step-in kind. Swimming was about all the family could afford, and he was a coach before long.

As he drove and talked, Scott pointed out the Manitoba border, which was difficult to miss. Leaving Ontario, the road divides into two two-lane tracks that blow straight ahead through the forest of Whiteshell Provincial Park.

Scott returned to his narrative, clearly happy to have an audience. Although he had been a star athlete, he had trouble in school. After failing Grade 8, he transferred to an alternative school and was put in with what he called "the bad ones." Only later, years later, did he learn he had attention deficit disorder.

"Here I was a jock. I was on all the teams. Didn't smoke. Didn't drink. And they put me with these other kids," he continued, as we left the park and began to cross the farmlands of southern Manitoba. It was like a vast frontier opening before us, the long, flat distances of the Prairies. I realized what I had just come through: two thousand kilometres of Shield, rising, falling and turning. I could not remember the last time I was able to see the road so far ahead.

Scott was still talking. "The only way to fit in was to smoke, do drugs, fight," he said. "I fought everyone. I started to sell joints because that seemed to be the person everyone looked up to, the guy who sold drugs."

His mother, working all day as a bookkeeper for $7 an hour, was rarely around to pull him back from the brink. Scott dropped out of school after Grade 9, taking up full-time work as a pusher. Selling joints in Castlegar's arcades, he made more than his mother ever did in an office. By sixteen, he was selling acid and soon found a ready customer in a girl who wanted to rebel against her church-going parents. Two months later, she was pregnant. When she delivered the baby, he came off a three-day drinking binge just in time to get to the hospital. He didn't remember the birth.

At nineteen, he switched to cocaine, "because that seemed to be the thing that grown-ups did." His father, who ran the mill equipment company and had stayed in touch from a distance, offered him a job in Prince George, but nothing changed for Scott, except he had more money for his addictions. He continued to snort coke and drink every night, until his father fired him. His girlfriend had already left him and taken the baby.

He went back to school for three months, "and then I found the crack house. Six months later, I was with the hookers." He was also doing piles of Valium, the cheap route down from crack's high, and slowly shifting to heroin, the junkie's preferred depressant. When he was near the point of no return, with his life fading in and out of consciousness, his old girlfriend found him in a crack house and took him to a recovery program. For some reason, he woke up. He was ready to take responsibility for his life. "I could blame school. I could blame my parents. I could blame a lot of things," he said. "I was the one with the problem. I see that now. Scott had the problem."

It had been two years since his father gave him a second chance in the company. He had not had a drink or a whiff of drugs. His biggest crime was speeding. In his first month on the job, he racked up $600 in tickets. He gave the credit to AA, which he attended religiously, at home or on the road. He had been to a meeting the night before in Kenora and had recently attended an alcoholics' jamboree in Minneapolis. "It's bigger than any church," he said of AA. "No church meets every day."

By the Steinbach turnoff, twenty minutes east of Winnipeg, the real Prairies were a reality in every direction—so flat and long it looked like you could see tomorrow. "This is it till you hit Jasper, man. Flat to the horizon," Scott said. He laughed, as he did with almost every comment, no matter how serious he was trying to be.

Winnipeg sat visibly in the distance, like a cluster of grain silos crowded together on the horizon. Before we approached the city, Scott wanted to stop at a big service station to load up on gas, cigarettes and junk food. He planned to stay the night in the city, where he had a sales call to make, but he did not relish the chance to drive its streets. Winnipeg drivers, he said, were the worst in Canada. He swore he had yet to see a driver there who would allow others to slip in front of him. "They'll pull up beside you, a foot behind the next guy, just to make sure you don't get in," he said, not laughing this time.

We were soon in the city, making our way downtown to the rejuvenated Forks, which I wanted to see. Scott agreed to drop me there, before he headed to a customer's office, a local cabinet manufacturer he hoped would be interested in new saws to help their expansion into the U.S. market. He gave me his cell phone number and said to call if I wanted a ride to Edmonton in the morning. He would be busy that evening, he said, at AA.

The Forks in downtown Winnipeg was more than a historic site where old railway lands and parks had been turned into a tourist destination. It represented the many transformations of what we know as Canada. At the muddy confluence of the Red River and Assiniboine River, the flat banks were used by local Indians as long ago as 4000 B.C. It became a natural trading post for the early voyageurs and an easy place to build settlements when waves of European immigrants began to arrive. Over the centuries, the north-western bank, where the two rivers meet, had seen Metis villages, French forts and Scottish camps.

Its terminal and big market also gave rise to Winnipeg's glory years, when the city was truly a Chicago of the North, with enough buzz and money to make people believe it should be the capital of Canada and commercial hub of the West. At one point, it claimed to have more millionaires than Toronto. But that was before The Forks watched the city decline, hammered by the opening in 1914 of the Panama Canal, which led to a continental economy based on east and west coasts. Although Manitoba's population doubled to 550,000 between 1901 and 1916, it had not doubled since then. More troubling was this: by the nineties, a third of Manitoba's revenue came from federal transfer payments. The city could not even maintain its beloved pro hockey team, the Winnipeg Jets, which in 1996 moved to Phoenix and became the Coyotes.

In another new century, though, The Forks was again seeing a changing Winnipeg. When I entered the old Market Building, which was bustling on a Tuesday afternoon, I was struck immediately by the diversity of faces and accents, and the aroma of spices and scents from every land. Hitchhiking through rural Canada, one can get the impression that every Canadian is white, drives a pickup truck, eats chicken burgers for lunch and considers Shania Twain a cultural icon. But in the Market Building of central Winnipeg, the first people I saw were part of an Ecuadorian band touring Manitoba. Beyond them and the crowd of people listening to their music were stalls selling Ukrainian borscht, Caribbean jerk chicken salad and South Asian chickpea curry. If I had thought my first meal in the West would be prime rib, I would have been sadly disappointed because my choice came down to Taste of Sri Lanka and Bindy's Caribbean Delight. I opted for Bindy's, figuring jerk beef would be an appropriate blend of old Prairies and new.

After lunch, I walked along a footpath leading down to the real forks, chatting with a young family from Trinidad along the way. They had moved a year earlier to Winnipeg. Another couple I met by The Forks had moved more recently from India's Punjab state, having heard that South Asians were fast replacing Ukrainians on the city's map. It was hard to imagine that Manitoba was once the crucible of Canadian intolerance, a largely Protestant province that openly discriminated against Metis, French and Catholic minorities.

From The Forks, I walked to the nearby downtown core and the old Exchange District, a rundown Edwardian quarter that was enjoying a reno boom. Winnipeg yuppies, led by their openly gay mayor, Glen Murray, were flocking to the airy turn-of-the-century buildings that made for perfect condos and art galleries. Farther up Portage Avenue, there were other signs of a rebirth. The Air Canada building, designed to shift jobs here from eastern Canada, had brought some equally needed chrome and glass to an imposing streetscape of stone and brick. More importantly, with fountains and an open square, it had reintroduced the notion of public space to a downtown dominated by enclosures: buildings running to the sidewalk's edge with a maze of skyways in between, draining the streets of their human flow.

But such changes were not plentiful. On a glorious afternoon, I had to search for an open-air café where I could bask in the sun and watch the city creep by. The café was crowded with international students from the nearby university, an encouraging sign for any city. But across the way was a far more disturbing, far more Winnipeg, sight: a small park crowded with natives, all of them visibly drunk. In winter or summer, this was the constant of downtown Winnipeg, the presence of inebriated Indians tossed like human litter against the city's walls, park benches and trees. This was Thunder Bay multiplied, a city that served as a magnet for any Manitoba native driven from a reserve by unemployment, boredom, violence or crime.

For more than a century, the city had welcomed the world. Yet the much smaller world around the city, the aboriginal world that had been on these banks for six thousand years, was not going to vanish. If Winnipeg was any indication, the monochrome Prairies were going to churn up the colours of a cultural torrent as two Canadian rivers, carrying very different visions and expectations, flowed into one.

Getting out of Winnipeg looked simple enough, seeing as Portage Avenue turned into Highway 1, the original Trans-Canada, which shot straight through to Vancouver. But Scott had a different impression. In the morning, after I found him by cell phone at his hotel near the airport, he picked me up and immediately started to complain about the city's roads. And that was just the start of it. At every light, he looked around and complained about signs being misleading, names being confusing and markings being inadequate. As if to prove his point, when we stopped at a drive-through for coffee, we somehow got lost trying to get back onto Portage. I thought Scott was going to lose his cool.

"The city is the worst to drive in. The worst!" he said, exasperated by the arrangement of one-way streets that had trapped us. "The roads, they're all named after people. They're not alphabetical. They're all one-way. And they go around in circles!"

For someone from Alberta, where streets are numbered, not named, and the grid pattern is more sacred than the oil rig, Winnipeg's roads were understandably a challenge. But on the Prairies, road challenges are always short-lived. Our coffees were still hot when we found Portage and, within minutes, were out on the open plains. As we left Winnipeg, the transition from city to country was as blunt as any I had seen. Five minutes out and the land was as flat as a billiard table, gridded by roads that met only at right angles. We followed a perfectly straight line for the next ten kilometres as Scott told me about his AA meeting.

The previous evening, while I was at the café reading *A Short History of Manitoba,* a book about the province written by Ed Whitcomb, a Canadian diplomat stationed in Asia, Scott had found a group, as he usually did, using the telephone book. It was a rau-cous affair. According to Scott, a wealthy Winnipeg man had shown up. The man was worth $10 million. He was also drunk. "He said we were all losers," Scott recalled. "Then, at the end of it, he was crying and saying, 'You know, I wish I had what you guys have.'"

At least that was better than the previous Saturday night when, during another stop in Winnipeg, Scott had found a meeting at the detox centre. Most of the participants were native. Some shuffled into the room in white institutional robes, reeking of booze and trembling. The detox workers laid out buckets in case they needed to vomit.

Although Scott said he was a firm believer in the twelve steps, he found honesty to be the most important tool in fighting an addic-tion. "I had to learn how to be an honest person. You have to learn how to deal with life on life's terms," he said. Whether with Indians in The Pas or millionaires in Winnipeg, Scott said he tried to be honest with everyone. It was hard on the golf course, with clients knocking back a beer every few holes while he, in the middle of a sales pitch, had to say he was a twenty-seven-year-old alcoholic. But nothing compared with the decision he and his girlfriend, also a reformed addict, had just made. When they found out she was acci-dentally pregnant, they opted not to have an abortion because they felt it would be dishonest to erase a consequence of their own actions.

Scott's puritanical approach, blaming himself for failures while assuming the strength to shape his own destiny, sounded very American. He wasn't surprised when I said this. At the Minneapolis jamboree, with seventy-five thousand American alcoholics in his midst, he felt as much at home as he once did on the ski hill. Like a lot of Westerners, he had grown tired of the Canadian habit of assigning blame. He just wanted to get on with it.

An hour up the highway, we turned off for Neepawa, where Scott planned to make another sales call. The community was once home to the author Margaret Laurence and had been described as the prettiest town in Manitoba, with its treed ridge and spacious

Victorian homes. It also had a thriving company in Prairie Forest Products, Scott's customer, which never saw its market for fences decline. He hoped the company would be interested in a new saw with its own radio-wave system and built-in computer that could assess the grain and knots in each piece of wood and then chart the most economical course for the blade to follow. The cutter cost $110,000, with another $150,000 for the scanner, and according to Scott it was selling like water in a drought. The American building boom had made timber so expensive, he explained, that every square inch of wood had value. I sat in the El Dorado while Scott made his pitch. When he returned, he said the company man wanted to think about it.

Not far to the west of Neepawa, just before we hooked up again with the Trans-Canada, I asked Scott to drop me at a fork in the road outside Minnedosa, about twenty kilometres ahead of us. I said I wanted to cut through some back roads to Saskatchewan and meet a few more Manitobans. He understood. He already had a tape ready for his cassette player. It was a recording of the best AA meetings he had attended.

⸺ ⸺ ⸺

The Minnedosa roadside was as hot and dusty as any I had experienced since Saint John. At mid-morning, the temperature had hit thirty and showed no sign of cooling. Rather than follow the main highway through farm country, right into Saskatchewan, I decided to head straight north, for a detour through Riding Mountain National Park, which sprawls across western Manitoba. The park covers nearly three thousand square kilometres of highland forest and lakes and was once home to Grey Owl, the socially concerned Brit who fooled the world into believing he was a wise native man.

I got a ride up Highway 10 to the park with Frank, a retired car dealer from Brandon who had moved to Wasagaming, a summer resort town on the edge of Riding Mountain, where he golfed every day in the summer and curled through the winter. When he dropped me at the park entrance, I felt like I was nowhere near the Prairies, at least not the ironing board Prairies that Scott had taken me across. The park is located on an escarpment that stretches down to North Dakota and looks as out of place as a wrinkle on an ironing board cover. At the south end, the forests are thick and untouched around Clear Lake, the main attraction that looked as tranquil as the lakes of eastern Ontario. Sailboats bounced along the playful waves while, onshore, sunbathers crowded a long, soft beach. Tennis, sailing and windsurfing were in full view, with not a combine harvester in sight.

Wasagaming's main street was straight out of the 1930s, a result of the park being protected from development. Rustic buildings made of stone and peeled logs were the dominant image, none more fetching than the Park Theatre, Canada's only log cinema. (Its saddle-notched log design, with exposed beams and rafters, did not look like it was created for *Mission Impossible II,* the advertised feature, but one never knows.) In another fit of nostalgia, the Parks Canada Visitors Centre up the road had planted a flowerbed that spelled out ERII. Strangely enough, it seemed appropriate. The farther I got from Winnipeg, the more I noticed its diversity slipping away, as the older— in some places, very old—Prairies began to crop up.

I was told all about this demographic shift on the way out of the park by a middle-aged driver named Barry who was headed to Dauphin, half an hour north of Clear Lake. He was a tribal council water manager, hired by local native bands to run their water systems. He was also one of the dwindling number of young whites left in Dauphin, having moved there for the good pay and security of working for an Indian band that had no one in its own population to fill the post.

Dauphin's population was so old, Barry said as we drove north, that you had to be careful at crosswalks, for fear of drivers mowing you down. He was serious. As a volunteer firefighter in the town, he had seen his fair share of accidents involving elderly people who hadn't stopped at lights or crosswalks.

Once we reached the farming town, I saw his point. Its broad, straight streets looked like they supported far more trees than people. Dauphin had a population of sixteen thousand, but felt like a place with a tenth that many. On the main road, most faces were very white and very wrinkled. But down some of the side roads, I noticed younger people on bicycles or pushing baby strollers, all of them with much darker complexions. They were the Indians, Barry said, who drifted into Dauphin from all over central-west Manitoba. Most of the non-native kids had gone farther west, to Alberta mainly, for work.

As lifeless as Dauphin seemed, the reserves around this part of Manitoba were worse, Barry explained. In his job as water manager to a group of First Nations, he said he had to get to the reserves before noon or else everyone in the council office would be drinking. He said the entire native population was too accustomed to having their needs, as basic as they were, cared for by the outside world. There was no incentive to do anything else. Anyone on the reserves recruited to replace him didn't last through the training period. One Indian he had trained for a year quit. The reason was usually the same: drinking. The tribal council always knew Barry, with a salary financed by the federal government, would show up.

"When you're spoon-fed for so long, you expect to be spoon-fed," he said. "You can't learn to work for money when it's free."

He dropped me off by Zamrykut's Ukrainian family restaurant and suggested I hurry out to the junction if I wanted to get a ride to Saskatchewan before sundown. I quickly walked around downtown Dauphin, hoping there was more to the place than retired farmers and Indians, but the only place I could find open, other than Zamrykut's, was the Parkview Lodge, a hundred-room retirement home. At eleven storeys, it was the tallest building in Dauphin, perhaps the tallest north of Riding Mountain.

——— ——— ———

Getting out of a small place like Dauphin can be as tricky as finding one's way out of a big city. I stood for an hour just past the western edge of town, on the main road from downtown. As the shadows grew beside me on the road, I decided to walk a bit farther, to the bypass road, where, within a few minutes, an old Ford Escort stopped. It had come off the main road where I had been standing for so long.

The driver was the kind Barry had warned me to avoid: old, a little dull in the senses and wholly out of touch with the basic rights of pedestrians. He was not even going to Saskatchewan, which I hoped to get to by evening. He was going only ten kilometres up the road, he announced a little too proudly, and would be letting me off at a remote, and infrequently used, intersection. By the time I could have shouted "Stop!" it was too late. Clifford, the driver, had already launched into what came across as a very well rehearsed speech on miracles—a subject that was suddenly of great interest to me as I was about to be dumped at sundown in rural Manitoba.

Since our time together would be short, Clifford hoped I wouldn't mind if he jumped straight into his favourite anecdote. Had I heard about a hitchhiker picked up in these parts by a man and woman?

I had to say no, I hadn't.

"The hitchhiker got in the car and after a few minutes said, 'Jesus is coming soon!'" Clifford said excitedly. "And then he disappeared. The man and the woman looked around the car but they couldn't find him, John."

I sat silently, staring at the very empty road ahead, not knowing where Clifford was going with the story. Would the hitchhiker re-emerge from the back seat with a chainsaw? Or was there some hilarious punchline, perhaps about hitchhiking on the road to Damascus?

Clifford continued, following the path I feared he would. "You know, John, I also believe Jesus Christ is coming soon. The way we're destroying the environment, God must be ready to do something soon. I think it will be an asteroid, eleven miles wide."

He had heard about this on a Texas radio show one evening. I wanted to tell him that in my view one of the great curses of the Prairies, egregiously missed by Margaret Laurence and W. O. Mitchell, was the vagary of late-night radio, when unregulated banter from the Deep South comes pouring across the border. But he was too wound up. Clifford wanted to tell me about his days working as a missionary in northern Ontario, among the Indians there, and the native man he knew who once dreamt of the Second Coming, and how horrified that man was to wake up and realize he was not prepared for the greatest moment.

It must be said that Clifford managed to make ten kilometres go a lot farther than anyone I had met, but the turnoff came eventually. When it did, he gave me a mauve-coloured pamphlet, which he had pulled from a bundle in his glove compartment. It was about the Resurrection, produced by Lamp and Light Publishers of Farmington, New Mexico. "This is something I have for all the hitchhikers," Clifford said, smiling. "God go with you on your travels."

The junction of Highway 5, which headed west to Saskatchewan, and Highway 10, going north to Swan River, was as deserted a place as I had been in twenty days on the road. There were small patches of scrub and woods on either side of the road, and, because the junction was in a bit of a dale, no grand Prairie view. If there was a farmhouse nearby, I wasn't going to see it from here. I thought about rolling out my sleeping bag in the grassy ditch, as ten and then twenty minutes passed without a vehicle appearing. But finally, an oil tanker truck came around the corner from the north. The driver stopped on the gravel shoulder, and a door, five feet off the ground, swung open. The last trucker who had stopped for me was Gilles, the Quebec driver who ditched me in the Charlevoix Valley. This was altogether different. I was already in the middle of nowhere.

As I climbed into the cab, I discovered the passenger seat was occupied by a small dog that was nearly blind. The driver, a middle-aged man, shooed him to the sleeping compartment behind the front seat and pulled away, climbing out of the dale. Clarence Hannotte said he was glad to meet a newspaper reporter. He read the *Globe and Mail* and *Financial Post* almost every day, to follow his investments, and wanted to know immediately which business columnists I knew. I got the sense he was not going to be another Gilles. But then again, this was not the Charlevoix Valley. The road through western Manitoba was as deserted as the junction of 5 and 10. Not only were there few cars going in either direction, many small farms along the way were vacant or boarded up. If there was a population implosion underway in the Prairies, this was the epicentre.

"There's no new money to buy these farms," Clarence explained as he drove west, heading for his home in Yorkton, Saskatchewan. "The only ones who will come in are the corporate farms or maybe the Hutterites. Maybe we'll see big corporate farms like in Alberta. Maybe it will become like Kansas, when I was working there. They have big farms and a centre every sixty kilometres. In between, just a few whistle stops with a gas station. Our towns will be emptied."

Clarence had been around the Prairies more than a few times. He had drifted through the central United States as a young man and tried his hand at just about everything in Yorkton. He had owned a gas station for six years, until he realized he would never get as much money out of it as the time he was putting into it. He bought a truck instead and hauled goods all over western Canada, until he grew tired of that too. Now he drove for others.

He preferred to let his wife pay the bills. She ran a Hallmark store, working day and night to earn $30,000 a year. In Yorkton, it was a good income, though it did not compensate for what they had lost in terms of Prairie life.

"There's not as much people helping each other," Clarence said. "If you had a flat tire, people would always help you. That's not there now. Everything's seven days a week. The wages, the way jobs are full-time/part-time, mean both people have to work for a couple to get by. There's no time for socializing. Maybe you're tired and bitchy, too. People feel there's less security. Plus there's a depopulation of the rural areas. Thirty years ago, there was also more private business, small business. Now it's mostly corporate. I feel like the profits are going to Toronto or wherever headquarters is."

Except for his last comment, he sounded like someone from Toronto, where everyone was stressed out and dreaming of somewhere calm, somewhere they could find the serenity of a place like, well, Yorkton. How shocked my neighbours would have been to hear that no matter how far you run in Canada, the stress of modern life will follow.

Clarence knew that all too well. Two of his three grown children had left Saskatchewan for work, as had most of their friends. One daughter was a pharmacist in Yellowknife, earning $31 an hour at Wal-Mart. His other daughter was an office clerk in the Northwest Territories, where she earned $30,000 a year—as much as her mother, the shopkeeper, with a third fewer hours. Both girls hoped to get to Alberta eventually. His son, a plumber, had stayed in Yorkton.

"If I was that age, I'd probably move to Alberta, too," Clarence said. "Why would they stay here? The taxes are high. The cities aren't very exciting."

Clarence had just delivered a load of oil to a construction crew working up Highway 10, a route he followed often. Every time he crossed the Prairies, he couldn't imagine those crowded foreign places he read about so often in newspapers.

"There are places in the world so crowded they're falling over each other, they'd probably be happy here," he said. "There's got to be lots of immigrants who would want to come here. I don't know. If I was living in Serbia and someone said, 'You can work in a toothpick factory in Yorkton or stay here and get shot,' I know what I'd do."

The first good hint of human life along the road did not appear until just before Roblin, with a sign pointing to the Jackfish Bible Camp. We roared by it in the tanker truck, like a lone bison charging across the horizon. The road sneaked through more small dales and rolled over gentle hills, not the checkerboard picture of the Prairies I had imagined. There were patches of trees along the way, and then a big dip into a valley, across a still, narrow lake that ran as far as I could see in both directions. It was a branch of the Assiniboine River, which people here called Lake of the Prairies. Up the other side of the valley, we were into a new province. "Saskatchewan. Naturally," a sign read.

The first thing I should appreciate about his province, Clarence said, was the state of its roads. Now on another Highway 10, I could feel what he meant. Rural Saskatchewan was far bumpier than rural Manitoba, which away from the Trans-Canada was far bumpier than rural Ontario. Clarence blamed the grain trucks. Over the past decade, they had come to fill the secondary highways at harvest time, ever since railway companies began to abandon the spur lines that had once helped build the West. At one point, roads were so overburdened that the Saskatchewan government asked farmers to save some of their grain and ship it in winter. The banks said no. They weren't going to let farmers sit on their inventory for a few months just to save the province some road repair funds.

I was more taken by the straight lines. Away from Lake of the Prairies, we had re-entered grain land. The horizon, and there was but one, looked like it stretched forever, with the late sun sitting above it, no more than ten degrees from the edge of the earth. For a time, everything seemed frozen. Clarence did not have to move his steering wheel a titch. There was no reason to gear up or down. With an enormous crimson sun just hanging there, and no breeze to rustle the odd tree that we passed, I felt like we had driven into an Ansel Adams landscape and would rest there, contented, forever.

I was starting to nod off when the truck hit a rut so deep it bounced Clarence's blind dog from the sleeping compartment to the floor behind the stick shift. I feared Clarence too was drifting off and so began to ask him about the changes he had seen in Saskatchewan. Indians, he replied. He used to see them around their reserves, but now they were a fast-growing force in every small town and city across the province.

With so many non-natives leaving the province for work elsewhere, and the native birth rate still at a high level, I knew Saskatchewan was on course to become the first native-majority province, perhaps sometime in the middle of this century. I also knew how the two populations, native and non, did not have the best of relations. Which was why Clarence surprised me. A forty-nine-year-old white man, he was more likely than others to hold some strong biases. And yet, when he spoke of Indians and how they were changing the province, he did so with more sympathy than most people I had met on this trip.

Clarence knew about the drinking and corruption on reserves, and the ordinariness of crime in modern native life. "I used to own a gas bar. I'd always keep an eye on an Indian when he'd come in. I'd have to. You know they steal," he said. "How do you think they feel, to always be distrusted? How would you feel coming from a reserve, from a small patch of dirt, to town where everyone distrusts you? There's reason they hate the white man. But they have to understand that what the white man did to them was not this white man, it was four generations ago."

We stopped at a gas station so Clarence could buy a can of Coke. We were the lone customers.

The isolation and anger of Prairie natives was something Clarence understood. The Western notion of responsibility, both to oneself and to a society—he was not sure many natives understood that. Every native he had hired at the gas station ended up quitting. The ideas of commitment, between his world and theirs, did not balance.

Getting back into the truck, Clarence said he and his wife hoped to sell their five-bedroom house, now that the kids were gone. When the price was right, they planned to move to a smaller country house, perhaps one with land for a few cows. This was one story of the Prairies: a slow draining of its population, natives excepted, and lost with it a tax base and youthful spirit. There was another story, though, and it had just crept up on the horizon. I had to strain my eyes to make sure I saw it correctly. But there in the distance was a car dealership, with a farm field on one side and a shopping mall on the other.

As Clarence geared down for Yorkton, I gained some sympathy for his views on changing Prairie life. The eastern entrance to his town was a long strip of commerce, copied from the next town like a genetically modified seed. I had met up again with the Trans-Canada, which looked like it had rolled over Yorkton with a sign-making machine. Wal-Mart, McDonald's, Burger King, Smitty's, Tim Hortons and Canadian Tire were all there, along with a Days Inn advertising the oddest sight I had seen on the flat, dry Prairies: a waterslide.

8

Wheat Castles and Wal-Marts

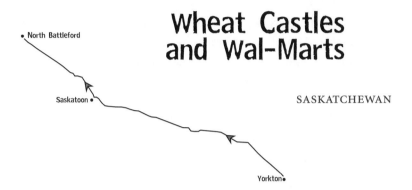

SASKATCHEWAN

Saskatchewan looked like a place in unrelenting decline, and I was barely sixty-five kilometres across the border. One farmhouse after another had been mothballed. And Yorkton, the biggest town in the southeast, had been redesigned as a drive-through community. Awkwardly, it still sported onion-domed churches but, like an old-timer trying to squeeze into his championship jersey, that was about all that remained of its proud past as a Ukrainian farming centre.

In the new Yorkton, every aspect of civic life catered to the Trans-Canada, which flowed like a mighty river through the town, the halfway point from Winnipeg to Saskatoon. Restaurants, motels, convenience stores—they all had big signs, as big as Prairie silos, to pull in cash-heavy travellers. Smartly, someone had erected a set of traffic lights on the highway that every few minutes drove home the point, so to speak, of Yorkton's convenience. It wasn't just the long-distance drivers the city was after, though. The small town, with a population of sixteen thousand, served a quarter of the province, having bled the retail life out of scores of hamlets and little towns in eastern Saskatchewan. This was the Wal-Mart effect, turning small towns and suburbs into

regional hubs that tower, like medieval castles, over their commercial fiefdoms.

At this hour, there was no hope of my getting a good ride. The
sun had set, and traffic on the Trans-Canada's Yellowhead Route had
thinned to a couple of trucks and a wayward car passing every few
minutes. Clarence dropped me at a motel, kindly pulling his rig into
the parking lot so as not to block the more considerable flow of
vehicles heading to Wal-Mart across the road. For the after-dinner
crowd, the mall was as good as Yorkton got.

I checked into the motel and took a copy of *Yorkton This Week +
Enterprise* to a Smitty's up the road. The local newspaper was full of
bland municipal news and grain reports, but something else caught
my eye. A guest column by Richard Truscott, provincial director of
the Canadian Taxpayers' Federation, gave an impassioned cry
against the province's massive brain drain. The writer said twenty-
six thousand people left Saskatchewan in 1999, while only twenty
thousand moved into the province. Worse, a majority of the
working-age migrants had gone to Alberta's oil patch and surging
farm economy, which Saskatchewan had not been able to match.
"Once again, Saskatchewan plays the farm team, educating people
for the twenty-first-century economy, at the expense of the
Saskatchewan taxpayer, and sending them off to build other
provinces," the column concluded.

I don't know if this was intentional, but right below the article
was a placement notice congratulating one Shelley Dawn Lewchuk
of Yorkton for graduating with a doctor of dental medicine degree
and accepting a job in Trail, British Columbia. A few pages later, the
employment section said far more than the Canadian Taxpayers'
Federation ever needed to. There were columns of want ads, offering
work for medical radiation technicians in Banff (and lots of room
attendants there too); carpet cleaners in Calgary; nurses in the
United States; a community newspaper reporter in Swan River,
Manitoba; steel fabricators in Alberta; journeymen in Lake Louise,
Invermere and Castlegar; and an A&W shift manager in Wetaskiwin,

south of Edmonton. A much shorter column advertised jobs in Yorkton at the real Canadian Superstore (up to $11.75 an hour), A&W ("uniforms supplied and a meal discount") and the repair shop at Canadian Tire. Who could blame Dr. Lewchuk?

In the morning, there was a hint of wheat in the air as I walked to the western edge of Yorkton, past the empty parking lots and the magnificent churches of its past. I hoped to get a good long ride, perhaps with someone who had just filled up at Smitty's and was going to Saskatoon. Or better yet, Edmonton. I had been on the road for three weeks and had little time any more for short hops and truncated conversations. I wanted to get somewhere. My determination lasted all of one hour. I was still looking back at the onion domes of Yorkton, thinking I'd be happy for a ride to the next concession, which was about where the BMW was going.

When the black sports car pulled over, I had to believe that it was a stunt in which the driver would speed off, spewing dust and gravel in his wake the moment I picked up my pack and headed for his car. He didn't. But he did offer an apology. He was going only to Springside, twenty-five kilometres up the highway. My heart sank. For a moment, I had imagined doing the Rockies in a BMW, only to realize we'd be at the driver's destination before he was out of fourth gear.

The middle-aged driver was an estate planner on his way to visit a client, a rather wealthy farmer who lived near Springside. Despite the perennial bellyaching of Canadian farmers, the estate planner said there was no shortage of wealthy ones in these parts. True, many, many farms had gone under, with families selling their land and moving to Yorkton, or beyond. But there were still farmers like his client who were buying land, investing in new farming equipment and high-tech growing methods, and reaping their reward. He said I might be surprised by the number of millionaires out this way.

He was not exaggerating. A study prepared by Forrester Research Inc., of Cambridge, Massachusetts, found Canadian millionaires to be as unprepossessing as American millionaires were not. According to the study, twenty-two per cent of Canadians with at least a million dollars' worth of assets, in addition to their primary residence, were blue-collar workers, including farmers. In the United States, the proportion was only six per cent. Moreover, only forty-two per cent of Canadian millionaires had a college or university degree. In the United States, it was seventy-two per cent.

As we talked about wealth in the comfort of a BMW, the estate planner slowed down for what looked to be a bad accident up ahead. Traffic was stopped in both directions, the first jam I had seen since Ontario. A van and a pickup truck had collided, and both appeared spun around. A U-Haul trailer had decoupled from one of the vehicles and was on its side in the ditch. But no one appeared hurt, judging by the drivers and passengers who stood by the roadside, chatting with each other as if they were at a summer barbecue. Creeping past the accident, we were directed by a highway police officer into the oncoming lane and around a scattering of glass before returning to a hundred and twenty, unmindful of what we had just seen. Tragically, the Springside turnoff was just ahead.

I stood outside the farming hamlet for an hour, at first hoping the bottleneck from the accident would lead to something. The steady flow of cars and trucks, by the time they reached Springside, was still slow enough for me to make eye contact with drivers. But then, once the broken glass was cleaned up and the damaged vehicles towed away, I was alone, watching the occasional car zip by at a hundred or more.

From the road, Springside hardly conveyed prosperity. The biggest structure was a grain elevator, which like so many on the Prairies looked doomed. Once known as "Wheat Castles of the New World," the vertical structures, which allowed wheat to be stored and then automatically poured into rail cars, had been etched in the Canadian imagination. Through generations of paintings and photographs, they became as iconic as the church steeple in Quebec. But with the decline of rail transport, and the rise of grain trucks that were grinding the back roads around Yorkton, the old elevators were endangered. There were just seven hundred or so of them left in Saskatchewan, down from fifty-eight hundred in the 1930s.

As the morning heat set in, my mind turned to thoughts of the nightmare scenario—walking twenty-five kilometres back to Yorkton—when a new Ford Pathfinder pulled over. It had been going at such a clip that it did not come to a stop until fifty metres beyond me. I grabbed my bag and jogged to the waiting SUV. A corporate logo on the Pathfinder's side told me I was in for another salesman, although not one like Nate Gardiner. With a plump face and ruddy cheeks, he was unlike any salesman I had met. At twenty-six, Nate was in charge of most of the Prairies for his American company, which made some of the world's most advanced planting and harvesting equipment. But that was not the half of it. Despite his cherubic look, Nate was among the last of the cowboys, and the first I had met on this journey. His resolve in life was strong. His opinions on just about everything were firm. And he wasn't going to shy away from telling me so.

No sooner was the Pathfinder back on the road than Nate was spitting on central Canada. Not literally, though his habit of chewing tobacco while he drove gave me good reason to lean away. You can never be sure what will happen when chewing tobacco is involved. But his views were pure venom.

"Doesn't politics stop in Ontario?" Nate asked. He sounded testy. He could not believe someone from Toronto really wanted to hear the opinion of a westerner. "I thought you guys didn't care what we thought out here."

Nate was on his way back to Saskatoon, where his company had transferred him a couple of months ago from British Columbia, his home province. Even though he was on the road much of the time, he chose to live on a farm outside the city—on eighteen hundred acres of land, to be precise, which he was renting. In addition to his day job, he raised cattle and horses and experimented with crops, but mostly he just wanted to be close to the land. "I honestly see farming as a way of life. The people are different," he said.

I asked Nate what might be the differences between farming and, say, running a hardware store. The question surprised him, but he tried to answer it anyway. He had this to say, by way of illustration: "Raising a calf, keeping it in your kitchen on a frigid night, then selling it in autumn. The independence, working alone."

We were racing along the straight and narrow of Saskatchewan, blowing by one farming hamlet after another. In between towns, the fields were rich and golden with a bumper crop, so much so they looked like a gentle sea flowing away from the road. The rain and sun had been just right that summer. This was the way the Prairies were supposed to be, the way Viscount Milton had imagined them on the eve of Confederation.

In 1862–63, Milton, an eccentric and wealthy young English gentleman, followed this route with his physician, across the Prairies from Winnipeg to Edmonton, and on through the mountains at what is now Jasper before finally following the Thompson and Fraser river valleys down to the Pacific Ocean. In *The North-West Passage by Land,* Milton's best-selling account of the journey, the two greenhorn explorers met with one trauma after another in the mountains. But on the Prairies, in the early days of their adventure, the vast open stretches of field clearly appealed to the twenty-two-year-old viscount's aristocratic sense of land. He wrote: "From Red River to the Rocky Mountains, along the banks of the Assiniboine and the fertile belt of the Saskatchewan, at least sixty millions of acres of the richest soil lie ready for the farmer when he shall be allowed to enter in and possess it."

Back home, the viscount's father, Earl Fitzwilliam, was one of the great Whig magnates of his day, with huge tracts to his name in Yorkshire and Ireland. His possession of sixty-six thousand acres at Coolattin in Ireland made him one of the great forces of Dublin, but here in Saskatchewan, the young heir was getting to see property in an entirely new proportion. "This glorious country," Milton wrote, "capable of sustaining an enormous population, lies utterly useless."

Five generations later, people were fleeing the place. Manitoba was hurting. Ontario, Saskatchewan and Alberta were worse off. According to Statistics Canada, those three provinces had lost ninety-six thousand farmers in just three years, or about one-third of their farming population.

I noticed a pillar of dust on the horizon that from a distance looked like a tornado. A bit closer, I could see that it was a combine at work. These were the kind of farms that excited Nate. He was keen to sell Saskatchewan a new range of high-tech combines that came with computerized moisture sensors and global positioning systems to track soil conditions, weeds and crop yields along each row, and adjust the irrigation, seeding and fertilizer accordingly. The machines were selling for $200,000.

For farmers who had paid $35,000 for their last combine, it was a big leap. But it was a leap, Nate liked to say, that European and American farmers had already made. Canadian Prairie farmers, he was finding, were more timid when it came to investing in land and technology, or experimenting with new crops and livestock. They didn't like what he called "precision agriculture." Of course, it didn't help his sales pitch when grain prices fell by half in one year, as they just had, or when the federal government rolled back subsidies, as it had just done, while the United States and Europe jacked up theirs.

As we drove along the fertile belt that so impressed Viscount Milton, Nate remembered the days of his youth when Canadian governments were more concerned with agriculture. He couldn't understand why Ottawa had changed its priorities. It was not like it didn't have the money, he said. He had read about taxpayer-funded reports on such absurd subjects as bees and bats, and on aid money going down the drain in Ethiopia. He wasn't aware that much of Canada's aid to Ethiopia was in the form of western grain, sent by the shipload to the hungry. But he still believed Ottawa was at the root of many of Canada's troubles. Gun control, for instance. New federal plans for gun registration were driven, he felt, by Toronto's fear of crime, with no concern for farmers who might need a gun to put down a horse.

"What's next? An armoury?" Nate asked. "Is it going to be a library where you have to check out your gun?" Why, he'd even heard talk around Saskatoon that the Toronto media, in an effort to whip up fear over guns, had used rhetorical tactics similar to those once employed by Hitler and Stalin. "At least that's what I've read," he said.

And then there were natives. He did not understand why natives were so frequently in disputes. "If my granddaddy wrecked your granddaddy's truck and my daddy didn't square up with your daddy, does that mean I owe you a truck? Where does it stop? I mean, 'Yeah, your guys had it pretty rough but that was then, this is now. You want a piece of the jungle, with no welfare, nothing? Here, have it.' But you see these guys driving around in new pickups, living in government-subsidized houses, getting welfare, then complaining they don't get enough. Where does it stop?"

Nate said he knew what would straighten out Canada. A Saskatchewan farmer—"simple and honest."

Himself, he had grown up on a ranch outside Stewart, British Columbia, near the Alaska panhandle. He started to ride rodeo at ten, just as his father had, because it was what made men out of boys. Through the sport, he'd learned to respect animals, his competitors and himself. "When you're eight and all you're doin' is eatin' candy and you get thrown from a bull, it hurts pretty good, and you realize you're fat and maybe you should do something about that. Too many kids in the city grow up soft."

The rodeo won him a full scholarship to Casper College in Casper, Wyoming. After an injury in second year, though, he decided to drop out and turn pro. He lasted until he was twenty-four, when a dislocated shoulder convinced him to hang up his spurs. The shoulder still pains him, just as his father's old rodeo injuries make it difficult for him, in his fifties, to sit down. "I'm not looking forward to turning forty, or even thirty," Nate said.

He and his wife settled in Cranbrook, in the Kootenays, where they bought a small farm with twenty-five cattle and some horses, and Nate began selling machinery for Agco Corporation, a Georgia company that took over the Massey-Ferguson line, once the very emblem of Ontario corporate dominance. That Nate was selling Massey-Fergusons on behalf of an American company would have been sweetly ironic if he did not believe the Canada–U.S. border was wrong to begin with. "It should have been the Mississippi," he said.

He turned up the radio. The grain price report was on. We had been driving close to three hours and the first signs of Saskatoon were appearing in the distance. This was a city, Nate said, where "you can go to a cattle show, a horse show and visit the mall, all in the same day."

I couldn't think of a better plug for a Prairie city. And then he dropped me at the worst place imaginable, at the very spot where two lanes expanded to four as the highway approached Saskatoon. We were thirteen kilometres from the city centre, at the turnoff to his farm. I was too far from the city to walk and too close for cars to want to bother with a hitchhiker. They would all be accelerating into the new lane, with no time to size up a stranger.

There were bugs everywhere, too, as bad as Labrador. Dozens of tiny bugs nipped at my exposed skin as I stood on the roadside writing more notes about Nate. I would have to spend the rest of the day walking to Saskatoon, I imagined, just to save my skin. But then, a few minutes after Nate went his own way, a tractor-trailer pulled over. The driver said he was going downtown, which was good news. I wanted to see some of this unique city that had cattle shows, horse shows and shopping malls to offer on the same day.

——— ——— ———

With two hundred thousand people and a modest skyline, Saskatoon looked like a metropolis to my eyes, which had adjusted to the evenness of the Prairies. But it was also small enough that the trucker, who used to be a university administrator, could drive his rig down one of the main streets and drop me in the city centre. He urged me to spend the night there, at the very least to go to Bud's on Broadway, Saskatoon's premier blues bar. He claimed it was the best blues bar west of Chicago.

I needed to keep moving, though, dreading the thought of another marathon wait to get beyond a city's limits. From downtown, there was no way to the open highway except by city bus. I found one that would take me to the farthest possible on-ramp, headed for North Battleford and on to Edmonton, not realizing how much of the city extended beyond that.

Stuck again in the suburbs, where too many cars were going too short a distance, I couldn't get so much as a friendly wave. I chose to walk, following the side of the divided highway past the next on-ramp and then another, and then another, until I had walked about five kilometres and was, at last, at a fork. The Trans-Canada headed one way, while the highway to Prince Albert in the north went the other. It had taken me three hours to get through Saskatoon, and I was still without a ride. It was also getting late, too late to hope I would get anywhere before dark and too late to walk back to the city. Standing on the gravel, I noticed how many dead bugs there were, hundreds in a small stretch: dead bees, flies, dragonflies and, if I looked closely enough, mosquitoes. The least appreciated form of roadkill, they crammed the roadside.

I was so bored with waiting that I was about to begin counting the dead dragonflies when an old brown Toyota station wagon pulled over and crushed my new-found collection. The driver said he was going to Edmonton, five hours away. The sun, directly to the west, was still strong enough that he wore welders' goggles over his regular glasses. But soon it would be dark, and he would need the company to stay awake.

Marcel Meersman had to get to Edmonton to catch an early morning ride to Fort McMurray, another 450 kilometres north of there, where the giant Athabasca tar sands project was transforming the landscape. A journeyman by trade, he had received the call only a few hours earlier, with an offer for steady work until winter, at $25 an hour. He left without saying goodbye to his girlfriend, who was at work, and stopped only briefly at his ex-wife's to see his two teenaged sons. He said he'd be back again in a couple of weeks, when he would be due for a few days off.

Prior to the call from his new employer, Marcel had been on a month's layoff from a project to build a pipeline through Saskatchewan. It had been a good job, he said, paying $23 an hour, but the work was not steady. He also didn't like all the Americans who seemed to be running the project and were creeping into almost every aspect of his life. He was getting tired of their brand of conservatism that was creeping into Saskatchewan, too. His province was once the bedrock of Canadian socialism, and Marcel liked it that way. Universal health care, welfare, unemployment benefits—these were things he said he valued as much as a job.

The '83 Toyota struggled to break a hundred, and when it did it shook angrily. That was not its only fault. The windshield was cracked and smeared with bugs. The car, Marcel explained, was out of wiper fluid.

As a young man, he had taken Pierre Trudeau's advice to his generation and travelled Canada. He hitchhiked and stayed in hostels, and was still proud of having gone east as well as west. He was one of the few westerners I had met who was not bitter toward central Canada, perhaps because he had seen it as a youth. He continued to see it not as an adversary but as an integral part of his Canada.

Marcel knew, however, that he was among a new minority in the West. Even in socialist Saskatchewan, the federal Canadian Alliance had made serious gains on a ticket of alienation and discontent. Provincially, the conservative Saskatchewan Party was on the rise, too. These were dangerous forces to a card-carrying union member like Marcel. But he knew the temptations of their politics. The same forces would keep him driving until midnight, just to get to a job that paid good money. In the age of affluence, little else was as important, especially with two teenaged boys to support and equip. Guitar lessons alone for his older son were costing Marcel $600 a year.

By the time we reached North Battleford, the bigger of twin towns that straddle the North Saskatchewan River, Marcel had put away his welders' glasses. The sun had set, leaving a mauve glow on the horizon framed by the silhouette of hills in the distance and a skiff of clouds overhead. Marcel said there would be just enough daylight left for a quick tour of the town. He had grown up around here and felt I should see the place if I wanted to appreciate some of the province's decline.

At half past seven on a Thursday night, the main street was deserted, save for the bingo hall that had taken the place of an old grocery store and seemed to be doing a steady business. The rest of downtown was littered with For Rent signs, used clothing outlets and one pawnshop. A big Woolworth's had closed, with no tenants to take its place. The old Beaver Hotel, a hot spot in the sixties, was a dive. Except for a liquor store under construction on the outskirts of town, the only new operation in North Battleford appeared to be the storefront office of Community Futures Development Corporation, a government agency designed to rescue towns that were beyond hope.

Marcel said a new Wal-Mart and a Canadian Tire on the outskirts had wrung the downtown dry. But the changing economy of rural Saskatchewan had played a role too. The big grain elevator, built next to a rail yard in the middle of town, was once a symbol of prosperity for the region. It now carried the look of an old car junked in a country yard. As in Dauphin and so many other Prairie towns, the biggest building was no longer the grain elevator. It was an old folks' place: the Valleyview Retirement Home, perched on North Battleford's majestic escarpment overlooking the river valley and gentle plains rolling from the other bank to Alberta.

Once we crossed the river and were up on the other side, where the road followed the CN line, Marcel said it would be another hour to the border, and a couple of hours beyond that to Edmonton. He fiddled with the radio but could not find anything worth listening to. He had hoped to get some Led Zeppelin going, to ease him into the twilight as the sky turned orange and pink. At forty-nine, Marcel was one of those aging rockers for whom Classic Rock stations were designed. More than the endurance of his generation's music, though, what amazed him was the enthusiasm that his seventeen-year-old had found for it. Zep, Stevie Ray Vaughan, Eric Clapton, ZZ Top, Chuck Berry—these were his elder son's musical heroes. The boy hadn't found them in his father's record collection. He spent hours every day on the Internet, looking for oldies to download.

"It brings tears to my fuckin' eyes, because the guys he's pickin' up are the gods of guitar," Marcel said, sounding like he was on the verge of tears. "He's playing 'Stairway to Heaven'!"

Eventually, he found a radio station from Lloydminster, an oil town that straddles the line between Alberta and Saskatchewan, and played it until we reached the boundary. For a guitar fanatic, the local station wasn't much: Blue Rodeo and the like. But twilight was fading fast, and Marcel seemed to need everything he could find to finish the journey. I wasn't going to be much help. I had told him I was going only as far as Lloydminster, hoping to see some of the oil town in daylight. I also had been on the road for twelve hours—half of it standing in the Prairie sun, the other half in strangers' cars and trucks—and was at the end of my hitchhiking rope. I had run out of things to say.

9

Life on the Fringe

Lloydminster (Lloyd to the locals) was visible from miles away, not by the glow of its motel and bar strip but by the lights of its enormous heavy-oil reducer, the biggest symbol this side of Winnipeg of the Mulroney government's desperate efforts to maintain western support. The oil complex, lit up in the evening, looked like a travelling carnival, with its stacks rising like the heights of a roller coaster—not an inappropriate image given the billions of dollars that taxpayers and investors had sunk into the place.

The town itself, straddling the provincial boundary, looked like a low-rent midway. By half past nine on Lloyd's main street, the base-ball diamonds on the Saskatchewan side were dark and deserted. But beyond a set of towers that marked the border, the Alberta side was lit up like the old Vegas, with bars, liquor stores and a couple of strip clubs doing a steady business.

Somehow, when I told Marcel I wanted to get a taste of the oil patch, I had expected Lloyd to be one of the great Canadian cross-roads. On one side of the town was Saskatchewan, home of modern socialism in Canada—birthplace of medicare, subsidies and high taxes. On the other side was Alberta, birthplace of modern conservatism, where the seeds of private health care, welfare reform and low taxes were planted. I thought I would find a hotbed of political debate. Instead, Lloyd was nothing more than a base camp for roughnecks. My first sight was a souped-up Trans Am with an Alberta plate screeching by, its stereo blaring something old from AC/DC. It was the sort of tune—heavy on bass, light on acoustics— that would not have impressed Marcel, whose '83 Toyota wagon seemed dwarfed by motel signs as it headed west into Alberta.

But Lloyd had a very different look in the morning. Where the Trans Am had raced by, two combines were driving down the main street. Leaving my motel through its parking lot that was full of mud-splattered four-by-fours, I walked to the western edge of town, past the First Truck Centre, the one with a big plastic steer mounted on its sign. This was more like Alberta, and it wasn't long before a red Dodge Ram four-by-four pulled over. The driver said he was going to Vermilion, a quarter of the way to Edmonton—not much, but it was as good a start as I had had since the Soo.

In jeans, a T-shirt and hiking boots, Barry Bartusek was obviously in the oil business. He ran his own small rig operation. He was also in a bit of a hurry, rushing to see a client and then on to a rig where one of his crews was working. As he drove, he ate a hot dog for breakfast and drank a coffee. In between bites, he smoked a du Maurier.

Barry lived in Lloyd but spent almost every waking hour on the road or on a rig, trying to make a bigger buck—a huge buck, perhaps—from the hardest end of the oil business. There were nine hundred rigs in western Canada, and he had three of them. His bigger challenge was finding people to work on his rigs, which I think was why he picked me up. He was always looking for new hands. "There are lots of rigs. There aren't enough men," he said, wiping his mouth clean of the convenience-store hot dog. "Our industry doesn't attract the overachievers. It's hard work. It's dirty. We get people who dropped out in Grade 10."

I thought of some of the people I had met along the way who had complained about the lack of good-paying jobs. Barry was in permanent need of rig workers starting at $16 an hour, ten to twelve hours a day. There was every prospect, he said, of making $25 an hour within a year. That was how he got his start, working on rigs for more than two decades until he realized he could run the operation better than his boss. But he knew the type of work was not for everyone—handling chains that whip around at dangerous speeds, being splashed with oil and cold water all day, listening to the incessant grind of engines and co-workers yelling.

"There's good money if you stick with it," he said. "Some guys don't want to work winters. Some guys don't want to work summers. Some guys just want to earn enough cash to go to the lake for a while. But younger kids today, they just don't want to work. Kids that come off the farm, even they don't want to do something. There's so much computers and technology, these kids today they don't know what physical work is. They complain when they break a sweat. I have to look at the over-thirty crowd, it's that bad."

With his three rigs each costing him a million dollars a year, and an itinerant workforce, Barry was always at the mercy of others, but none more than the oil companies that hired him to drill their holes. He pointed to the Motorola phone on his dashboard, which rang through the day with voices telling him to get his costs down because some obscure country somewhere had started pumping more oil.

"We're not nice people in this business," he said bluntly. "If we don't perform well, the oil companies say, 'Thanks for coming out. Now you're finished.'"

There was always someone else with a rig ready to go. That was the spirit of Alberta. It was not so much an ideology as an atmosphere of intense competition, right down to the rig, that resulted from the province's fortunes, more than those of any other, being tied to events in a bigger world.

Such a world seemed very far away from the overpass at Vermilion, where Barry dropped me. There were rolling green and golden fields in every direction, and more and more livestock. For the first time, I felt like I had left the Prairie grain lands and entered ranch country.

But one thing was the same: the roads were empty. I stood on the on-ramp, watching a herd of cattle for close to an hour with no more than a dozen vehicles passing. Most of the drivers looked at me coldly, as if I were an unkempt drifter. The particular scowl of one man in a cowboy hat pushed me to move to the highway, where many more cars were passing by on their way to Edmonton. Of course, they were all going over a hundred, but that too had its benefits: the scowls were far more fleeting.

After I'd waited ten minutes or so on the side of the highway, a beat-up hatchback pulled over, coming to a stop in front of me. The driver must have decided to pick me up well before he could get a proper look at me. Something else gave me misgivings, although I didn't fully appreciate it until I was trapped in the back seat: there was no easy way for me to get out. I had climbed in with some difficulty, after a teenaged boy in the front pulled his seat forward to allow me to squeeze through. Another boy, a bit younger and with a sedated look on his face, was already squished in the back between a couple of bags and the window.

Getting into a crowded back seat was breaking a basic rule of hitchhiking, the same one I had forgotten with Joe and Judy on the road to P.E.I. Should the man and two boys pull something strange, I had no way to escape; at a hundred kilometres an hour, I couldn't even jump out. The back was so cramped that I would not even be able to wave frantically at passing cars—that is, if they could see me through the cracked windshield. For the next two hours, maybe much longer, I would be a prisoner. If there was any mercy, it would have to come from the driver, a big, bug-eyed man who spoke with a Cape Breton lilt and had a large gap between his front teeth.

The driver introduced himself as Cliff, a welder from Sydney who lived in Lloyd with his two sons. This didn't ease my worries. I now realized I was trapped inside a car with a family of drifters on their way to Edmonton to party. "I'm forty-six, with twenty-eight years of partying experience," Cliff said proudly, soon after giving me his name.

When I told Cliff I had spent the night in Lloyd, he turned around and looked me in the eye, not losing a click on his speedometer. Had I seen any bar fights? He seemed disappointed when I said no. Back in 1979, when he first moved to this area, there were bar fights every Friday night between the boys in cowboy hats and the boys with funny accents. There still were, he said, though they tended to be about women rather than accents.

"They used to complain that the boys from Down East were taking all the good jobs," Cliff said. "I used to laugh. The local people didn't want the jobs."

They'd fight just the same, the cowboys and the Newfies. Around Lloyd, everyone from east of Quebec was a Newfie, even a good Cape Bretoner like Cliff.

Once I was settled into the back seat, I noticed the boy in front of me had a bald patch on the back of his head. The boy beside me sat with his mouth open, looking dazed. Neither had said much since they picked me up, preferring to stare out the window. Their few words with their father were occasional grunts and mumbles when one wanted to bum an Export A.

The boys seemed hypnotized by the car's loud rattling as Cliff tried to keep it at a steady hundred and twenty. We passed Vegreville and its big sign for *pysanka,* the world's biggest Easter egg. Made of aluminum and painted, it measured nine metres high by five and a half metres wide. Cliff continued talking, not taking notice of the egg. He used to hitchhike between here and Sydney, he said, usually taking four days to make the trip. He was disappointed it had taken me three weeks.

"What's going on in Edmonton?" I asked.

"Pot," Cliff said, turning around again as he drove so I could hear him.

Every weekend he had off, he took his boys to Edmonton to buy four ounces or so of marijuana. In Lloyd, he had to pay $300 an ounce, but in the big city he could get the same stuff for $240. He wasn't worried about the risks. He had been charged twice in Lloyd

for possession and fined $100 each time. Cliff laughed at the innocu-
ous nature of his crime. While he harmlessly smoked his dope, Lloyd
had become an unpleasant hard-core drug town. Ecstasy and crystal
meth were big among the roughnecks, as was crack. "It's not like it
used to be," he said. "You now get crackheads in these small towns."

As we passed Elk Island National Park, reputed to be one of the
West's best wildlife sanctuaries, Cliff changed the subject. He asked
if I knew anything about prophecies. The car was rattling so loudly
I could not hear what he said next. I think he mentioned the
Learning Channel. I think he mentioned Sartre and Nietzsche. I know
he said something about Leon Uris because he lifted a copy of *Trinity*,
which he kept in the front seat.

I tried to draw his sons into the conversation, if only to make
sure they were alive. Nigel in the front seat, who was eighteen, told
me about his job at McDonald's. He was earning $6 an hour and
finding it hard to save enough to pay the $120 fine he owed for
underage drinking.

The boys used to live in Sydney with their mother. When they
moved to Lloyd, Nigel tried to stay in high school but eventually
dropped out. "I went to school stoned every day," he said. "I still got
average marks."

"Sometimes he takes my advice, sometimes he doesn't," Cliff
interjected, speaking over the engine's rattle. "I told him, if there's
one thing you do, don't go to school stoned."

Through the cracked windshield, I could see the tips of
Edmonton's skyline. The city was still twenty minutes away.

Jason, who was sixteen, said he dropped out in Grade 7, back in
Sydney, after a teacher drove him to hate school. He said the last
straw broke when she gave him permission to go to the washroom
and then chastised him in class for being slow about returning.
"Yeah, I had to take a crap," he said.

After leaving school, Jason was jailed for a year for assault and then,
two days after his release, arrested again for break-and-enter. It was at
that point he and Nigel decided to move to Alberta, to join their father.

I asked Cliff's boys what they wanted to do with their next few years. Nigel, the elder one, hoped to return to high school and then enrol in a welding course, to follow his father's footsteps. Jason couldn't think of a quick answer. "Trying to stay out of jail," his father said.

This was Cliff's fourth tour of Alberta and looked like it would be the longest. He had been coming out here since he was a child, when his own father was working in Alberta and the Northwest Territories. Five of his seven brothers and sisters had done the same thing, moving to Alberta and British Columbia. Of course, ever since he had brought his boys out here to live, they had missed the beaches of Cape Breton, among the finest on the East Coast. "The water was so cool you could keep your beer in it!" Cliff said nostalgically. In Alberta, the lakes were coated with a green slime left by poplar pollen. The bottoms were mucky. They all got swimmer's itch when they went in.

But after three years in the oil patch, working at various rig jobs, Cliff doubted he could go back to the Maritimes. "I'll probably be here forever," he said. "There's nothing for me Down East, no jobs. Besides, when half the country sinks into the ocean, Alberta will be the place to be."

He turned again to me, laughing so hard the gap between his upper front teeth seemed to grow.

We were soon crossing Wayne Gretzky Drive, past the Northlands Coliseum where the all-Canadian boy had played so many games. On the way downtown, Cliff promised to drop me near his dealer's house. From there, I'd be able to catch a bus across the river to Old Strathcona, the neighbourhood where Edmonton's Fringe Festival was underway.

To other Canadians, the city was probably best known for its hockey team, right-wing governments and gargantuan, forty-eight-hectare mall, perhaps the only one in the world with a wave pool, ice-skating rink, dolphin show and theme streets. The city was also home to North America's first mosque. But the Fringe was what really set Edmonton apart. With ten days of theatre, dance, mime and music that drew thousands of performers, it was as good a festival of its kind as any on the continent.

⸻ ⸻ ⸻

Edmonton had always been a corporate town. Created by the Hudson's Bay Company as a fort and trading post, and then expanded as a gateway to the North for prospectors and miners, the city came into its own as an oil town, with big new companies servicing the likes of Cliff the vagabond and Barry the entrepreneur. I spent the afternoon walking around the downtown core and was struck by the number of corporate buildings, including many high-tech companies. Equally striking, though, were the big gobs of public space—an art centre, parks and a beautiful riverside trail. Quite remarkably, Edmonton had set aside more land for parks than any city of its size in North America. It had also invested in the Fringe. In 1981, when the festival was launched as the first of its kind in North America, it sold seventy-five hundred tickets. In 2000, the number reached eighty-one thousand. Close to 300,000 more people came to the open-air section of Old Strathcona that was blocked off for free theatre and street performers.

The Fringe was one of those things that made Edmonton the most non-American of English Canadian cities. Geography helped too. No other city big enough to have a team in the Canadian Football League was so far from the border—550 kilometres—or from a major American city. You'd have to drive ten hours to get to the nearest National Football League game, in Seattle. Such distances weren't trivial. They had protected Edmonton from a deluge of local U.S. television, the kind that Toronto suffers from Buffalo and Vancouver from Seattle. And they ensured that anyone coming to Edmonton was serious about the place.

I had crossed the river to Old Strathcona and was only a few steps into the Fringe when I saw how different the city was. At the entrance, a young boy played violin while beyond him were a ventriloquist and his puppet; a magician; and Doug Pruden, the Push-Up Man, who was closing in on the world record for lifetime push-ups. The thirty-seven-year-old was about to do his four millionth, having already set a new Canadian record of ten thousand in a single day. Deeper into the festival, an entire avenue of plays and concerts opened up, the most fanciful being *Shakespeare: The Lost Episode.*

After an evening at the festival, watching hilarious skits and inspiring performers, I was getting ready to walk back to a bed and breakfast where I had left my bag when I stopped for a moment to absorb the scene. It was one in the morning. The local streets and boulevards hummed with street performers, festival-goers and thousands of bar-hoppers cruising Whyte Avenue, the trendy axis of Old Strathcona. Canada was beginning to feel hip. Montreal was easily North America's sexiest city. Saskatoon had one of the best blues bars going. And here in Edmonton, here in the last gateway to the North, a theatre festival was drawing close to half a million people. It hardly felt like a nation of lumberjacks.

The next morning, I took a local bus past the West Edmonton Mall to the city's last interchange on the Trans-Canada. Except for the monster mall in the distance, which resembled one of those industrial complexes I had passed in Quebec, it felt like the outskirts of Saskatoon. All that was missing were the dead insects. An hour passed before a car stopped, just as dark storm clouds overhead were about to break. The old Hyundai reminded me of Cliff's car. Even the odour inside was familiar.

The driver said he had just dropped off his wife at the Edmonton airport and was returning to his rural home and llama farm near Evansburg, forty minutes up the road. "I just smoked a joint so I'm driving a little slow," he said, introducing himself as Murray. "Do you toke? There's a roach somewhere in there if you want." He pointed to the ashtray.

Murray appeared to be a throwback to another age—an age that no one would identify with northern Alberta, especially not the red-neck Alberta that dwells in many Canadian imaginations. But here he was anyway, a pot-smoking hippie on his way home to a llama farm to tend to his garden. On most days, Murray worked in a coal mine, operating heavy equipment. It was why he smoked pot, he said. To relieve muscle pain. But the garden was his real pride, he added, eager to persuade me of the joys of a green lifestyle. I'm not sure if it was my jeans and T-shirt, or perhaps a well-fed look that suggested I had just consumed a sixteen-ounce slab of Alberta beef, but Murray believed I needed persuading.

Back in Evansburg, Murray and his neighbours had just fended off a feedlot—the giant pig and chicken operations that were all the rage in rural Alberta. Thousands of animals on one farm would have threatened the entire local water system, he explained. And for what? More McNuggets? It was like the Edmonton Eskimos game that he and his wife had gone to the night before. There was so much advertising he couldn't figure out what it was all for.

"There's so much materialism in our world, it makes me sick," Murray said. "Why does one person need to control so much land? Why can't people grow their own food? You go to cities and in apartment blocks people are going hungry."

As we cleared the last traces of suburban Edmonton, Murray began to tell me how he got to this point. The story promised to be long, seeing as he had slowed down further to accommodate the steady rain that had begun. He had started to raise llamas, next to his organic garden, as part of a demonstration project, in hopes of saving people from their own destruction. He wanted to set an example for his grown children, and the children he saw devoting their lives to shopping and entertainment.

"Mankind would be healthier living," he said, "rather than just chasing this Wal-Mart dream. I believe this is the way people are going to live in the future, not working forty hours a week—maybe twenty hours and then producing for yourself, whether it's food or art."

I glanced at a road sign to make sure I was in Alberta. Murray, though, was not of Alberta. He had grown up in the small city of Peterborough, outside Toronto, when it was stuck in the age of Robertson Davies. In 1966, as a teenager frustrated with a community clinging to its past, he drifted to Toronto's Yorkville district and on to the lower mainland of British Columbia, with an old car and sixty-two cents to his name. By 1969, he was in Berkeley. The People's Park riot broke out the day he arrived. LSD was everywhere. He was not yet twenty.

Murray lasted awhile in northern California and then, with his girlfriend, drifted north to Vancouver and the psychedelic hangover of Kitsilano. They had a baby, and then two more. That was enough to make the young hippie discover he needed more than love. He needed a job, and on the West Coast that meant logging.

I said I was surprised to meet a hippie who had become a logger and now worked in a coal mine.

"I'd rather hug a tree than cut it," Murray said. "But when you've been through years of drug abuse and you get your girlfriend pregnant and then have three kids, you gotta do something to put bread on the table. You can't live on the beach and go in to town to collect a welfare cheque and raise a family."

You can't change character overnight, either. Murray went through ten years of Narcotics Anonymous. He and his girlfriend split up, which was when he moved to Alberta and remarried. Improbably, Murray's wife was an accountant—"from another planet," he said.

As we passed the mine at Wabamun, where he worked, earning enough to keep going, he suggested I visit his llama farm. For some reason—the second-hand smoke, perhaps—I agreed.

We followed a secondary highway off the Trans-Canada for a few kilometres and then turned down a dirt road to his three-hectare lot. Murray and his wife kept a trailer home there and around it the makings of a small working farm. From the car, I could see some of the animals, but didn't get an appreciation for the llamas' size until I got out and stood near one. It looked like it could knock me over with one head butt.

Murray had four llamas, largely to protect his seven sheep from coyotes. There were also five pigs and a chicken. He showed me his garden—the rain had stopped—and a patch of forest he had cleared in hopes of renting it out to city-dwellers in search of a country garden. He couldn't imagine how all those people at the West Edmonton Mall would not rather spend a few hours on this land. The rain started again, so heavily that it drove us inside the trailer. Murray made some coffee and suggested I wait until the downpour stopped. There was no point standing by the highway, getting wet.

We continued talking. His own kids had turned out okay, although one had gone through several years of heavy drinking, and they all still spent too much time watching television, in his view. Everyone did. His neighbours, down the dirt road, did little else when they were home. In the Evansburg area, he knew only five people who toked. He thought the low number reflected poorly on the community.

When the rain stopped, at least enough for me to believe I could get another ride, Murray kindly agreed to take me back to the highway. He said he had some shopping to do in Evansburg, although it was usually the saddest part of his week, having to enter the retail world. He dropped me just outside the town, where most westbound traffic was headed for the mountains. I let the first wave of cars pass, preferring to watch Murray drive in the other direction, very slowly, toward a grocery store.

For those coming from afar, the Rockies were close enough that I doubted anyone slowed down to see Evansburg, or me standing at its edge. Only the afternoon drizzle, which began a few minutes after Murray dropped me off, stirred some compassion in Kenneth Preston. A true Scot, he knew what it meant to stand in the rain.

Kenneth was driving an old red Chrysler Sundance, with a cracked windshield, but I was more taken by what was in the back: a baby seat, with a sleeping child in it. This was my first ride with someone travelling with an infant, and I felt immediately at ease, telling Kenneth about my children before he could tell me about his.

He was on his way to Grand Cache to pick up his other son, a five-year-old, who had been staying for a few weeks with his mother's parents. He would then take them home to Edmonton and wait for his wife to return from Fort McMurray, where she was working for the summer at the big oil sands project before returning to teachers' college.

From his voice, I knew Kenneth was new to Canada, though I was surprised to hear him describe himself as an immigrant. Scottish immigrants sounded like something out of the nineteenth century, when New Glasgow and retail banking were hot. Kenneth was short and well built, with a solid voice, dry wit and pragmatic mind, which was both Scottish and Canadian. He had come to Canada four years earlier, on a whim, after meeting a Canadian woman on a train in Europe. She raved about her homeland, which intrigued him. At seventeen, he had just finished school, qualifying to be an electrician, and was eager to see new places. "I knew Canada had some Great Lakes, a few mountains and some Scottish people who came over here in the 1800s—that's it," he said. "I couldn't believe the vast expanses, how much room there is here to house people."

The humming engine was enough to keep the baby asleep, so Kenneth continued talking. Travelling around Alberta, he met a single mother and fell in love. They moved in together, married and had a child, the one sleeping in the back of the Sundance. As an electrician, he had no trouble finding work. He was currently on a project to build a shopping mall in Edmonton, which I suggested was like shipping coal to Newcastle. He gave me a stern look. His father had been a coal miner until Margaret Thatcher sold the mine in the 1980s and England began importing cheaper coal from Eastern Europe, which was another reason Kenneth decided to emigrate.

The Yellowhead had become a dual carriageway, with straight lines, little traffic and nothing other than wandering wildlife to slow us down for the next hundred kilometres. Kenneth still could not get over the distances here. As a child, his family car trips lasted no more than five hours. In six, they could cover Scotland. "In Scotland, you couldn't go ten kilometres without hitting five villages," he said. Now, he lived in a province that could fit all of Great Britain inside it. When some English friends came to visit and he offered to drive them to Thunder Bay, he thought the journey would take no more than a day. Two days later, they were still driving. "Wow, we could be in Russia by now," the English friends said when they reached the corner of Arthur Street and the Trans-Canada.

By the time we reached Edson ("Slo Pitch Capital of Canada"), the rain clouds had passed over, and there on the horizon, as we came over a crest, was the first glimpse of mountains. Their snowy peaks glistened in the afternoon sun, a sight that to me, after so many weeks on the flatlands of central Canada, looked as inviting as an oasis in the desert.

Kenneth returned to what he liked about Canada. With two children, a house and a car, he already had achieved the Canadian dream, and he was just twenty-one. Once his wife finished school and began teaching, they hoped to buy a bigger house and a better car, which he took as the new Canadian dream. "I guess I want more for my kids than I had," he said. Back in Scotland, his buddies from technical school still lived in small apartments, and none had a car.

I asked Kenneth about his wife and what drove her to take a job, even for the summer, so far away from her children. The pay, at $30 an hour, was hard to beat, but there was more to it than money. She was an Indian, he explained, who had her first child when she was a teenager—a common occurrence in many native communities, but one that she did not want to hold her down. Her mother was a lawyer, one of the first female native lawyers in Alberta. That inspired Kenneth's wife. She was determined to make her own life too.

As a newcomer to Canada, he was impressed by the close bonds of this and other aboriginal families but also dismayed by their social expectations. Natives enjoyed a hiring quota at the tar sands project because it was being developed on lands claimed by First Nations. His wife also got free tuition and books at college, as part of a government effort to boost native enrolment. Kenneth, who grew up in a struggling coal miner's family in Scotland, could not understand why aboriginal groups were so restless. "I know they had a lot of rights taken away from them," he said. "But—and I guess this is politically incorrect to say—they've had a lot of opportunities, too. I've seen that. There's no reason a lot of them can't have jobs."

I wondered how his wife's family felt about his own Scottish ancestry and if they knew how Scotland had been treated by history, specifically English history. I thought there might be some shared themes of oppression and disenfranchisement to share. The very suggestion made Kenneth laugh loud enough to stir the baby.

He had told his wife about his childhood and being taught the English royals were "the root of all evil." The government in London was even worse, he believed. As a young boy, he joined the local coal miners in their protest marches and once got to throw an egg at Margaret Thatcher's car. He was four at the time.

So what did his wife say?

"She loves the royal family," Kenneth responded with a note of despair. "She has a collection of Princess Di memorabilia. She keeps it in a special box."

Once he suggested throwing out the box. That ended the conversation, and they had not discussed the royal family since. The box stayed.

The Yellowhead dipped and rose through river valleys and thick forests as we approached Hinton. The town was probably best known still for the horrible 1986 collision between a freight train and passenger train that killed twenty-three people. But the closer we got the better Kenneth was able to illustrate his view of Hinton as a quiet workers' paradise. Beyond the far end of town were the first mountains that form the northeastern gates to the Rockies and the entrance to Jasper National Park. At the near end was a smaller range of subdivisions, packed with big houses and wide driveways that each held at least one all-terrain vehicle and one four-by-four. It looked more like an affluent suburb in the American South than a mill town in the Canadian North.

According to Kenneth, just about everyone in Hinton made at least $70,000 a year at the local paper mill or two nearby coal mines. He knew guys pulling in far more with overtime—"a hundred and sixty thousand a year," he figured. It was the sort of scene that left him in awe of Canada the moment he arrived, and still did. "It's hard to believe a country could have all this," he said.

After Kenneth dropped me by a strip of fast-food outlets, where I could grab a late lunch, I walked west toward the mountains, figuring there was nowhere else for anyone to go. Sure enough, within a few minutes a sporty four-by-four pulled over. It was the kind common to the other side of Hinton, but the driver was not a mill worker. He was a travelling salesman from Edmonton, on his way to Jasper to pitch a new line of high-end sunglasses to tourist outlets. The town sold so many sunglasses, he said, that just a few sales calls made the three-hour drive worthwhile.

Twenty kilometres beyond Hinton, we passed the majestic face of Pocahontas, and then followed the banks of the unassuming Athabasca into Jasper National Park, where the river finds its source. The diversity of Jasper Park was breathtaking, from marshy river-banks to alpine forests to snowy peaks, all in half an hour. But the scenery could not compete with the sheer drama underway in Jasper town. Since the creation of a national park in 1907, the community—named for Jasper Hawes, an early North West Company clerk—had been a ward of the federal government. Parks Canada held responsibility for every public decision and all municipal services. If the town needed a new stop sign, a recommendation had to go to Ottawa.

In the early decades of the twentieth century, few local residents minded the arrangement because the town was largely inaccessible to outsiders. But the coming of the Trans-Canada Highway eventually put Jasper on the same path as Banff, the other big Alberta mountain town that was in many eyes a travesty of development. Rents soared. Business operators clamoured for better services. The locals got angry.

In 1986, the 4,500 people of Jasper held a plebiscite on independence from Ottawa and voted overwhelmingly against it. But now, another referendum was looming, and every indication suggested the freedom fighters would win. The federal government, which owns all the land in the park, was already preparing to negotiate self-government with the town, although it was firm about maintaining control over land-use planning, development and environmental regulation. These issues aside, the sleepy little town of Jasper was about to declare independence.

For political spirit, a better microcosm of the West could not be found. Jasper's struggle for some autonomy would be sure to find support across the Prairies, not only from a bunch of redneck libertarian yahoos, though I had met a couple, but also from some of the most diverse communities in Canada, dope-lovers included. What these people wanted was to be heard, be it on gun control or aboriginal rights.

The Prairies' greatest problems lay not with Ottawa, however; they came from within. Away from the oilfields, the countryside that for centuries had defined Manitoba, Saskatchewan and Alberta was being hollowed out. Whole villages were disappearing. In prosperous towns as well as the bigger cities, the uniformity of North American suburbs had taken something from the West, which downtown efforts such as The Forks or the Fringe could not replace. Like the imprint of grain elevators that had been erased by shopping malls, the region was seeing its identity erode. If this kept up, it was at risk of becoming like Jasper—clear in ambition, cloudy in purpose.

When we reached the town of Jasper, I got out on the main street and blended in with the crush of tourists, leaving the sunglasses man to do his rounds. There were so many postcard stands and T-shirt racks creeping onto the sidewalk that it was impressive anyone managed to get to where they were going, which in most cases seemed to be an ice-cream store that was overflowing with customers. I could see where the anti-separatists were coming from. Should the ice-cream vendor become mayor of an independent Jasper, there was no telling what would become of the town. It already looked like a theme street in the West Edmonton Mall. What was to stop the whole mall from shifting here?

The Great Pig Race

BRITISH COLUMBIA

The approach to British Columbia turned out to be the easiest leg of my journey. After a quick walk around Jasper, I returned to the Trans-Canada and got a ride through the Yellowhead Pass in no time at all. A park official picked me up on her way home to Valemount, an hour over the mountains in B.C. Sharon was a middle-aged blonde who looked like she had been hiking in Jasper for decades, which of course was true. But she and her husband were trying to ease out of Jasper life. After he retired from the park service the previous spring, they had moved to Valemount. The housing was cheaper and the community, oddly, was more at peace with nature than were those who lived inside the park. In Jasper, Sharon said, new houses were going for $350,000, which attracted a certain kind of person.

The two-lane highway through the Rockies had little traffic at the end of the day and the end of the season. Two nights ago, Sharon said, it had snowed on the ridge above her home in Valemount. But now, as we passed through the Yellowhead into B.C., rain clouds were reaching down from the sky like a veil over the mountains.

We came around a deserted bend to see a big motorhome with American plates thundering in our direction. It passed with the force of a freight train, its tailwind rattling Sharon's old GMC van.

I did not appreciate how heroic the construction of the Yellowhead route had been until we skirted around the next bend and along the wild shores of Moose Lake. The choppy waters, stirred by the passing storm, seemed to fill every bit of the pass except for two narrow lanes of road that had been carved out of a rock face.

This was the pass that nearly cost Viscount Milton his life in 1863, as he travelled on horseback and foot hoping to make the case for a railway pass through Jasper, instead of the more popular route to the south. I had been loaned a century-old copy of his memoir, *The North-West Passage by Land,* by Douglas Gibson, the head of McClelland & Stewart, who was in the process of publishing the account of a re-creation of the journey by Michael Shaw Bond, one of Viscount Milton's descendants. The Victorian traveller was a foul-tempered and pampered young man who came to Canada largely to make a name for himself. After he returned to England and wrote up his account, the story of his incredible journey, made more so by the fact that he was epileptic, went through several print runs and made him the toast of London society, even though the CPR eventually opted for a southern route, at Kicking Horse Pass.

My mind had wandered to Milton's crossing of the pass when a shot of light pierced its way through rain clouds and stole my attention, causing me to miss, for a moment, what lay ahead. Beyond the lake, a pickup truck had collided with a camper van, and both lay in a ditch. Sharon kept driving. A police cruiser had arrived, and no one appeared hurt. She said accidents like that were not uncommon in the area, where drivers were usually staring at mountain peaks or wildlife instead of the road. Two weeks earlier in the park, a driver had stopped to photograph an elk, leaving his car on the road, where it was promptly crushed by a semi coming around the bend. No one was hurt. "I understand their excitement because some of these people have never seen an elk or a bull, but it's kind of scary how they drive," Sharon said.

Whenever she stopped to pick up litter, she usually found half a dozen cars and vans stopping behind her staff truck, their drivers assuming she had spotted some wildlife. In some spots, where there actually was wildlife, she had to direct traffic because so many people stopped to get out of their vehicles. If only Milton could have imagined the fate of his passage, I thought: motorhomes, tour buses and photo ops.

We soon passed a towering wall that formed part of Mount Robson, which at 12,972 feet is the highest point in the Canadian Rockies. And that was it. We had cleared the range and were following the upper reaches of the Fraser, a placid little river that a thousand kilometres from here would heave its mighty weight into the Strait of Georgia and on to the Pacific Ocean. At this rate, I figured I would be on Vancouver Island in two days.

In the next valley, at Tete Jaune Cache, Sharon agreed to take me off the highway and down a little side road to where the Fraser merged with a smaller river from the Cariboo range. She wanted me to stand on an old wooden bridge for a few minutes and listen to the two rivers fighting the rocks that lay in their way. She pointed to the water below, to dozens of salmon swimming furiously against the current, stopping occasionally behind a rock for rest, and then darting forward a few metres in their great swim upstream, to the next resting point. I was not sure who learned more from their journeys: humans or fish. But when Viscount Milton emerged at the same spot, this was what he observed: "The view from The Cache looking westward is, we imagine, one of the most wonderful in the world. Away as far as the eye can reach—north, south and west—are mountains packed behind mountains, separated only by the narrowest valleys, most of them snow-clad, and apparently stretching away to the Pacific. . . . We were assured by Mr. Fraser, of Victoria, who had visited both the Andes and the Himalayas, that nothing could compare with these hundreds of miles of mountains in British Columbia."

For Milton, the bliss was short-lived. Not long after Tete Jaune Cache his party ran dangerously close to starvation. They ate their last pemmican along this stretch and had only a quart of flour left for the journey to the fort at Kamloops, which would take weeks. To their horror, there was little wildlife to be hunted in this area, and so, out of desperation, they ate their horses.

Sharon dropped me at Valemount for the night. I gulped when she recommended a local restaurant that was well known for its steak.

The next morning, there was a chill in the air when I set out early for Kamloops, thinking I could cover the three-hundred-kilometre distance by lunch and be in the balmy Okanagan by evening. But after such a good run through the Rockies, I quickly found myself stuck in Valemount. Cars, vans and trucks roared by, not in great numbers, but not sporadically either. After the first hour of waiting, I went into a gas station for a coffee, to warm up. After the second hour, I went back to the gas station to get something to eat. After the third hour, I returned again to check the bus schedule. There was nothing to Kamloops until evening. After the fourth hour, I began to walk south along the side of the highway. It was a stupid thing to do. There was nothing ahead of me but forests and mountains. But if Milton could walk through forests and fields to Kamloops, I figured I could get around the next bend. There might be another gas station, or a set of lights in the middle of nowhere, or a turnoff to somewhere that was not on any of the maps I was carrying.

I was probably no more than two hundred metres south of the gas station, turning and holding out my thumb whenever I heard the whir of an approaching vehicle, when a new PT Cruiser pulled over. In the front were two women who said they were going to Blue River. I had no idea where that was but got in anyway. In the mountains, there is nowhere to go but upriver or downriver, and we were pointed downriver.

The women were on their way back to the tiny resort town where their husbands worked as Cat operators, clearing a mountainside for an ambitious new ski resort. They said they usually didn't pick up hitchhikers but felt sorry for me. An hour earlier, when they were on their way north to buy a few things in town, they had passed me standing in the same spot.

It was good I didn't walk any further, the driver said. There was nothing between here and Blue River except a hundred kilometres of forests, river valleys and bears. Now I was in comfort. The car felt like a sled on fresh snow as we glided around one mountain after another, each blanketed by thick forests and separated from the next by a rushing brook flowing into the North Thompson. When we reached the big river itself, the trees ran straight down to the water's edge, all of which Milton had to traverse on foot, while hungry. It was on this stretch that his party slowed down to five kilometres a day. In the PT Cruiser, we were covering a hundred and forty kilometres every hour.

"Isn't that beautiful?" the driver exclaimed.

Ahead of us was a snow-covered rock face stretching down to a forest and meadow. The snow was fresh, and here we were, not even at Labour Day. But as we got closer, I realized something quite extraordinary. The meadow was nothing of the sort. It was a vast tract of clear-cut forest. The driver, who had introduced herself as Kelly Mortimer, said I didn't need to express any dismay. The logging industry around here was dead and buried. She and her husband, both in their late thirties, used to run a thriving business opening and closing logging roads. They'd cut their way through a forest to make a road. When the clear-cut was finished, they'd go in by helicopter and drop logs and rocks on the road to keep vehicles out, and then a few seasons later clear the path for another logging crew. But they hadn't reactivated a logging road in five years, she figured.

When I asked about Blue River, Kelly and the other passenger, her mother-in-law, Cathy Leblanc, gave me an entirely different story. The hamlet used to be a CN town, with a wheel house and some small logging operations in neighbouring valleys. During the Second World War, an internment camp was built up the river. The logging operations expanded greatly after that, at first clearing the North Thompson valley to make way for the rail line, and then cutting and sawing trees for the West Coast housing boom. But when lower prices and U.S. trade barriers combined to close the mills, Blue River seemed doomed.

That was when the service economy kicked in. Using helicopters and Cats from the logging companies, a savvy ski operator was able to turn Blue River into a base camp for heli-skiing. He built a small resort, with luxury rooms and cabins and a tennis court, added a great chef and massage centre, and was charging guests—Americans and Europeans for the most part, with the occasional star like Kevin Costner—about $7,000 a week. "You have to book three years in advance," Kelly said with some pride.

And that was only the beginning. A golf course was going in, along with a second lodge, with 250 rooms. (This in a hamlet of 250 people.) Up on the hills, a team of loggers, including Kelly, her husband and his father, had been hired to clear a mountainside of forests to make way for a new alpine ski resort. Eventually, Blue River would have lifts to the top of Saddle Mountain, with twelve kilometres of trails coming down.

With no such development in sight, we continued through a series of stunning valleys. In one, a waterfall cascaded out of a mountainside and down through a forest to the North Thompson. It looked like there was no end to the beauty or bounty of the area. As much damage as the loggers had done over the past half-century, the forests kept rolling, on all sides in some valleys. I was now sitting in the middle of the back seat, leaning forward to hear what each woman had to say and to get a better view of the scenery. I marvelled at how little logging appeared to have been done in one valley when Kelly pointed out that it was Blue River. Clearly, I had not seen the hill ahead, on the left. It was naked down the middle, with a Cat crawling up its side. Kelly said the operator was her husband, cleaning off a ski run that soon would be the widest in the world.

"Blue River's going to take off, just like Whistler," Cathy said from the front. "When I first moved to Whistler, in '87, there was nothing there."

It was a strange comment, since fashionable Whistler was such a bane to the hard core of B.C., rednecks and greens. I asked Cathy if Whistler was what she wanted to see here. No, she quickly answered. Whistler was what she called "snotty." She once worked in a grocery store there, as a cashier, and had to deal with a beautiful blonde who looked like a Hollywood star. She thought it was Kim Basinger. The woman tried to butt into the line. "Don't you know who I am?" the star asked, hoping to get a few groceries rung through before the line of people behind her raised a stink.

"I don't give a shit who you are," Cathy replied. "These people are in line. Don't you know it's lotto day and they all want to play their numbers?"

Cathy and Kelly got a good laugh from the story. Then they insisted on a quick drive around town, showing me the first lodge, tennis courts and several construction sites, as well as a very empty-looking railway depot and a gas station on the highway, where they dropped me. It was the first since Valemount, they said, and a sure bet for rides.

———— ———— ————

Blue River was identical to Valemount in one respect: there seemed to be no hope of escape. After an hour by the roadside, I skipped my routine and went straight for the bus schedule. It was the same bus coming from the north—in the evening. I tried walking down the highway, only to find myself in a secluded spot, as if I were lost in the forest, and quickly followed my tracks back to Blue River. Finally, after three hours of this, with a motel staring invitingly at me, a big yellow boat of a car pulled out of the gas station and stopped in front of me. At first, I thought it was a police car—a very old one—so bright was its yellow and wide its front. As I got closer, though, I realized the only way the driver could be a cop was if he was an undercover narc. A young man, he wore a patterned shirt, jeans and a captain's hat that did nothing to hide his ponytail.

Corey MacDonald was a veteran tree planter, as much a part of the forest as a twenty-year-old could be. He picked me up because, he said, I looked tired and angry. We weren't out of Blue River, and already I liked his judgment. Corey was on his way to Kamloops from his house outside Dunster, a hamlet north of Tete Jaune Cache. He used to hitchhike all over the province, at least enough to know that Valemount was the worst place in B.C. to get a ride, with Blue River a close second. Once he was stuck on the roadside at Valemount for four and a half hours—and he lived in the area. "It's all rednecks, giving you the finger," he said, laughing.

Corey smoked du Mauriers as he drove the Parisienne Brogue, which he'd bought from a Kamloops taxi operator for a thousand dollars. He had grown up in the forest, in a granola-eating, tree-planting family. He and his twin sister dropped out of school in Grade 8 so they could work in the summers, ski all winter and travel in between. They had been through Central America and most of Asia with their parents, who were divorced but lived on the same property and remained close friends. "We have an alter-native family," he said, dropping his butt in the ashtray below a taxi meter he still kept on the dash. "You'll probably never meet one quite like us."

The previous year, Corey had built his own log cabin on the property, next to the Fraser River. He lived alone there. Last month, he had bought his first television. "I believe in simplicity," he said.

Corey had followed his father into tree planting, starting his first job when he was fifteen. He could make $300 a day in the good summers and go on unemployment insurance in the winters. The previous winter, he had collected $9,000 in UI while skiing almost every day. His father had pulled off the same trick for decades, and at fifty-one was still pulling it off. He preferred, though, to spend his winters overseas, often working in a Mother Teresa centre in Calcutta. Once, he took Corey and his sister along, figuring a winter in South Asia would do more for their minds than a winter in a Canadian school.

Outside, the North Thompson valley was still narrow and steep, so much so that the CN line seemed to hang from the opposite bank. The water below raged like a mountain stream.

"I learned a lot about the world and a lot about myself," Corey said of his travels. "I feel very privileged to be alive at this point of time, to see so much change. Life for us is so easy. We have everything here, especially when you see other parts of the world when they have nothing and they're getting poorer and poorer."

Corey had been off work for a month after slicing open two tendons in his left hand with a machete while trying to cut a tree branch. Now, driving with one hand, he was on his way to Kamloops for a doctor's appointment in the morning and listening to a homemade tape of reggae, grunge and a few old rock groups. It was now on to something from The Clash. Corey and his friends liked seventies rock, even though it was made before they were born. He said they had played a lot of it the previous night at a music festival in Dunster to raise money for the fight against logging in the Fraser Valley.

"Logging?" I asked, with some disbelief in my voice. My last two rides, one with a naturalist, the other with a couple of trailblazers, had led me to believe that logging in these parts had disappeared with the last century. Corey shook his head and told me to brace myself for the next several valleys. Sure enough, there were entire mountainsides ahead that looked scarred, stripped of forests on top with patches of planted trees down the side. Where the woods had grown back, they looked spotty, like sutured hair. But the greatest damage, Corey said, was up the valleys, away from the North Thompson. "If you can't see it," he said, "it's definitely being logged."

Oddly, what remained of the local logging industry was doing little for communities along the North Thompson and Fraser. Dunster and McLeod, the villages closest to his cabin, were on their way to becoming ghost towns. The local mills had closed, as logs were cut in the forest by portable mills and then shipped elsewhere for processing. Nor was there much replanting. Dunster used to have four planting companies. Now it had one.

Corey was not against the logging industry, obviously; his livelihood depended on it. He just wished that B.C. had not been so rapacious. To protect forests against disease, it could have gone with a greater variety of trees than just spruce. It could have followed a more balanced planting pattern, too, as many Scandinavian countries did. With more space and more time, the trees would have grown to greater heights. But it wasn't even the forestry practices that worried him most. It was the people behind them—executives, regulators, consumers, pretty much everyone. "Clear-cutting is not going to be the end of humanity," he said solemnly. "It's the way people treat each other that worries me."

I asked Corey about tree planting, knowing it was the hardest physical work out there, hunched over little holes all day with a sack of seedlings on your back. He said the biggest problem was bears. He ran into them a lot, usually when he was alone planting trees. Bears almost never attack groups of two or more people, he said. Not even territorial grizzlies.

Corey's advice on dealing with bears was worth noting. Never run, he said, except downhill, which bears find awkward. He'd never seen anything like a bear running through a flat forest. "Nothing gets in their way," he said. If a bear comes close, hold your ground. They usually charge and then stop a few feet away, backing off a little and circling you to sense your mood. That's when he would raise a shovel and make as much noise as he could, preferably growling. He had worked with an African-born tree planter who once was charged by a grizzly. The man shouted African chants at the bear, and it backed off. The same thing happened the next day, again with a grizzly, and again the bear backed off.

"They won't kill you for food," Corey said. "Humans taste terrible. We're all sweat."

At Clearwater, an hour south of Blue River, the North Thompson widened and deepened as it followed a big curve, leaving its raging currents behind. The first farms emerged, around the spot where Viscount Milton had at last found a trail and rejoiced. A short while later, at Barrière, a few horse farms and cattle ranches joined the scene, and then, just before Kamloops, the picture turned to desert. In the last valley before we reached the city, I was shocked to see thorn bushes along the road's edge and parched brown hills that lacked any serious tree cover but were rich in earth tones. In the last golden moments of sunlight, in between the pools and suburban gardens that spotted each hillside around Kamloops, the soil burned with a red glow, as if we were entering Phoenix and not somewhere on the same latitude as the northern tip of Newfoundland.

When he reached the same point, Milton was impressed. Just outside Kamloops, scarcely able to believe he was alive, he wrote, "The country around had assumed a California aspect—the colour of a lithograph—rolling swells, brown with bunch grass, and studded with scattered yellow pines. The more sandy hills were covered with small spruce, and there, too, grew quantities of bilberries as large as English grapes, and of delicious flavour."

Corey kindly drove me to the far end of the bilberry city, beyond where the three big rivers—the Thompson, North Thompson and South Thompson—come together, to a place where I would be able to find a motel and, in the morning, catch a ride to the Okanagan Valley. I had been on the road ten hours and travelled only 350 kilometres. Only by Viscount Milton's standard had the day been anything short of miserable.

—— —— ——

I was so accustomed to waits of two, three and four hours that the next morning, when a big old Chevy pulled over just five minutes after I had started hitching, I felt unsettled, even a bit cheated. I thought of turning down the ride. The car was crowded, with a middle-aged man at the wheel, a teenaged boy in the front seat and another in the back, next to a box of groceries. They reminded me of Cliff and his boys on the road to Edmonton. And they were going only to Kelowna, a mere 163 kilometres away. Perhaps I could hold out for Penticton, Osoyoos or even Vancouver, I thought for a moment. Fortunately, the moment didn't last. The younger boy in the back moved the grocery box to make room for me, and we were off, briefly east along the Trans-Canada and then southeast along a rural highway, through ranchland, to the Okanagan.

The driver, Paul Razeau, was taking his son and a friend fruit-picking outside Kelowna as part of a charity drive for their church. The fruit was to be boxed and shipped to Vancouver for canning and then sent on to hungry people in the developing world. I figured that, living in southern British Columbia, Paul knew all about the perishability of fruit, and I didn't want to bore him with the dangers of giving people acidic, foreign foods. The issue of can openers was another question best left unspoken. He was the one giving me the ride, and I was now more concerned about a book I had spotted on the dash. It was *The Book of Mormon.*

Paul began talking about the book as soon as we turned down Highway 97, toward Vernon. "I was searching for a long time for what was happening in the world, and why am I here," he said.

He was a big man, big enough to look cramped in the front of a Chevy. At forty-five, he had also been through two marriages, four kids and several lifetimes of experiences, which he was quick to unload on me. Paul had come west as a young man from Cornwall, in eastern Ontario, to find work in Alberta. He did odd jobs in the oil patch and then hitched around the United States for work.

It was awful, he said, to be exposed to American highway justice. Once, an American driver dumped him in the middle of an express-way, for no apparent reason. Both sides had high fences. The driver, before speeding off, told him to walk. When a police cruiser eventu-ally stopped, Paul was told through a loudspeaker to freeze. He explained his story to the highway patrolman, who was sitting alone inside the car. The patrolman put him in the back and drove him to an on-ramp, where he was ordered to stay on the cement. "If you move, I'll put you in jail," the patrolman said. Paul later watched the same cruiser drop two other hitchhikers on the opposite on-ramp. When the pair moved to a better position, the cruiser appeared from nowhere and took them away. Paul gave up on American drivers when one asked him if he carried a baseball bat, knife or gun. "You should," the driver said.

He ended up in Fort St. John, on the Alaska Highway in northern B.C., with a wife and kids. After nine years, the marriage fell apart. His wife would not let him go to college, where he wanted to study to become a home care worker. His heavy drinking didn't help. Moving south for a better climate, he enrolled in Kamloops' University College of the Cariboo, got a certificate in home care nursing and promptly discovered there were no jobs available. He remarried and settled outside Kamloops on a one-acre spread where he kept a chicken, four rabbits and a grove of apricot and peach trees. The area's forty-degree summer days were not nearly as oppressive as Fort St. John's winter nights.

Here, I sensed, was where his story was about to get to the point of our shared journey. Knowing Paul had some personal troubles, a friend invited him one day to the Church of Jesus Christ of Latter-day Saints. As a non-practising Catholic, he felt at ease with the informal services and active discussions about belief. "I felt at home," he said, looking at me in the rear-view mirror. "It's a lot less rigid, I find, than other churches."

"And it's not a cult," the boy beside me said.

The landscape had changed abruptly, from the desert valleys around Kamloops to forests and rolling green hills that were ideal for big cattle farms.

"Now I feel I'm not alone," Paul went on. "I do have people I can talk to. I can go and pray."

He and his second wife attended church together and made time for a night out alone at least once a week as suggested by the Mormons. Family, I noticed, was at the core of almost everything Paul mentioned. He considered everyone to be a brother or a sister.

"I also learned we all have to conquer the wrongs in the world by conquering the wrongs in ourselves," he said.

"Our church doesn't believe in strong fluids like coffee or body piercing," the younger boy said, for no apparent reason, though I feared he had a sixth sense because I was yearning for a coffee.

I looked in the box of groceries next to me. It was their lunch: a loaf of bread and several cans of Safeway cola, which I guess did not get the "strong fluid" rating.

The boy beside me was twelve. Paul's son in the front seat, from his first marriage, was thirteen. They both smelled like they hadn't bathed in days, which was becoming a bit of an issue for me as Paul would not roll down the windows, even though the car was getting plenty hot as the morning wore on.

I asked Paul what he did for a living, since home care hadn't worked out. He said he had found work as a chimney sweep in Kamloops, earning $9 an hour. I wasn't aware that chimney sweeps still existed. Neither was the younger boy.

"Like in *Mary Poppins*?" he asked Paul in a voice of genuine curiosity. It was that magical moment when, as a child, you discover what a friend's father or mother does for a living, and you think it's cool. Paul said there was nothing cool about $9 an hour. He wasn't able to make ends meet and planned to go out on his own in the fall. Either that or he would have to move again, probably to Alberta.

The boy beside me was no longer interested in stories of employment and began whittling a stick with a knife that he had pulled out of a bag.

At Vernon, the highway merged with another and took on the feel of an urban route, with malls, drive-throughs and all the big hotel chains. The road then climbed over a hill and there before us was Lake Okanagan, aqua blue and sparkling in the summer sun, as disjointed from the shoreline, with its parched yellow grass running up either side, as the hillside swimming pools had been in Kamloops.

After a long journey through the mountains, I felt like I had burst into a Shangri-La of recreation. The shore was lined with docks and boats, and in the middle a lone water skier was carving his way up the long, narrow lake, as if he could go on forever. Which was almost possible. He would have to stop after a hundred kilometres, unless Ogopogo, Lake Okanagan's fabled creature of the deep, got him first.

Paul continued to talk about his greatest concern: the family. I'm not sure what had put him onto the subject. Perhaps it was a Holiday Inn billboard offering a family discount. "The breakup of the family: that's what is hurting North America," he said. "If we could find ways in Canada to make the family a stronger unit, Canada would be a strong country. There would be no corruption. The family unit is the basis of our society. People are looking instead at cars or houses. They're individuals within a family unit. There's too much emphasis on individual achievement, from schools right on through. There's too much emphasis on 'It's okay to have a broken-up family.' There's too much support for broken-up families, without any support to help them get back together as a family."

Neither boy appeared to be listening any more, their eyes and minds fixed on the summer weekend unfolding outside. I told Paul that just about everything we were passing on the road was geared toward families. Hotels were built around indoor waterslides and games rooms. Every other restaurant advertised that kids ate for free. Every big trailer park I had passed had incorporated kids as a major part of its appeal, along with parking spaces for RVs. These were not what Paul had in mind, but when I reminded him of the Holiday Inn deal, the boy beside me snapped into the conversation. He had once stayed in a Holiday Inn with his mother. "It was awesome," he said. "I told her I never wanted to leave."

Paul restated his point with a reference to ads promoting condoms as a way of fighting AIDS—ads that he thought promoted promiscuity. It sounded like the subject of this week's discussion group at church. "Why is it wrong to say abstinence is possible?" Paul asked. I don't think he expected me to answer. "Some of the world's best athletes have stayed away from sex until they were thirty. It's possible to stay away from sex until you are married."

He went back to the importance of marriage, not for sex but for spiritual support. Nothing, he said, could be more important, yet nothing in our society got shorter shrift. "We have a lot of freedom and liberty to try things to see if they make you happy," he said. "It turns out marriage is one of those things they try out for happiness. For me, I thought I needed to get married to someone who was attractive. I realized later friendship was more important as a basis for marriage. Attraction is not enough. My first marriage, I did it because I thought it would bring me happiness. I needed it. What I needed was to grow up."

Paul was so worked up that neither of us noticed we had reached Kelowna. A sign for the city said "Welcome to the Sweet Life." We followed Highway 97 through the centre of the city, past its lively bars and waterfront, where crowds of young people were gathered around the marina and boardwalk. Paul continued on a bridge over Lake Okanagan to the Westbank First Nation, an Indian reserve, and let me off at the first turn. The orchard where he and the boys were heading was down a side road.

Before I got out, Paul offered me his copy of *The Book of Mormon*. He said they were free at his church, where he could get plenty more. I would have accepted the gift but had no spare room in my pack, now that I was back in summer clothes. Nor did I want the extra weight. Paul understood. He took my card and said he would mail me a copy.

As I watched the Chevy follow a side road away from the highway, I felt some admiration for Paul and his boys. Back in Kamloops, they had struck me as white trash, derelicts with little to show for what they had been given. Yet they seemed to hold stronger beliefs than most of the people I had met. Even the boys, who were not old enough to drive, talked independently about Jesus and their church. They reminded me of Corey, the tree planter, who in his own way was equally spiritual. All those days alone in the forest, and those months wandering through very foreign lands, had done him good, for he had a more balanced view of life than people I had met who were twice his age.

It was hardly surprising that I had come across such people in the B.C. interior, where the quest for spirituality had always been strong. This was the one part of Canada where you could find Mormons, Doukhobors, Tibetan Buddhists, Sikhs, Baptists and nudists, all in growing numbers. The interior's splendour, with gentle mountains and cascading rivers, had something to do with the cerebral air. So did the region's isolation from North America's manic urban culture. But there was something more. Out here, on the outer islands of North America's sea, the entire Okanagan seemed unhinged from earthly concerns—that is, if you ignored Saturday morning traffic.

Although there was no Wal-Mart, I figured the spot where Paul had dropped me was beyond the city limits. There was little except orchards and scrub to be seen, aside from a series of subdivisions sprouting from a hilltop in the distance. But then I followed the road over the hill, frustrated at not getting a ride for half an hour, and saw that there was a lot more city ahead. Like all valley towns, Kelowna kept extending in two directions because it had nowhere else to grow. The Westbank reserve had been transformed as a suburb, with strip malls, drive-throughs and trailer parks. I kept walking, only to find that over each hill and around each turn—and the Okanagan is nothing but a series of hills and turns—there was always another intersection and more development. With so many distractions it was impossible to get a driver's attention, so I kept walking. And for two kilometres, the suburban sprawl continued, with auto-body shops, tire stores and, finally, a Wal-Mart. The only development beyond it was an RV sales centre.

I was just past the Wal-Mart when a car with Washington plates and a Hertz bumper sticker pulled over. I was shocked. This was the first American to pick me up, I thought nervously, remembering Paul's hitchhiking experiences in the States. And then I heard the driver's voice. He was all Alberta.

Don was returning to Penticton from a quick Kelowna shopping trip. He was on vacation, from a small town outside Calgary, but had come here through the United States, where he had met up with an Australian friend in Tacoma, Washington, rented the Hertz and driven to the Okanagan for the Canadian triathlon, second biggest in the world after the Ironman event in Hawaii. Back in southern Alberta, Don ran a couple of water-pipe businesses, which were thriving. He spent a good portion of the drive to Penticton raving about the province's booming economy and how its Conservative premier, Ralph Klein—ha, ha, ha—was to blame. As we passed through Peachland and Summerland, I pointed out that this area was an even greater bastion of conservatism: the home of Stockwell Day and breeding ground for the Canadian Alliance. "Isn't it great?" Don said, beaming.

I was grateful for the ride because I could have still been walking. Easily. The lower Okanagan was one long stretch of intertwining country and city. Where there weren't dense orchards and vegetable fields, there were strip malls and "adult communities" that drew retirees from across Canada. Every square inch above the waterline seemed to be accounted for. Even the white bluffs at the southern end of the lake, outside Penticton, had been scraped away to make room for a subdivision.

Don dropped me in the middle of Penticton, near Main Street, where there were more astonishing bodies, male and female, than I could have imagined. The triathlon had attracted fourteen hundred athletes to a city with a few hundred hotel rooms. As I walked around the small city on a glorious summer's day, it was hard not to feel that this was the capital of fun, with an abundance of parks and a bike path along the river that runs through town. In the only bookstore on Main Street, there was an entire section near the front devoted to rock rappelling, and nothing on Canadian politics.

The contrast with the traditional West—rural Saskatchewan, for example—was startling. Penticton's population had grown to thirty-one thousand from thirteen thousand in 1975, with its wealth appearing to grow faster still. There were probably more fine cars per capita than anywhere else I had been. At one intersection where I stood, a few BMWs, several convertibles, an IROC-Z and a new banana yellow Beetle rolled by in the course of one light change. But the town was not driven by youth, despite all the tanned abs on display. Its growth had come largely from the aging—not the sort of elderly folk you'd find in the Dauphin retirement home, but boomers taking an early retirement, to slow down in a place where they could, at various times of the year, golf, ski and sail. They were the people in search of Pen Tak Tin, the original Salish name for "place to stay forever." They were also the people motivated by fear—fear of aging and dying, fear of change, fear of being in a place where the eighteenth hole was not always the same. They were the new conservatives.

Despite their demand for change in Canadian politics, these were the people who least wanted change in their lives. Comfortable as can be, they wanted the predictable, and Penticton provided just that. The town advertised that it had six hundred hours of sunlight every summer—ten hours a day on average, which, according to just about every brochure I found, was more than Honolulu got at this time of year. I could only imagine what the people of darkened Labrador Straits would think.

If Penticton was staid, though, it was not from isolation. This outer island had plenty of bridges. Down at the waterfront, there were flags for every province in Canada, Quebec included. I took note of this because you would be hard-pressed to find a B.C. flag anywhere in Quebec. As I tried to make my way out of town on foot, I found local residents to be exceedingly courteous, too. They offered the most detailed directions with more politeness and genuine concern than I had met elsewhere in Canada. These were the sort of traits I had come to expect from Americans. But then I followed a riverside footpath to the highway and assumed my role again as hitchhiker. Immediately, every driver was hostile. As big SUVs and deluxe pickup trucks roared past, several men gave me the finger and mouthed words that appeared to be neither polite nor concerned. It was my first encounter in Canada with mass road rage toward a single hitchhiker. I remembered only once before experiencing such a deluge of resentment, and that was many years ago on an interstate in Oregon.

Despite waves of curses and foul gestures, I got a ride out of Penticton within an hour, just when I was beginning to think I might be there for a week. The driver tried to explain that people around here had trouble with outsiders, partly because there were so many of them. Phil Knox looked like one of the boomers in town, an *arriviste,* perhaps even a contestant in the triathlon. He drove a red Nissan Pathfinder and was dressed like an athlete heading home from a game, in shorts and a T-shirt that hung loosely from his sweat-sprinkled muscles. He was a newcomer, for sure.

From Quebec originally, he quickly let me know that he was also a member of that other tribe of the B.C. interior: the born-again Christian. Phil was a single father, living in Penticton with his kids and working on a big pipeline project south of here, which was where he was headed. He seemed to be doing well by the society around him. He also didn't like it. Everything, to Phil, was wrong. There was economic decline and rampant immorality and a Catholic prime minister who voted for abortion and presidents who had messed around with drugs and young women. "If you look at the history of empires and giant nations, they're all close to God and then lose their way," he said. "I believe in God. I believe God leaves us to our own devices. Look at what happened in the Roman Empire, in Babylon."

His short hair and clean-cut nature gave him the look of an evangelical preacher. Or an Alliance candidate. Either way, he pointed to forest fires raging in the United States and fighting in the Middle East as further evidence that "some strange things are going on." Strange indeed. Before I could get a word in, he was quoting from the Books of Daniel and Revelation. "Every prediction in the Bible has come true," he said firmly.

The road was following a spectacular course around Skaha Lake, part of the water system that stretches from Lake Okanagan down to the Columbia River. On one side, the lake was flanked by a hundred-metre-high cliff. On the other, the neat symmetry of apple orchards ran, patch-like, up the slope, their lines interrupted only by the jerking spray of sprinklers that looked like they were set to run through the night.

Phil loved it here, for the intriguing beauty of deserts and orchards that co-existed so easily. He still couldn't figure out why the Okanagan had not become another Silicon Valley. The climate was ideal for any company dealing with computers and communications, and who would not want to live here, minutes from warm water in summer and powder snow in winter?

He was raised in an altogether different Canadian experience, as a Catholic in Montreal. It didn't take long to grow disenchanted with the formalities of the Church. Confession was absurd when he was free to repeat his sins and again beg forgiveness. He went on to become a national-level wrestler and rugby player, which explained his athletic appearance. But he also fell into drinking and drugs. It was only after a divorce, which gave him custody of his children, that he sought something more lasting, something more solid than himself. He tried Buddhism and some New Age beliefs but gravitated back to Christianity, in its evangelical form. He gave up drinking and handed over his soul. "If you are obedient," he said, "you won't have to go through as much abuse in life."

Phil dropped me in Oliver, an orchard centre about half an hour north of the Washington border. There were rows of apple trees in the middle of town, several fruit stands for passing motorists and a Kingdom Hall. The late afternoon was eerily quiet, the only sound being the jit-jitting of irrigation sprinklers. I walked south a hundred metres to the edge of Oliver, where the landscape turned to small hills and rolled to the horizon with orchards and vineyards. Everywhere the grass, even under drooping apple trees, was as green as a well-kept fairway in Georgia. The air was also dry, like a desert, a good indication that the parched bowl of Osoyoos could not be far away.

——— ——— ———

I was out of Oliver in about as much time as it took me to walk from the centre of town to its edge. And it was just as well. The driver, a young man named Vern in a Suzuki Jeep, was all the proof I needed that the Okanagan was not a theocratic state. As soon as Vern was back on the road and had shifted into high gear, he took a swig from a beer bottle that was resting between his legs. He said he always drank on the way to work. It kept his mind loose on the overnight shift as a security guard at Phil's pipeline project.

I guess I was lucky. Vern had passed me once and doubled back after looking at me in the rear-view mirror and deciding I did not pose a threat. More to the point, he said, I didn't look like an Indian. The Okanagan band was entangled in a series of land disputes running up and down the valley, from Westbank, where they wanted more control over the land leased to trailer parks, to the Penticton airport, which they claimed as theirs, to the Apex ski resort, which they had blocked off the previous winter as part of another land claim. When it came to native rights, the Okanagan was a hotbed of dispute.

We weren't around the next bend and Vern was letting me know his true thoughts about the native question. He believed the solution was to put the Indians in their place. "One day, me and the boys are going to go down there with Uzis and finish the job," he said bluntly.

When he failed to see any reaction on my face, he tried a joke: "Why don't Indians take Aspirin?" he asked.

I shrugged.

"'Cause they're white and they work."

Still not getting much of a response, he switched gears to hitch-hiking. Once when he was hitching around here, he ended up with a driver who insisted on stopping to buy a six-pack for himself and Vern. Back on the road, Vern realized the driver was drunk when, passing a semi on a curve, they saw another truck coming straight at them. Both trucks quickly swerved to the side, away from each other, allowing the car miraculously to squeeze through.

"My heart was up here," Vern said, raising his open hand to his neck. He laughed. "I got out of that car real fast!"

Vern was driving fast enough that we were in Osoyoos in about ten minutes. He dropped me by the bridge across Lake Osoyoos, just north of the border, where a sign warned boaters not to drift inadvertently into U.S. territory. I could not remember a place in Canada so beautiful. The setting sun left a glow on the desert hills that tumbled down to the edge of the clear, warm lake. The water was so placid that it carried the reflection of rocky slopes and spots of cactus, until a boat pulling a tube full of children raced over it.

Although Osoyoos had long been a quiet gem of retirement living, with an arid climate and golf courses priced in Canadian dollars, it had developed its courses enough to become a golfing destination for Americans. With tourism money pouring in, parts of the town had been redone in a Spanish motif—not an inappropriate design next to a pocket desert on the east bank of Lake Osoyoos, where rattlesnakes, painted turtles and coyotes can be found. The little Canadian desert is part of a topographical belt that stretches down to Mexico.

I watched families play on the lake, on their Jet Skis and in their boats, before strolling through a waterside park, where a family of ducks was bedding down for the night. I left the town's mundane main street to the end, after the sun was gone, following it to Osoyoos's only serious intersection, where one highway led to the United States and the other to Vancouver. Even in darkness, on a Monday night, trucks were rumbling south to the vast American market. In the morning, I would be going the other way, on the final leg of my journey—over the mountains behind Osoyoos, along the bank of the Fraser and out to Vancouver Island for one last run, to the sea.

The rain had been coming down for several hours when I set out for Highway 3, and the wind was whipping with such ferocity that a huge Canadian flag at the Husky truck stop, across from my motel, sounded like it was going to rip. Wisps of cloud hung so low over the desert mountains that the lake and hardscrabble hills were not visible from any distance. With one look at the wet road leading out to the Fraser Valley, I decided to head for the truck stop and breakfast. The parking lot full of semis suggested the pros were going to sit it out too.

Hoping the storm would pass, I tried to drag out breakfast for as long as I could, reading every newspaper the restaurant offered and drinking enough coffee to know I would regret it should I be wedged into the back seat of another hatchback for two hours. I returned to the roadside when rain gave way to drizzle and was exposed just long enough to be soaked through two layers of clothes. Miraculously, a tiny pickup truck pulled over, although I'm not sure the driver had a choice. Halfway up the hill behind Osoyoos, where I had walked in hopes of getting above the rain, his old truck had slowed to such a crawl that he could not escape the guilt of my long gaze.

The driver was a small man, bald except for some long strands flowing down the back of his neck, which, as he explained, made his journey odder than mine. Having borrowed the pickup truck from a friend in Rossland, nearly three hours east of here, he was on his way to Vancouver for a haircut. He made the trip twice a year because his barber in the city's Chinatown was the only one he trusted with the remaining strands. It also gave him a chance to pick blackberries, usually on the way home.

The driver, Michel Germain, said he picked up hitchhikers whenever he could, because he liked to rebuild the karma that every long-distance hitchhiker understands. He had made it around the continent a few times by thumb and never knew when he might have to resort to the roadside again. The last time Michel picked up a journalist, he said, it was a writer who claimed to be from *Cosmopolitan* magazine, on the most unlikely of assignments. He had been commissioned to travel to five countries—Japan, Turkey, India, China and Canada—to find a virgin in each one and have intercourse with her, without paying for it. Michel still believed he was on the level. That was part of the karma, he said, to never doubt the person who gave you a ride or the one who accepted one from you.

Michel was a chef from France, who still carried traces of his native accent, although over the past twenty-five years he had drifted to almost every part of Canada and worked in many of the country's top restaurants. Fed up with the mainstream, he settled in Rossland, where he lived in a cabin, gardened and did odd jobs for cash. The previous year, his net income was $1,747, which he said was all he required. "With a big garden, peace comes to you."

Highway 3 climbed over the Okanagan Highlands and into a new climatic zone, where more desert valleys and vineyards were visible all the way to Keremeos, the next town. The rain was well behind us. As the pickup rolled down the other side of the highlands, gaining enough speed to rattle my door off its hook, Michel turned his mind to the next valley, which was full of Quebec fruit pickers, the hardest workers in the B.C. interior, he said. Over the years, the migrants had given the valley a distinct culture, with its own patois, nightlife and food. The same was true all along southern B.C., from the Fraser Valley to the Kootenays, Michel said. Each valley had its own identity and eccentricities, much like the districts he remembered back in the French countryside. They were like cantons, really. But that was changing, for the worse, as big companies took over local industries, as new technology weeded out the burst of local ingenuity and as people everywhere became less rooted to ideas of community.

Around Rossland, where Michel lived, the local tradition of picking was gone, with the work passing to the hands of seasonal migrants. Up the road in Trail, where a huge smelter had drawn Italian workers since the nineteenth century, the image of a Little Italy withered long ago. It was just another blue-collar town. In Castlegar, hometown to Scott the reformed coke addict, the berry farms and cottage jam shops were now centrally owned. Even Castlegar's infamous Doukhobors, the Christian pacifists exiled to Canada from Russia in 1899 with the help of Leo Tolstoy, had faded into the bucolic landscape. Certainly, no one talked any more about Doukhobors running around naked, as they did decades earlier.

We continued along the Upper Similkameen River for a while before the road climbed up through the clouds and then dropped down through thicker and thicker forests. Mining towns began to pop up with regularity, while the Okanagan's pastoral calm, and its horti-culture, faded behind us. We were back in blue-collar B.C.

Michel said that after a quarter-century in Canada, he still found the country's dichotomies hard to understand. Having grown up in Burgundy, where he apprenticed as a chef, he moved to Montreal in 1975, at the age of twenty-two, because he was told it was the land of opportunity. Once here, he found the French-English divide easy to appreciate. Artisans in one valley and coal miners in the next became more of a challenge to his ideas of nationhood. He still could not understand why such a masculine country, defined by woods and water and those who toiled in nature, could throw up such feminine writers as Margaret Atwood, Michael Ondaatje and Rohinton Mistry. Relationships. Feelings. Humanity without nature. It was like Victorian England.

I pointed out the obvious, that Ondaatje and Mistry were immi-grants, and the more contentious idea that Canada had moved beyond Farley Mowat. We had become a much more human place—perhaps one with a feminine side, if he wanted to put it that way. Michel disagreed. He too was an immigrant and had worked in one of the more emotional industries: the kitchen. He believed

Canada was drowning in the vanities of urban life, having surrendered much of what had made this nation unique. Those berry farms in Castlegar, for instance. It was why he had quit the chef's life and retreated to a cabin, to be human as Canadians are human.

"The West is more the kind of place I wanted to be," he said. "The link with nature—two or three bears in my yard, and mountains and more mountains, as far as you can see. The city, everyone is racing, it's like a drug. Well, maybe nature is a drug, but it's a good drug. It's like marijuana, when the city is on LSD."

At Princeton, the highway forked, with one branch heading north through mining country and the other cutting south through the sixty-six thousand hectares of Manning Provincial Park. It was like the continental divide of B.C. society, with one side exploiting nature and the other side enjoying it. Several young hitchhikers were on the road, going east, probably for fruit-picking jobs in the Okanagan. One young couple had a puppy with them. Michel was always picking up these types on his way home from Vancouver, usually runaways and itinerants who liked to lap up the city's party scene until their welfare money ran out.

I pointed to a logging yard, the first I had seen since Kamloops. "It's a scary town," Michel said of Princeton. "When you go inside, you'll see. A lot of inbred people. It's like that place in northern Ontario. What's it called? Wawa?"

I shocked Michel with my Wawa story. He had been hitching for more than two decades in Canada and had never heard of anyone getting out of Wawa in one day. Sixty seconds—he could not believe it.

"America, it's the craziest place I've ever been," he said of his own experiences on the road. "Maybe China is second."

It's true, the lunacy of hitchhiking in America. I once made it down the West Coast to San Francisco and vowed never to do it again. The guy with a shotgun in the front seat did it for me. He kept saying, "You should never go anywhere without your gun," and then insisted on giving me a tour of his county. At least I got to see several large marijuana farms disguised as horticulture operations.

Michel was once picked up in Corning, New York, by a driver who was drinking beers at the wheel. When another car cut them off, Michel's driver gave chase, undeterred by the man who kept throwing beer cans at them. Michel's driver pulled out a gun from under the front seat and pointed it over Michel at the other car. Michel asked to get out. He didn't care that they were in the middle of nowhere.

His next ride was more welcoming. A yuppie couple headed to the Midwest promised to get him halfway to California. But then, for no apparent reason, they stopped the car in the middle of the night and told Michel to get out. He had to sleep in a ditch. Eventually, he reached California, only to discover most of his rides were with couples who wanted someone to mediate their quarrels or at the very least observe them. In one car after another, a couple would sit in the front seat and argue about something domestic, money usually, as Michel watched silently from the back.

We came over another hill to a wide view of Manning Park, with its vast horizon of towering cedars that looked like they ran to the top of every mountain. The road carried on like this for several kilometres and then dropped so fast on its way down to the Fraser Valley that my ears popped. As the highway reached a plateau, four SUVs raced by us, their drivers looking eager to get somewhere. "All right, there they go. The rat race has begun," Michel said in a mocking tone. "Who's going to win? Who's going to get to the city first?"

We joined the Trans-Canada at Hope and were soon in another canton, the one of "adult living" neighbourhoods, shopping centres and rows of billboards that told us we were back in consumer-land. We were not yet in Greater Vancouver, and Michel was beginning to feel it draining him. At a service station where we stopped for gas, everyone's face was long. No one said hello. It was worse on the highway, where Michel pointed to grief-stricken looks in just about every car, as if we were in the middle of a long funeral procession.

The Trans-Canada remained divided, with an embankment of trees on each side, right to the edge of Vancouver. The first glimpse

I caught of its skyline, it was rising through the mist like a Pacific Oz, with gleaming office towers backed by mountains and the lush rain forest of Stanley Park. Once we found an off-ramp, my eyes turned to something much closer at hand: a man, dishevelled and gaunt, standing on the roadside. He was facing traffic, holding a sign that read, "Homeless. No Welfare. No Work." Michel shook his head in dismay.

⸺ ⸺ ⸺

As we entered Vancouver's East Side, Michel didn't know where to drop me, and I had no idea where I was. Just to be sure, he said he would take me to his friend's house, where I could get directions downtown. I was catching on. It was part of his karma.

When we reached the house, his friend was around back in his organic garden, putting the last touches on an organic sleeping hut made of clay, stone and straw. It wasn't clear exactly what he was growing next to the hut, but his Hemp Growers' Association T-shirt suggested one possibility. He gave me directions just the same. With any luck, I'd make it downtown in time to meet a friend for dinner, before heading off in the morning for Vancouver Island and the end of the road.

From the East Side, the bus that Michel's friend recommended drove past some unimpressive displays of cultural diversity—a Chinese auto-body shop, and the derelict Raja Cinema, which was showing a Hindi film—and wound its way down to the Lower East Side, the worst of Canada's skid rows. A tiny park known as Vancouver's crack haven was packed on a Tuesday afternoon with teenagers who looked like the ones hitchhiking at Princeton. For the next couple of blocks, every store and pawnshop seemed to have window grates. Either that or they were boarded up.

Then, over a small ridge and past the Salvation Army, everything changed. The heart of Vancouver felt like the most progressive, upbeat place I had been since, well, Montreal. Everything pointed outward. Rows of new office towers and condos were coated with glass, their large windows opening to views of mountains and beaches. Even on Granville Street a panhandler carried a sign reading "Need $$$ for pot." Vancouver had long since outgrown the days when it was a bizarre cross between Lotusland and the Klondike, when you were either a Kitsilano hippie or a Shaughnessy timber baron. A couple of decades of intense immigration and an influx of new industries, most notably filmmaking, had transformed the city. And yet its most striking characteristic, amidst all this beauty and opportunity, was crankiness.

Touted in the nineties as a new capital for the Pacific, a city that could rival Singapore, Hong Kong and San Francisco, Vancouver had hit a rough patch, as had its province. Despite its natural wealth, B.C. was growing poorer, hit by a long and hard recession in mining, fishing and logging, its three staples. The province's income was now below the national average, which was one reason more people were leaving than coming in—11,300 more in 1999. I had heard that one place in Vancouver embodied this decline more than any other and decided I had to see it before moving on. Besides, it was the end of summer. The Pacific National Exhibition was as natural a destination as an orchard in autumn.

The PNE was in its last great days at Hastings Park, the site where for more than ninety years it had been the great exhibition grounds for the Canadian West. This was where the rotary-dial telephone was introduced to Vancouver, and where the Beatles played, and where in 1954, at the British Empire Games, Roger Bannister ran the Miracle Mile. Although the exhibition had fallen on tawdry times, those were the days when it was a symbol of the greatest age Canada had known, the decades between the Second World War and the dawn of cable television. It was a time when we were on top of the world and knew how to share that feeling. At country fairs and big-city exhibitions, we knew how to come together as a nation.

There were the historic fairs, big and splashy, of course: Expo 67 in Montreal and Expo 86 in Vancouver. But far more important to our national identity were the humbler exhibition and county fair that allowed Canadian kids to do a victory lap for summer. On the eve of autumn, just before the arrival of new hockey sticks at Canadian Tire, these exhibitions were how a young nation marked its transition from one season to the next. And they were dying. The PNE was preparing to move to Surrey, in the suburbs, in one last desperate attempt at a revival. Its amusements had been crushed by the age of video games, its special shows had given way to pay-per-view and its original calling, as a marketplace, had been overrun by late-night television and the Internet. As if that were not enough, the PNE was also under attack by the Christian right.

Trouble started when the exhibition, desperate to attract young people, took a chance with its latest marketing campaign, relaunching its Playland carnival as "The Second Coming." The hottest new rides were called The Hellevator, Hell's Gate and The Revelation. Its big TV ad for the summer featured a turnstile clicking through at number 666.

Some local Christians were furious, saying they would not allow their faith to be mocked like this. A few weeks earlier, another John Stackhouse had appeared on the front page of the *Vancouver Sun*—its Saturday edition, no less—condemning the sacrilege and calling for a boycott. He spoke with authority: he was an evangelical and noted professor of theology at the University of British Columbia's Regent College. And there he was, dragging our common name into the biggest scandal running in Vancouver. How would Jews, he asked, feel about a ride named The Holocaust Horror? Or Muslims react to a roller coaster named Mohammed's Mania?

John raised a fair concern, and he was not alone in targeting the PNE. A local member of the Green Party had gone after the petting zoo for its treatment of animals, labelling it the Evil Petting Zoo. Now, you know when the evangelicals and environmentalists have a common enemy that it's either the most fun place you could ever imagine or it's on its last legs. Having found a place to stay down-town, I convinced my friend to cut dinner short and head to the PNE. Rod agreed. He too had followed the satanic scandal. Besides, the old fairgrounds were just down the street from his house, and I had offered to pay for a cab.

As soon as we stepped foot into the flames of Playland, we real-ized it was not the most fun place either of us could have imagined. The Revelation, with a ticket price of $19.95, was getting by. But no one was lining up for the $39.95 package of ride, video and T-shirt. Clearly, hell had its limits. Rod said that apart from the troubled Playland, there were only two other events to keep the exhibition going: Superdogs, the dog show that drew over 300,000 people a year, and Richard Humphreys's pig races. We opted for the pig race.

We found Richard Humphreys and his four little pigs near the entrance, on a horseshoe-shaped track where four times a day the farm animals exerted all the energy they could muster for the grand prize of one mini-donut. It was a futile and inhumane pursuit but as Humphreys told the large audience that had gathered, each of his racers would enjoy a long and well-fed retirement. For a pig in America, it sure beat the alternative.

An old-time carnie from Hot Springs, Arkansas, Humphreys was in firm control of the audience when we got there, ten minutes ahead of race time. He divided us into four cheering sections and assigned a pig to each one. And, he insisted in his deep southern drawl, no wagering.

"We're at a pig race, not a funeral!" he barked at the crowd before the starting gun went off.

Once the pigs were released, they covered the track in about ten seconds. The winner was Albert Einswine, nudging out Magnum P.I.G., Tammy Swinette and Hammy Faye Bacon.

After the race, Rod and I walked through the PNE's Marketplace, the one venue that showed most clearly why the age of exhibitions was near its end. Up and down the near-empty aisles were booths marketing items you might never live to see, or use, were it not for the magic of the annual fair. Where else would you find the Professional Spatula and Miracle Shammy? Or Longevity's Missing Link (one capsule equals ten glasses of pure orange juice)? Somehow I doubt I ever would have learned about buckwheat pillows were it not for an extremely knowledgeable salesman from the Great Canadian National Buckwheat Pillow company. Contrary to popular belief, he told me, buckwheat pillows were not a Canadian invention. The Chinese were using them in the fourteenth century.

Sadly, these dedicated and eager hawkers were not aware that the infomercial—the Frankenstein of cable television—had cornered the market on every dubious invention ever made.

"I'm feeling very, very alone," said a woman from Canadian Tire.

"There's not enough people here to fill a quorum," added a man who was giving out free samples of eyeglass cleaner.

Most of the fairgoers, we discovered, were outside, in the biggest lineup at the PNE. Young and old, they were filing through the main prize in the exhibition's annual ticket draw: a $750,000 dream home that came with property outside Vancouver. The crowd marvelled at the home theatre and a sunken bathtub in the middle of the master bedroom. As we left the fair, the viewing lineup was out the front door and around the corner, longer than anything we had seen at the Hellevator.

If the sun is out and sailboats are skimming along Georgia Strait, the ferry ride from North Vancouver to Nanaimo can be like a gentle, soothing withdrawal from urban Canada. There is something about the big city fading behind a ferry, appearing transitory in this world next to Grouse Mountain and Stanley Park. There is something, too, about the length of the trip that gives it a sense of journey, and about the approaching scenery of Vancouver Island, with mountains, open waters and forests, that tells you a different Canada awaits.

Not at Nanaimo, though. A former coal-mining centre, it was hoping to transmogrify. Its waterfront, away from the ferry docks, was lined with yacht basins, stylish new condos and fashionable pubs and bistros. Up the hill, the old coal town had been gentrified a degree further and renamed the Old City Quarter. But change was coming hard to the island and Nanaimo. There was not much old about its Old City Quarter. The brick sidewalks and stone arches were new additions and about as authentic as the menus at Dar Lebanon and Café Vinifera inside.

I hoped to get quickly beyond this Vancouver Island gateway, walking a couple of kilometres to a shopping mall that looked like it marked the western edge of town. With the Pacific now within easy reach, I was expecting this to be my last day on the road. But I didn't expect such competition. The roadside was already claimed by a couple of young people, with long hair and more beads than some islanders might care to see in their cars. This was not the land of ruffian hitchhikers any more, where the roadsides saw nothing but men looking for a free ride to their next job. This was rave country, where the roadsides saw nothing but teenaged kids looking for a free ride to their next party.

When I found a place of my own to thumb, a young woman walking up the road in search of a place to hitch stopped to chat. She was from Vancouver and hitched all the time on the island. I'd have no problem getting to the west coast, she insisted. That's where she was heading, hoping to make Tofino by nightfall for a beach party. She would have got there the previous night, she said, but was diverted by a rave in Vancouver. She then put her hand on my shoulder and wished me luck, her tie-dyed shirt and skirt wrap flapping in the wind as she walked away.

A few minutes later, a teenager named Joe stopped by. He too was going to Tofino and wondered if we should team up. He suggested it would be "symbiotic." I said it would be confusing—me in my khakis and Joe in his frayed jeans, beaded necklace and struggling beard. He agreed, having given me a closer look, and tried to catch up with the tie-dye girl, who had disappeared over a small ridge ahead on the road.

Soon after Joe headed off, an old Corsica with a licence plate reading TOURBUS pulled over, cutting across a lane of heavy afternoon traffic to reach the shoulder. The driver was a woman with short hair, a hardened face and forearms that looked as firm as iron pipes. I felt I was getting closer to the island.

We rounded a bend and passed Joe and the tie-dye girl, who were hitchhiking together and looked—what was his word?—symbiotic. I was more concerned with what lay ahead, though. There seemed to be no end to Nanaimo, sprawling as it was along an unending progression of intersections, each anchored by a McDonald's, Burger King or Boston Pizza.

The driver—a former arm-wrestling champion who had lost her job as a heavy-equipment operator after a highway accident in India damaged her back—dropped me at an intersection five kilometres up the Trans-Canada. It felt like I was still in Nanaimo. It looked identical to the place where the arm-wrestler had picked me up, as if, on some stunt, she had looped back and left me at my starting point. Then again, the intersection looked identical to one I had stood at in Saint-Hyacinthe. Only the mountains and tall firs in the distance reminded me of where I really was.

It took me another quick ride with an unemployed fisherman to get out of the city, a trip long enough to hear in detail how he lost all his government assistance by investing in a bird shop in the small town of Bowser, up the coast. Those who wanted birds or bird supplies just drove to Nanaimo, he cursed, to the Wal-Mart or Costco. But at least he got me to the open road and heading inland to Port Alberni, across the central mountains to the sea.

I was beginning to see what the tie-dye girl meant about the ease of hitching on the island when, within a few minutes, a van stopped. The two men in the front asked if I would mind sitting on the metal floor in the back. At least they offered a can of Bud to hold me over until Port Alberni.

I sat cross-legged on the floor, a beer in my hand, watching the island's beauty through the front window alternate between pristine and rugged. At Cameron Lake, the road turned dark as we passed through Cathedral Grove, a sanctuary of towering, ancient Douglas fir and red cedar that local natives consider sacred. Farther on, there were waterfalls, lakes, more thick rain forests and, in the distance, snow-capped peaks. Amazingly, Russ, the driver, warned me that after this great run of beauty we would hit his hometown, Port Alberni, "the second ugliest town in the world." The first, he said, had to be Cumberland, an old coal-mining centre about a hundred kilometres northwest of Nanaimo. "Actually," he corrected himself, "I was just in Cumberland and they've really improved the place. I guess that makes Alberni the ugliest town in the world."

Port Alberni was the centre of everything great and bad on Vancouver Island. Clear-cutting had gone on for generations around the town, and the harbour was still crowded with boats that had stripped the rivers and sea of their salmon. It also served as a launch pad for some of the best hiking trails and kayaking routes in western Canada. From the back of the van, I couldn't tell if the town was really that ugly, but from Russ's description it didn't seem eager to change. Port Alberni's two big mills were still running day and night. I could see that much, from their plumes of smoke. The fancy four-by-fours in front of us suggested the locals weren't hurting, either. I was relieved. After Nanaimo, I had begun to worry no one on the island worked. Russ said many of the townspeople were making six-figure incomes. His own brother, who had a job in one of the mills, had paid off the mortgage on his $250,000 house and had a pickup and a boat to boot. But most people knew that the forests, just like the fish, weren't going to last, no matter how much they heard about sustainable forestry.

"There's a lot of rich people here and a lot of poor people here," Russ said, "but not a lot of smart people."

The two men offered to take me to the western edge of town, but first insisted that I see Port Alberni's newest tourist attraction. It was a rusted Chinese refugee boat that had been seized by the Canadian coast guard and towed here, while its passengers were taken to a detention centre. To get to it, we drove past a row of wharfside restaurants and on to the town's main pier, where the West Coast's great salmon fleets once docked. The rusting boat looked like a mothballed fishing vessel. Russ suspected many more were on their way, enough that Port Alberni, he said only half-jokingly, might have found itself a new growth industry.

——— ——— ———

It was a short hop to Sproat Lake, the last hamlet before the coast, which I made with the help of a retired man who was heading home from Port Alberni. But I was no longer convinced I would reach the Pacific tonight, not as I stood alone on the roadside, watching the day's light fade on the placid lake as a gentle chorus of crickets and bullfrogs filled the early evening air. After nine thousand kilometres on the road, the last ride, if indeed my next one did get me to Tofino, was beginning to look like the hardest.

A couple of cars raced by, coming around a curve without enough time to slow down for a hitchhiker. And then long minutes of emptiness. I had no choice but to wait: there was no traffic heading back to Port Alberni and no place other than the ditch to stay. Another car sped by, then ten more minutes of nothingness before a small car emerged, this time at a safe enough speed to stop. Two young men in the front were on their way home to Ucluelet, a fishing town at the opposite end of the coastal road to Tofino. If I took the ride, I wouldn't finish the journey tonight, but I wouldn't be stuck in Sproat Lake, either.

Aaron Mundy had just picked up a trunkful of flatbread for his family's restaurant in Ucluelet, and that was about all he wanted to say. He and his friend Willie had a Vancouver rock station playing at such a decibel that I couldn't hear them anyway, even if they had been talking. I sat back and watched. The road followed Sproat Lake as it narrowed and became a sliver between two mountains, one of which we climbed to the Sutton Pass. At 750 feet, the pass lifted us over the island's great hump and placed us on a chute of tight curves racing down to Kennedy Lake and on to the sea. At first glance, I thought the lake, vast and swirling with whitecaps, was the sea, but Aaron corrected me. He turned down the music and told me about the land and water. It was, he said, his people's land and water. Aaron and Willie were members of the tribal council of the Nuu-Chah-Nulth, who for all intents and purposes had lived in this area forever.

The road skirted around Kennedy Lake and dipped back into a stand of firs, their branches twisted and bent by a lifetime of winds whipping off the water. We continued through the forest as if we were floating through clouds, without a bend to contest or a trace of humanity to consider. We had not passed another car in either direction since Sproat Lake. In fact, the only evidence of human life, apart from the road, was a sign left by the old Vancouver company MacMillan Bloedel, which had been one of the many household names to be swallowed by corporate America in the 1990s. "Replanted, 1953," it said.

Just before the Pacific, Highway 4 reached a T-junction. To the north, through Pacific Rim National Park, lay Tofino and the glories of Clayoquot Sound. To the south sat Ucluelet and its gateway to the West Coast Trail. Aaron's and Willie's families lived on a reserve, across an inlet from Ucluelet. Such geographic divisions are common between aboriginals and non-aboriginals across Canada, but Aaron said in Ucluelet they stopped at that. He and Willie grew up with the town kids. They went to school and played hockey with the town kids. They still went to raves on Big Beach with the town kids. They'd spend the night there, drinking Lucky beer and surfing in the moonlight, Aaron said fondly. I asked him why there was so little tension. It was unlike almost every other place I had been to in Canada. His reply struck me, for its simplicity and depth: "We all know each other, I guess."

The boys dropped me at their restaurant and pointed to a motel where I could stay. Any hope of this being my last day on the road had faded with the setting sun.

The next morning, sure that it would be my last day on the road, I walked through Ucluelet—a town not big enough to support an

independent post office but tough enough to keep a liquor store—
and headed to Big Beach for my first glimpse of an ocean since I was
in Newfoundland. From a back street of bungalows, the path to the
ocean led through a thick forest that dripped with moisture and was
filled with the screeching life of who knows how many birds. The
beachside forest had grown dense enough that in some places there
was so little daylight on the floor that it felt more like evening than
morning. In other spots, bursts of sunlight broke through the upper
branches, only to be blocked by the lower layers. There was no direct
route to the forest floor.

The trail to Big Beach seemed to run for miles, dwarfed as it was
by trees. But finally, through a small gap between the great cedars, I
spotted a splash of blue. The Pacific was calm, almost tranquil, compared to Kennedy Lake, as small swells broke into waves at the low-tide
mark, crashing against a final wall of rock and beach. I sat on a
bench carved from a huge log, in the shade of trees that looked like
they could reach the sky. Behind me, the sun had cleared the island's
central mountains and was shining directly on the sea. In front of
me, on a dirt path leading to the beach, an enormous snail, perhaps
four inches long, began crawling through its day. This was Canada,
great and small, reaching up and down and to the horizon, with no
sense of boundary and no limit to speed. A giant snail next to a giant
tree, dwarfed by a giant mountain, under a giant sun.

——— ——— ———

My ninety-seventh and final ride began back at the T-junction,
with two men who were headed to Tofino for work. They drove a
van and offered me a seat in the back, on the floor. This time, there
was no Bud.

Roy Hines and Dave Pederson ran their own engineering company, which serviced fish farms. It was turning out to be a good
business and said as much about B.C. as anything I had encountered. With the collapse of the commercial fishery, there were now
twenty-five salmon farms in the Tofino area, and plans for more.

"There's no way around it, you have to feed the world," Ray said, quite proudly.

"It's bigger than the movie industry," added Dave, referring to Vancouver's big job creator that had generated so much media attention.

It was also politically explosive. Aquaculture promised to maintain the West Coast's fish production through technologically sophisticated farms that could float in the calm sounds of Vancouver Island, each breeding thousands of fish a year. But to the eco-warriors of the West Coast, it was as evil to the ocean as pesticide was to land, polluting the sounds and inlets of Vancouver Island with salmon waste, allowing alien species to escape into the local waters and ravaging delicate ecosystems under the sea. David Suzuki, the Nuu-Chah-Nulth Indians, Greenpeace, Friends of Clayoquot—the forces against fish farming were formidable.

So were the proponents. The company Roy and Dave were going to see in Tofino was owned by a Norwegian conglomerate that operated salmon farms in every corner of the planet, from the Baltic Sea to Chile and New Zealand. The fate of Clayoquot Sound, I thought, was probably as significant to head office as Rhodesia was to the British Empire. But Roy felt quite the opposite. The Norwegians, world leaders in farming salmon, had brought with them capital and technology, from feeding practices to huge pens that floated in the Sound, at a time when both the Canadian government and local investors seemed too willing to write off the fishing industry. The foreign company had enabled a small Vancouver Island operation to become internationally competitive and had everyone in the business talking about expansion.

I was not in a position to disagree. Sitting in the back, on floorboards, I was being thrown left and right, like a bucket of fish, with every twist in the road. During the straightaways, I did my best to catch a glimpse of the stunning forests and beaches that rolled by, but then it was back to turbulence. Roy continued to talk about his company, which had been saved during the lean years by aqua-culture. Instead of facing collapse, he was now working beyond capacity on the West Coast and had opened an operation on the East Coast.

"There hasn't been such a fast-growing industry like this in years," said Dave.

"It's a great industry," Roy added from the driver's seat.

The two middle-aged men talked that way, picking up on each other's sentences, like a couple who had been married long enough to know the other's thoughts.

Roy was starting to talk about the dangers of the pendulum swinging against his industry—squandered jobs, lost investment— when we reached the outskirts of Tofino. New subdivisions appeared to be going in where chunks of forest had been cleared. More shops and hotels were also going up.

The great folly in Canada, Roy began to say, was in our rush to one point of view or another. Nowhere did this seem greater, to me, than in B.C. The forestry industry had enjoyed a free reign for decades, as it cleared one mountainside after another, harming the province's interests and eventually eroding its own as inevitably there were fewer forests to cut. The same thing was happening with aquaculture. In the eighties and early nineties, almost anyone with a line of credit could open a fish farm. Then, when environmental problems emerged, a moratorium on new farms was announced, and there was growing pressure for harsher measures. The farms were the new pig race.

"We've been under continuous threat of being shut down," Dave said, still astonished that anyone would think so badly of his line of work as to want it eliminated.

"You can't have the pendulum swing too far the other way," Roy added.

They could have gone on for hours, I suspected, but we had reached the wharf where their client was based. For me, it was an odd way to end a journey, landing up outside a corporate office in an environmentalists' haven. Perhaps the pendulum hadn't swung too far. But I had my eyes on another sight. Beyond the fish plant was one of the most gorgeous views I had seen, a sweep of Clayoquot Sound and its inlets, and beyond them forested hills that climbed up the sides of mountains, and a blue sky so clear you could count the treetops against it.

I followed the last road signs to the centre of Tofino, down a gentle hill and past a row of conspicuously priced native art shops to the First Street Wharf, where I found a small sign, with a whale's image on top, marking the western terminus of the Trans-Canada Highway. The end of the road. It was a humble landmark, hardly an indication that this was both the beginning and the end of the world's greatest highway. But I suppose that was the point, for beyond the sign there was a clutch of kayakers dipping their vessels in the Sound. They would soon be heading into the gentle waves of Clayoquot and on into their country, proving with each dip of the paddle that the road in Canada never ends.

Epilogue

While the paved road ends in Tofino, the mystical Trans-Canada Highway continues on Meares Island, across the inlet, where you step off a boat and into the wilds of another century, following a winding cedar-plank boardwalk, rustic and erratic, that leads you deep into the jungle.

As daylight recedes, the only sound is the hollow step of a rubber sole against cedar, and then you step off the walkway and onto a narrow mud path that cuts through the undergrowth, respectfully skirts the oldest cedars, rising three hundred feet above you, and dodges the giant stumps of their fallen cousins. The trail blazes through the forest, deeper and deeper into a primordial darkness, cutting over, through and, in places, under those fallen cedars that are the size of railway cars. And then it stops, slamming right into an upright cedar—until you notice a trap door, a little opening beside the tree that leads you to the other side, where a tunnel has been formed by the remaining branches of a fallen tree.

You watch the trail closely as roots and mud do their best to bring you closer to the dim floor of the forest, and you wonder if the sun is gone, except you know it isn't because way up there, where the sky should be, a few green feathery tips waver before a hint of blue sky. There is light.

Your shoes and pant bottoms splattered with mud, you stop and listen to the creaking of an old cedar twisting in the wind, the rocking chair of the forest, and in the distance you hear the incessant push of an afternoon tide, rising, rushing, pouring into vacuums, filling every nook of the Sound.

Exhausted, you stop where a path of mud and dirt and sticks meets a towering cedar that was here before we were, long before Canada was here. And you find a curve in one of that cedar's roots— its long, serpentine red roots that run right over the next tree's roots, like a giant tapestry on the forest floor. And you sit on that root that was here before we were, before the white man, before Canada. And you stare at all these glorious trees, like those New Brunswick trees that brought so many dreams to the other coast.

In the thin light of afternoon, with only the sounds of a creaking tree and rising tide to fill your ears, you can sit in peace and wonder at what we've done with all this. And you can be sure that if there had to be an end of the road, this would be as fine a place as any.

Conclusion

From a window seat on Air Canada, I could see stretches of the Trans-Canada Highway and marvelled at how long it had taken me to get from one town to the next along its path. The flight, crossing four thousand kilometres from Vancouver to Toronto, took less time than my extended morning journey along the North Thompson, from Valemount to Blue River. From the air, this gigantic country that had been so difficult to cross looked like nothing at all.

It didn't take me long, though, to come up against a different Canada on the ground. No sooner was I back in Toronto, and connected again to the country through the World Wide Web, than I began to see the many rich veins that run beneath the Canadian surface. Almost every instalment of the daily "Notes from the Road" diary I had written in the *Globe and Mail* seemed to have tapped into a deep sentiment—sometimes hostile, sometimes passionate, sometimes endearing. There were Canadians who were in love with their country. There were Canadians who were fed up with their country. But there were not many Canadians who were complacent about their country.

One of the first comments that caught my attention was a column in the *Winnipeg Sun,* under the headline "Suck eggs, Stackhouse." The columnist, Laurie Mustard, took offence to my methodology, and especially my views of his city: "He hitchhikes into town, which does make sense—who would pay this boob?—and with amazing skill, straps on his blinders, and paints the most putrid picture of our city he can put to paper, based apparently on what he hears from his guide (the salesman he is riding with, originally from B.C. nonetheless, and now an *Albertan*), and from what he sees after walking a few short blocks of Portage Avenue."

Then I heard the mayor of Winnipeg had also taken me on, labelling me "racist" for writing about drunk aboriginals on his city's streets. And he was being polite. A Winnipeg radio show tracked me down at home to allow listeners to berate me further about the arrogance of Torontonians writing about their city in a negative light. One elderly woman went on at such length that I thought for a moment I was a caller on hold for her show. When the host finally cut the woman off, he went on to a call from a former Torontonian living in Winnipeg who was sick of his neighbours criticizing his hometown while never accepting a negative word from that city. This went on for nearly an hour.

A Toronto policeman called the newsroom to ask why I was promoting such a dangerous pursuit as hitchhiking. The mayor of Port Alberni wrote to me to express her shock and horror at my description of her town as clear-cut and ugly. Dr. Shelley Lewchuk, on the other hand, wrote to say how much she enjoyed living in Trail, B.C. The taxes were still high and the economy unstable, the recent dental college graduate from Yorkton wrote, but what a view from her patio! In the country's crankiest province, it took someone from Saskatchewan to celebrate the view.

Others wrote to share their hitchhiking experiences, as if they had found a home page for memories of their youth. One man from the Toronto area, Tony Hill, sent me a newspaper article he had written in 1961, at the age of sixteen, about his recent summer experience on the road. He had hitched north and west to Manitoba, and then back east to Halifax before returning home. Along the way, he slept in tents, abandoned cars and one night in a jail in Sault Ste. Marie.

In *Alberta Report* magazine, the publisher Link Byfield devoted a column to his own hitching experiences from the early 1970s, noting how much the country had changed since then. It being *Alberta Report*, the column also explained how these changes illustrated the need for political reform.

"I sense that the mood had indeed changed dramatically," Byfield wrote. "Most people in 1970 seemed to want and expect life to get looser and easier. Today they want it tighter and more self-disciplined. Three decades ago, there was a strong, indulgent desire for tolerance, and to get rid of authority and religion. Not today. Now we want standards, predictability, effort, absolutes, faith, and above all a restoration of the family. This attitude kept coming up; and it seemed to be felt more keenly among the young than the old. People aren't mean about it; they just want everyone, especially the government, to get real."

Speaking of people who wanted the government to get real, Bernard Morency, the '79 Dodge owner from Quebec, wrote to tell me he was at last on his way to Costa Rica. (The letter was written on a blank invoice, and I was grateful to see it didn't itemize any damage to his Bryan Adams tape.) A man from North Bay sent a short note, attached to a clipping of my article on Newfoundland's moose problem. It was annotated with Newfie jokes. From Brampton, an eighty-year-old Jehovah's Witness wrote to give his own opinion about why I had seen so many Kingdom Halls along the road, and why Father Norm—the priest who took me from North Bay to Sudbury—was struggling to fill pews. To make his point, the letter-writer included a bundle of newspaper clippings about sex scandals in the Roman Catholic Church.

And then there was Diane Ollman, a mother from Hamilton, Ontario, who wrote for no other reason than to tell me about her own family's driving trips along the Trans-Canada Highway. In

Calgary, she was surprised to come across people who, seeing the Ontario plates, shouted obscenities at her car. The same thing happened in Nanaimo. In Courtenay, on Vancouver Island, a store owner told her and her husband and their two daughters that they "smelled" like they were from Ontario. Diane finished the unsolicited five-page letter with an analysis of the country's drivers. Ontarians, Albertans and Québécois were the most reckless, she wrote, while Winnipeggers were the most generous—the very opposite of what Scott the AA disciple had said. Cape Bretoners were the slowest on the road, she remarked. British Columbians were the worst. "They disregard every traffic sign. Drove all over the road. I think they let anyone drive who can reach the wheel."

But Diane saved her best observation for last: "When our trip ended this year and we were driving along the 401 towards home, we decided that even with the influence of 'American' life we are still very much Canadian. We encountered a definite Canadian feel in our trips and we feel very lucky to have experienced our country."

I felt the same sort of good fortune for having been able to experience the country and felt more confident about its Canadian feel at the end of my trip than I had at the beginning. In Saint John, driving with Lloyd so very slowly into the city from the airport, I had harboured some serious doubts about the road ahead. Everywhere I had looked since returning to Canada from so many years overseas, I saw the United States swallowing us, economically, politically, culturally, and there seemed to be little resistance from Canadians. The Donald brothers reaffirmed my fears, they having watched their Canada return to its former self. For them, the Maritimes was less the eastern end of a nation than the northern edge of a seaboard. They went south for shopping and health care, and west with their discontent.

The idea of a receding national spirit continued to present itself along the way, in places that were deeply Canadian but no longer felt like Canada. The Kanata Centrum, for instance. Or Dryden's enormous American-owned mill. Or inside Johann St. Pierre's car, talking about American movies on the road through separatist country. Or cruising through the Okanagan with a parade of yahoos. It felt less like Canada and more like America North.

Of course, the country was far different from the one of my childhood and our family vacations along the Trans-Canada. For one, the dominant issue of that Canada (our linguistic divide) had faded as a concern, even in Quebec. Our position in the world was no longer vague, either: we were joined at the hip with the United States.

In this increasingly urban nation, no one much cared about the hinterland—the North, the farms, the fishery. Travelling through long stretches of rural Canada, I was disturbed, even frightened, to see the gutting of places that once were central to the nation's identity. Cape Breton, Quebec's north shore, the Hemlo goldfields, rural Manitoba: you'd expect to find their images on the back of a five-dollar bill, and yet they were struggling to stay on the map.

I fear this decline of rural Canada—psychologically as much as economically—is changing our country in ways we don't fully understand. As much as we are a people shaped by nature and its myths, fewer and fewer Canadians have much to do any more with the rocks, water and wildlife that the rest of the world so often sees as us.

More disturbing is my impression that, despite our skill at mass communication, we also have less contact with each other. Our sprawling country was once something to be explored, developed or just understood. But on my journey I sensed Canadians were more in retreat from their vast land than they were out to embrace it. In just a few decades, our immense dominion had become a collection of city-states, each believing it was independent from the next, like a desert kingdom with its own economy, identity and demands. Of course they are not city-states. They've just come to rely far more on North America than on Canada.

Between the twin forces of continentalism and urbanization, our desert kingdoms had become the new forces of division and yet the new sources of identity in our country. Being from Edmonton or Montreal had become more important than being from Canada. Parochialism is not unique to this country, or to these times, but with the enormous distances between our big centres and the strong tug felt by each from the south, it can lead to a drifting state of nationhood. And it has: not the sort of resentful drift that I grew up knowing from Quebec or the West, but the drift of indifference, the kind realized only when someone like Davis Marcoux from Tête-à-la-Baleine wakes up and discovers he has more in common with Bob Barker than with Bernard Lord.

This sort of drift is not irreversible, not by any stretch. We can count on the curious Canadian mix of pragmatism and passion that went into the Timbit and so many other Canadian creations, from international peacekeeping to Second City. I came across it many times, in places like Labrador Straits and its remote communities that were clinging to their heritage through tough times and were happy for it. They knew their region had a unique identity, which informed their individual identities. But they also knew they were part of something bigger.

I have to believe it is the same for Canada. Almost everywhere I went, I came across people, places and things that were uniquely Canadian and had nothing to do with health care, hockey or the absence of handguns. Dina's kofta stand in Moncton, Edmonton's Fringe Festival, Michel the chef's pickup truck, Joe's marijuana break on Confederation Bridge, beer-drinking truckers on the MV *Caribou*, Aaron and Willie pointing to their ancestral waters while listening to rap music in their car: these would not exist in the United States, or anywhere else. They were uniquely Canadian in their blend of eccentricity and unpredictability, and their openness to competing ideas.

This didn't happen by chance. More often than not, the best parts of Canada I encountered had some form of strong federal involvement. Whether it was listening to CBC Radio with Murray as he smoked a joint in Alberta or enjoying the serenity of Pacific Rim National Park or listening to families talk about being able to stay close to their roots in rural Quebec, there was a bit of Canada in everything—even the road I spent most of my journey on.

But there was also a fierce demand for more local control over this Canada. From the angry old men of Newfoundland to the residents of Jasper National Park, the Canadians I met wanted a much greater say in the public decisions that were affecting their lives. And what's new about this? On one level, not much. The push and pull between Canadians and Ottawa is as old as the nation. But on another level, there is something new: the magnetism of America that came with both free trade and the satellite dish has drawn Canadians in yet another direction.

It is a very real threat to our identity, but it can also make the country stronger. In many ways, the forces we have felt from the United States, through television, war, trade and migration, have given Canadians a much better sense of who we are. I keep thinking back to Kyle Haygarth, the young engineering student working in Chalk River who believed he could go just about anywhere and do just about anything, and remain Canadian. He was right to believe that tolerance and fairness were more than ideals; they had become national traits. They had made Canada more than a place to live; they had made Canadian a thing to be.

My ancestors came to Saint John in search of those traits. More than two centuries later, newcomers like Kenneth Preston, the Scottish electrician, and Michel Germain, the French chef, were still finding those values in Canada. And they were making them a part of their ethos. It's why they picked up hitchhikers, and why they wanted to live in a country where people picked up hitchhikers.

More than anyone else I met along the way, they seemed to know that being Canadian is not just about giving rides. It's about accepting the rider no matter where they're coming from, sharing the journey no matter what kind of car you drive, and not worrying too much about the destination, because you'll get there eventually. Even on the world's greatest stretch of highway, you'll get there eventually.

Acknowledgements

The seeds for my journey, and this book, were planted by my parents, Margaret and Reginald, who share a boundless curiosity about this country. Decades ago, they took me and my sisters on long car trips to museums, battlefields and national treasures like the Gaspé. They shared with us their friends tucked away in every nook of Canada, who always made the country seem far smaller than it was. My parents, rightly horrified that I would hitchhike along roads they drove, at least never discouraged me from exploring the country. It was, they said, what Canadians did.

I probably would not have hitchhiked beyond university, though, were it not for the urging of Richard Addis, editor of the *Globe and Mail* from 1999 to 2002. He brought to the job an enthusiasm for adventure as well as for innovative journalism—anything to draw smart people's eyes to words—and I am grateful to him for pushing me to a higher standard and for giving me the time to write this book.

On the road, I was helped by many more drivers than are mentioned in this book, and, of course, by other hitchhikers and travellers. I am indebted to each of them, as well as to those I've written about. They took a chance in stopping for a stranger, and in sharing their views of Canada with a journalist. Since completing the trip, I've been asked by many people if I would recommend hitchhiking. The answer, I'm afraid to say, is no. The risks are bad enough; the waits are awful. But to those who did pick me up, thank you.

Two *Globe and Mail* writers who helped me along the way were Anne McIlroy in Ottawa and Rod Mickleburgh in Vancouver. I appreciated their company, humour and advice. At the newspaper, two exceptional feature editors, Jerry Johnson and Jerry Kinoshita, helped me write thousands of words about the journey on very short notice.

Turning the trip into a book was another challenge altogether. I wanted to record the journey in full, adding the texture and perspective that space would not allow in a newspaper series. I also believed Canadians should read about their country in a new light, or at least from a different angle. Anne Collins at Random House Canada was an early believer in the idea that a hitchhiker's journey could be turned into a political travelogue, and guided me in both thinking and writing. Despite the awkward delays that resulted from the September 11 terrorist attacks and their aftermath, the book benefited from the efforts of Tanya Trafford, Wendy Thomas, John Sweet and Pamela Murray. When the project finally returned to a normal course, Craig Pyette at Random House kept it that way, for which I am grateful.

During my absences from the foreign desk, assistant foreign editors Kathryn Maloney and Guy Nicholson had to assume my responsibilities, often over intense periods of world news. The fact that few people noticed my absence is a tribute to their skill.

But no one sacrificed more for this book than my wife, Cindy, who dissected each draft and made it better, and our children, Matthew and Lauren. They put up with my long absences on the road and then at a computer, as well as the distractions that any writer drags into a house like mud on a shoe. That they did so with love and patience was more than I could ask for. I owe this book to the three of them.